Key management ideas

Thinkers that changed the management world

3rd edition

Stuart Crainer

FINANCIAL TIMES
PITMAN PUBLISHING

FINANCIAL TIMES
MANAGEMENT

LONDON • SAN FRANCISCO
KUALA LUMPUR • JOHANNESBURG

*Financial Times Management delivers the knowledge,
skills and understanding that enable students,
managers and organisations to achieve their ambitions,
whatever their needs, wherever they are.*

London Office:
128 Long Acre, London WC2E 9AN
Tel: +44 (0)171 447 2000
Fax: +44 (0)171 240 5771
Website: www.ftmanagement.com

A Division of Financial Times Professional Limited

First published in Great Britain 1998

ISBN 0 273 63808 4 (Paperback)
ISBN 0 273 64114 X (Hardback)

British Library Cataloguing in Publication Data
A CIP catalogue record for this book can be obtained from the British Library.

10 9 8 7 6 5 4 3 2 1

Typeset by Pantek Arts, Maidstone, Kent.
Printed and bound in Great Britain by Redwood Books, Trowbridge, Wiltshire

The Publishers' policy is to use paper manufactured from sustainable forests.

About the author

Stuart Crainer is the author of numerous business books. He is editor of *The Financial Times Handbook of Management*. His books include *The Future of Leadership* (with Randall P White and Philip Hodgson); *The Tom Peters Phenomenon*; and *The Ultimate Business Library*.

He contributes to magazines and newspapers around the world including *Strategy and Business, Across the Board, Management Today* and the *Financial Times*.

Contents

Acknowledgments

While I have received assistance from a variety of quarters, any omissions or inaccuracies are entirely my responsibility.

Grateful acknowledgment is given to the *Harvard Business Review* for permission to include extracts from the following:

B Shapiro, "What the hell is market oriented?," *Harvard Business Review*, November–December 1988. Copyright 1988 © By the President and Fellows of Harvard College; all rights reserved.

P Drucker, "The new productivity challenge," *Harvard Business Review*, November–December 1991. Copyright 1991 © By the President and Fellows of Harvard College; all rights reserved.

L Hirschhorn and T Gilmore, "The new boundaries of the boundaryless company," *Harvard Business Review*, May–June 1992. Copyright 1992 © By the President and Fellows of Harvard College; all rights reserved.

R Pascale, A Athos and T Goss, "The reinvention rollercoaster," *Harvard Business Review*, November–December 1993. Copyright 1993 © By the President and Fellows of Harvard College; all rights reserved.

W Taylor, "The logic of global business: an interview with Percy Barnevik," *Harvard Business Review*, March–April 1991. Copyright 1991 © By the President and Fellows of Harvard College; all rights reserved.

Key for symbols

The following icons and the concepts they represent
have been used throughout this book.

 Key idea

 Thinker

 Checklist

 Further reading

Introduction

"Just do it," trumpets Nike's advertising. To the vast majority of managers, management is about action rather than ideas. They are motivated by the sense of achievement when they raise profits, successfully introduce new products into the marketplace, record a sale or bring in a new customer. Their language is direct, snappy, and peppered with talk of the bottom line. To them management is not a passive, studious, desk-based art, but something which is immediate and active. Management lives in the here and now.

Theory is what MBA students amass at business schools. The MBA covers ideals and dry case studies which invariably lack the direct immediacy of real management. It is theory without substance. It is one thing obtaining an MBA but, it is argued, quite another to convert what you have learned about a concept, such as strategic management, into constant practice across an organization.

The managers are right. Management is active, not theoretical. It is about changing behavior and making things happen. It is about developing people, working with them, reaching objectives and achieving results. Indeed, all the research into how managers spend their time reveals that they are creatures of the moment, perpetually immersed in the nitty-gritty of making things happen.

But, management is nothing without ideas.

"Nothing is so practical as a good theory," psychologist Kurt Lewin noted. Ideas drive management as surely as the immediate problems which land on managers' desks or which arrive via their e-mail. Decisions have to be based on ideas, as well as instinct. Without ideas managers flit desperately from crisis to crisis. They cannot know where they are going, why they are doing something or what they will achieve, without the vital fuel of ideas.

This observation of the economist Keynes holds true for management: "Practical men, who believe themselves to be quite exempt from any intellectual influences, are usually the slaves of some defunct economist. Madmen in authority, who hear voices in the air, are distilling their frenzy from some academic scribbler of a few years back."

Ideas count. Look at the post-war resurgence of Japanese industry. Its growth was based on the precept of quality – this was largely based on the ideas and research of two Americans, W Edwards Deming and Joseph Juran. While the duo were listened to in Japan their ideas were all but ignored in the West until the 1980s. By then it was almost too late. The Japanese converted theory into practice and became a huge industrial power thanks, in part, to their highly effective implementation of the ideas of Deming and Juran.

The Japanese have a tradition of revering ideas and being able to translate them into dynamic practice. Early management thinkers, such as Frederick Taylor and Mary Parker Follett, were widely acknowledged in Japan while receiving only tepid reactions in their home country. In contrast, ideas in the West tend to be seen as distractions and are categorized as instant solutions or as simply impractical. There is often an unwillingness to try to understand or to try and make them work. The requirements of the moment take precedence in a world beset by ever-increasing demands on time, energy and money.

Paradoxically, though managers appear to be bogged down in the minutiae of the moment, they are hungry for ideas, new perspectives and fresh approaches. Management books sell in their millions. Managers want to know and learn more. The problem is that they simply don't have the time. Research by the Management Training Partnership found that three quarters of personnel directors buy at least four management books a year. However, only one in five is actually read.[1]

Beyond the quest for one best way

That management books tend to be decorative is not the only problem. The key ideas which have shaped and continue to drive management are often regarded as inflexible. They concentrate on the "one right way" to carry out a task or achieve an objective. In reality, managers know that it is unlikely that one particular approach will solve all their problems. Reengineering, the latest in a long line of corporate saviors, was the idea of the early 1990s. It has since become buried among the detritus of ideas past their use-by-date.

Ideas count, but they are not off-the-peg solutions. No matter what consultants might suggest, there is no panacea. Faced with a crisis, a manager cannot reach across for the file on "How to implement strategy" and hope for instant results. Achieving success involves a multitude of ideas, approaches and skills.

> *Ideas count, but they are not off-the-peg solutions. No matter what consultants might suggest, there is no panacea. Faced with a crisis, a manager cannot reach across for the file on "How to implement strategy" and hope for instant results. Achieving success involves a multitude of ideas, approaches and skills.*

The trouble is that managers appear addicted to the idea of the quick fix. There is still an air of desperation in the way that managers cling to new ideas. Fads and fashions emerge in a fanfare of superlatives only to disappear almost as quickly.

The learning organization was another of the fads of the 1990s. Peter Senge's *The Fifth Discipline* led the way. An international bestseller, it propelled the MIT professor to international renown. By 1995 Senge was receiving a less enthusiastic response. "It's part of the fad cycle," he told the *Financial Times*. "People consume then drop fads and ideas all the time and corporations are no different."[2]

Ironically, blame for this obsession with the latest trend can be partly attributed to the professionalization of management. Once management became regarded as a profession, it was assumed that there were a number of skills and ideas which needed to be mastered before someone could proclaim themselves a professional manager. The skills of management were regarded like a bag of golf clubs. When the occasion demanded a particular skill it was extracted from the bag and put to work. New skills could occasionally be added to the managerial bag of tricks when, and if, required.

Unfortunately, managerial life is no longer so straightforward. Typically, work by the UK's Management Charter Initiative to identify standard competencies for all middle managers emerged with several hundred. Simplifying the complex is never easy. (And, when they are simplified, competencies become meaninglessly generic.)

Despite this, the faddishness of managers continues as they seek out new skills and new solutions to perennial problems. "It has become professionally legitimate in the United States to accept and utilize ideas without an in-depth grasp of their underlying foundation, and without the commitment necessary to sustain them," observes Richard Pascale in *Managing on the Edge*.[3]

The fad industry has emerged and the chief beneficiaries are management consultants and business schools. The search for the secret of management has taken managers and organizations through bewildering loops and has spawned an entirely new vocabulary. Managers have embraced brainstorming as a useful tool; they have explored Douglas Macgregor's Theory X and Theory Y; negotiated Blake and Mouton's "Managerial Grid"; been driven on by "Management by Objectives"; discovered strategic management through Igor Ansoff in the late 1960s; been converted by Tom Peters and Robert Waterman's *In Search of Excellence*; and have, no doubt, also tried their hand with quality circles and various forms of Total Quality Management. And yet, there is no single best way to manage – simply a rag-bag of shared experiences, short-lived best practice and high expectations.

It is not that these various ideas are poor concepts. Many do work, but they are not set in tablets of stone. They have to be flexible, and used when needed, rather than as all-encompassing "solutions." "Management has always been beset by fads and fashions, gurus and demagogues. But never before has there been such a sheer volume of new approaches," says Edward Lawler of the Center for Effective Organizations. "This has led many managers to reach one of two incorrect conclusions: that the new approaches are all hype with no substance, or that a particular program is the answer. The reality is more complex and challenging."[4]

Using this book

So, where does this leave managers? Often, the answer is confused and cynical. They have heard the fanfares so often that it is hardly surprising that their pulses don't race with excitement when they hear the next big idea.

Yet, they remain hungry for knowledge. This book aims to satisfy their hunger. It provides a potpourri of the ideas and the pioneers who have shaped management and which affect the behavior, expectations and aspirations of managers every day of their managerial lives. The ideas are not quick fixes. But, if they are understood and applied at the right time in the right environment, they can help bridge the gap between theory and practice.

The principal ideas covered in *Key Management Ideas* are organized under eleven headings:

- The new world of management
- The new world of organizations
- The challenge of technology
- Creating and implementing strategy
- New ways of managing people
- Careers and working life
- The quality revolution
- Reinventing marketing
- Leadership
- Learning and development
- Global management.

The wide-ranging nature of modern management means that managers need constantly to bring in concepts from among the plethora of leading edge ideas now at their disposal. This book aims to make these ideas more accessible, fitting them into place amid the pantheon of management pioneers and thinkers. For quick reference, the Glossary includes an A to Z of key management thinkers with details of their main ideas and publications.

The third edition of the book has been substantially updated. It includes new sections on subjects including intellectual capital, lean production and the balanced scorecard. There are two entirely new chapters on The challenge of technology (Chapter 3) and Careers and working life (Chapter 6). Future editions will ensure that *Key Management Ideas* remains as up-to-date and as practically useful as possible.

While the nature of managerial work changes constantly, the fundamental truth remains unchanged: management continues to represent a huge challenge to those who put it into practice every day throughout the world. This book will not lessen the challenge, but may help to make the trends, influences and people behind them, more intelligible. The acid test is action. Can managers translate the ideas in this book into activities and initiatives which change the way they do business? In the hyper-competitive business environment there is no choice. Concepts must be made to work. To be the best, managers and their organizations must learn from the best.

Stuart Crainer

References

1 *Financial Times*, 12 September 1994.
2 Quoted in Griffith, Victoria, "Corporate fashion victim," *Financial Times*, 12 April 1995.
3 Pascale, Richard, *Managing on the Edge*, Penguin, London, 1991.
4 Lawler, Edward, "New logic is here to stay," *Financial Times*, 28 January 1994.

The new world of management

"The old organizational life which may be comfortable and predictable is disappearing rapidly. The new logic is not like the fads and fashions that have gripped management over the decades. Instead it represents fundamental change in the way organizations will operate. People who develop the skills to be effective in organizations which follow the new logic will thrive. Those who do not will be just as obsolete as poorly skilled production workers in a high-technology manufacturing facility."

Edward Lawler[1]

From the machine age to the information age

The roots of modern management lie in the machine age of the nineteenth century, though the practice of management has far more historical antecedents. Commentators repeatedly observe that the machine age is fast being replaced by what is called the "information age." In the words of futurist Alvin Toffler, the "brute force economy" is being superseded by a "brain force economy."

This new era presents revolutionary challenges to the way managers manage and how they think about those they manage. "The closer we get to the information age, the more questionable become the traditional practices and precepts of Management. (In most companies management still comes with a capital 'M')," says Gary Hamel, co-author of *Competing for the Future*. "In the machine age a manager was a professional... Managers were given credentials... A manager was an analyst (value chain analysis, segmentation analysis, cost structure analysis). The act of management took place within the boundaries of industry convention, company tradition, vested authority, national context, functional specialization, the demonstrably feasible, and the here and now. Management was by the rules, by the numbers and by the book. That was then, this is now. The boundaries are gone. The game has changed. The rule book is out of date."[2]

Of course, there was never an actual "rule book" of management. But, like an unwritten constitution, there were ways of doing things and expectations which shaped every single aspect of managerial activity.

There was no hallowed ring-binder, but the "rule book" of machine age management was based on a number of precepts:

- **Command and control** – management was exercised **on** people through a kind of benign dictatorship. Inspired by military role models, the manager told people what to do and then supervised them.

- **One right way** – the instructions of management were assumed to be right. The role of those who were managed was not to question or suggest alternative approaches. There was a belief in one right way to undertake tasks.

- **Subjugation not subversion** – the machine age was built around subjugation. Contrast this with the positive encouragement of what would once have been regarded as plain subversion in some of today's more innovative companies.

- **Labor not human resources** – the workforce was "labor," hired hands with no stake in the organization. Laborers were generally in plentiful supply and the company did not owe them anything, though they were expected to demonstrate loyalty to the company.

- **National not global** – perspectives were generally national, sometimes regional, and rarely international.

- **Security not insecurity** – while employees were not offered recognition or responsibility, there was an unspoken contract built around security. Companies had a feel of permanence, dominating towns and their markets. The future seemed predictable and their place in the future even more predictable.

F W Taylor
Management as science

If there was any one creator of the machine age rule book, **Frederick Winslow Taylor** (1856–1917) should probably take the credit. Today, the name of the American inventor and engineer is now known by only a few practising managers. And yet, his work forms the cornerstone of much of the management practice of the twentieth century. The man may be forgotten, but his legacy lives determinedly on and, once described, would be instantly recognized by most managers.

Taylor was the originator of what became known as "scientific management." To the eyes of the late twentieth-century observer, scientific management would be considered anything but scientific. Taylor's science was built around minute observation of the best way a task could be undertaken and completed. Having found the best way, people could then be made to follow it, to the second, in the prescribed manner.

Scientific management

Based on the notion that there is a single "best way" to fulfil a particular job; and that it is a matter of matching people to the task and supervising, rewarding and punishing them according to their performance. Under scientific management, the job of management is to plan and control the work.

"Hardly a competent workman can be found who does not devote a considerable amount of time to studying first how slowly he can work and still convince his employer that he is going at a good pace. Under our system a worker is just told what he is to do and how he is to do it. Any improvement he makes upon the orders given to him is fatal to his success," observed Taylor.

Taylor sought to dehumanize work. In doing so, he laid the foundations for the mass production techniques which speedily emerged after his death. "His unforgivable sin was his assertion that there is no such thing as 'skill' in making and moving things. All such work was the same, Taylor asserted. And all could be analysed step-by-step, as a series of unskilled operations that could then be combined into any kind of job. Anyone willing to learn these operations would be a 'first-class man,' deserving 'first-class pay.' He could do the most advanced work and do it to perfection," Peter Drucker has accurately observed.[3]

Since the rise and fall of labor-intensive, highly functionalized, mass production, Taylor's ideas have been routinely derided – treating workers as unthinking robots able to carry out carefully prescribed tasks *ad infinitum*. Similarly, in Taylor's philosophy the role of managers and supervisors appears to go little beyond holding the stop-watch and admonishing – or speedily sacking – malingerers or poor performers. Taylor also emphasized quantity rather than quality, something which is increasingly out of line with today's management practice.

Five steps to scientific management

1 Find, say 10 or 15 different men (preferably in as many separate establishments and different parts of the country) who are especially skilful in doing the particular work to be analyzed.

2 Study the exact series of elementary operations or motions which each of these men uses in doing the work being investigated, as well as the implements each man uses.

3 Study with a stop-watch the time required to make each of these elementary movements and then select the quickest way of doing each element of the work.

4 Eliminate all false movements, slow movements and useless movements.

5 After doing away with all unnecessary movements, collect into one series the quickest and best movements as well as the best implements.

It would be easy to underestimate the impact of the era in which Taylor lived and worked on his ideas. Indeed, the significance (and continuing impact of his ideas in many businesses) is hardly appreciated. In addition, the fact that some of his insights do genuinely translate into the modern environment can be overlooked. In *Scientific Management*, for example, Taylor writes: "It becomes the duty of those on the management's side to deliberately study the character, the nature and the performance of each workman with a view to finding out his limitations on the one hand, but even more important, his possibilities for development on the other hand." This idea is continually echoed in much of today's management literature.

Similarly, comparisons can be made between a modern concept such as reengineering – which breaks down organizational processes into their constituent parts – and Taylor's attempts at analyzing each and every aspect of the production process.

As Peter Drucker has observed, Taylor's concepts may appear to be inhumane and limited to the modern manager, but he was the first person to really begin to think about the actual act of work rather than taking it for granted. For all his addiction to the stop-watch, Taylor was a truly remarkable man. He patented numerous inventions, excelled at tennis and (perhaps his most significant legacy) persuaded baseball pitchers to throw overarm rather than underarm because, typically enough, it was more efficient.

FREDERICK WINSLOW TAYLOR

1856–1917

American

Engineer, inventor and consultant

Education: Stevens Institute of Technology, Hoboken, New Jersey.

Career: Apprentice at Enterprise Hydraulic Works; chief engineer Midvale Steel Co.; general manager at Manufacturing Investment Co.'s paper mills in Maine; 1893 set up as a consulting engineer in New York.

Books: *Shop Management*, Harper & Row, New York, 1903; *The Principles of Scientific Management*, Harper & Row, New York, 1913.

Henri Fayol
Defining management

In Europe the first steps towards identifying what management entails were taken by the Frenchman **Henri Fayol** (1841–1925), a still underestimated figure in the fledgling years of management theorizing. While Taylor gained attention (and later notoriety) for his "scientific management," Fayol's work is generally forgotten. Yet, Fayol pursued a much broader path than Taylor and his codification of what he thought management involved remains valuable.

In his *General and Industrial Management*, published in 1916, Fayol laid down 14 principles of management. These were:

1 **Division of work** – tasks should be divided up and employees should specialize in a limited set of tasks so that expertise is developed and productivity increased.

2 **Authority and responsibility** – authority is the right to give orders and entails the responsibility for enforcing them with rewards and penalties; authority should be matched with corresponding responsibility.

3 **Discipline** – is essential for the smooth running of business and is dependent on good leadership, clear and fair arguments, and the judicious application of penalties.

4 **Unity of command** – for any action whatsoever, an employee should receive orders from one superior only; otherwise authority, discipline, order and stability are threatened.

5 **Unity of direction** – a group of activities concerned with a single objective should be co-ordinated by a single plan under one head.

6 **Subordination of individual interest to general interest** – individual or group goals must not be allowed to override those of the business.

7 **Remuneration of personnel** – may be achieved by various methods and the choice is important; it should be fair, encourage effort, and not lead to overpayment.

8 **Centralization** – the extent to which orders should be issued only from the top of the organization is a problem which should take into account its characteristics, such as size and the capabilities of the personnel.

9 **Scalar chain (line of authority)** – communications should normally flow up and down the line of authority running from the top to the bottom of the organization, but sideways communication between those of equivalent rank in different departments can be desirable so long as superiors are kept informed.

10 **Order** – both materials and personnel must always be in their proper place; people must be suited to their posts so there must be careful organization of work and selection of personnel.

11 **Equity** – personnel must be treated with kindliness and justice.

12 **Stability of tenure of personnel** – rapid turnover of personnel should be avoided because of the time required for the development of expertise.

13 **Initiative** – all employees should be encouraged to exercise initiative within the limits imposed by the requirements of authority and discipline.

14 *Esprit de corps* – efforts must be made to promote harmony within the organization and prevent dissension and divisiveness.

> *Fayol – unlike Taylor – recognized that* esprit de corps *is a vital ingredient in any organization. To Taylor any identification with fellow workers was a distraction rather than a motivation.*

Fayol – unlike Taylor – recognized that *esprit de corps* is a vital ingredient in any organization. To Taylor any identification with fellow workers was a distraction rather than a motivation.

Fayol also divided a commercial organization's activities into six basic elements: technical; commercial; financial; security; accounting; and management. The management function, Fayol believed, consisted of planning, organizing, commanding, coordinating and controlling. It is likely that many practising managers, even today, would identify similar elements as the core of their activities.

HENRI FAYOL

1841–1925

French

Engineer and manager

Education: National School of Mines, St Etienne, France (graduated 1860).

Career: Manager and later managing director of mining company, Commentry-Fourchamboult-Décazeville.

Books: *General and Industrial Management*, Pitman, London, 1949.

Beyond scientific management

Scientific management spawned a number of corrolaries. One of the most influential was the work of **Max Weber** (1864–1920). Weber took Taylor's highly practical supervisory form of management and sought to apply it to the organization as a whole – if there is a best way to do a job, there must also be a best way of running an organization.

Weber's conclusion was that the most efficient form of organization was mechanical. He labelled the ideal organizational form "rational-legal" in contrast to the less reliable "charismatic" and "traditional" organizations. Weber's long-lasting legacy is the image of the organization as machine – a mechanical and bureaucratic institution driven rationally and inexorably forward.

Bureaucratic organization

The ideal mechanical means of organizing a business characterized, according to Max Weber, by "precision, speed, unambiguity, knowledge of files, continuity, discretion, unity, strict subordination, reduction of friction and of material and personal costs." Weber framed this more as a Platonic ideal than a likely reality.

While it is easy to ridicule the bureaucratic organization envisaged by Weber, his analysis was probably right for the time. The charismatic type of organization, led by an outstanding individual, has always proved problematical – though the need for charismatic leaders to provide persuasive visions of the future is now widely acknowledged – and the traditional family company, where management was by hereditary right, had outgrown its usefulness even then.

Scientific management could also be said to have produced one of the most enduring rules of management, Parkinson's Law. Created by a British academic, **Northcote Parkinson** (1910–1993), the law takes an ironic slant on Taylor's conclusions. Parkinson's Law observes that work expands to fill the time available for its completion – something which Taylor well appreciated. Parkinson took the thinking a stage further observing that organizations have an inbuilt drive to grow regardless of their productive output. Even if nothing results, the number of staff increases, creating unnecessary work for each other so that everyone becomes even busier. Parkinson's ironic genius was to identify management and the business world as irrational. Applying rationality to the irrational produced humorous results – unfortunately, this is not something widely appreciated by management writers.

Parkinson's Laws

Work expands to fill the time available and expenditure rises to overtake income.

Parkinson's observations were part of the slow process of humanizing the more extreme thinking of the machine age (a process which has conspicuously failed in many organizations). But, in the decades since the Second World War, the key ideas have become more humanized as management thinkers have turned their attention to what motivates people and how managers can transform their roles from ones of supervision to leadership.

Even so, the virility of machine age thinking can be seen in the conclusions reached by **Louis Allen** in his 1973 book *Professional Management*. Allen's research began in 1953 and aimed to establish which management methods were most effective and what companies should do to manage more effectively.

Professional Management put forward four functions of management based on a belief that managers think and act rationally – planning, organizing, leading and controlling.[4] Allen broke these functions down into 19 management activities:

1 **Planning function** – forecasting, developing objectives, programing, scheduling, budgeting, developing procedures and developing policies.

2 **Organizing function** – developing organization structure, delegating, developing relationships.

3 **Leading function** – decision making, communicating, motivating, selecting and developing people.

4 **Controlling function** – developing performance standards, measuring, evaluating and correcting performance.

The echoes of Taylorism are there, though they are refined and developed. Indeed, in the eyes of many, Taylor's legacy lives on. More recently than Louis Allen, **Konosuke Matsushita (1894–1989)**, founder of the Japanese electronics giant which carries his name, has observed that Western firms remain "built on the Taylor model. Even worse, so are your heads. With your bosses doing the thinking while the workers wield the screwdrivers, you're convinced deep down that this is the way to run a business... We [Japan] are beyond the Taylor model. Business, we know, is now so complex and difficult, the survival of the firm so hazardous in an environment increasingly unpredictable, competitive and fraught with danger, that its continued existence depends on the day-to-day mobilization of every ounce of intelligence."[5] The truth of Matsushita's damning observation is only now being fully explored and uncovered – but only by those brave enough to do so.

The mythology of managerial work

Scientific management was not interested in mobilizing every ounce of intelligence, simply every ounce of **necessary** intelligence and energy to complete a particular task. It helped nurture a myth of management which usually bore little relation to reality. Managers are not always right. Nor do they think and act rationally all of the time. Scientific management encouraged managers to believe in their own propaganda.

Henry Mintzberg's book, *The Nature of Managerial Work*, published in 1973, proved a significant step forward in that he cast aside many long-held, but idealistic views.

Mintzberg found:

1 A similarity in managerial work whether carried out by the company president, the health service administrator or the general foreman. He categorized it into ten basic roles and six sets of work characteristics.

2 While differences exist arising from functional or hierarchical level they can be described largely in common roles and characteristics.

3 The managerial job is made up of regular and programed duties as well as non-programed activities.

4 The manager is both a generalist and a specialist.

5 The manager is reliant on information, particularly that which has been verbally received.

6 Work activities are characterized by brevity, variety and fragmentation.

7 Management work is more an art than a science, reliant on intuitive and non-explicit processes.

8 Management work is increasingly complex.[6]

Mintzberg's model of managerial work identified three overall categories and specific roles within each:

1 **Interpersonal category**
   (a) the figurehead role where the manager performs symbolic duties as head of the organization
   (b) the leader role where he/she establishes the work atmosphere and motivates subordinates to achieve organizational goals
   (c) the liaison role where the manager develops and maintains webs of contacts outside the organization.

2 **Informational category**
   (a) the monitor role where the manager collects all types of information relevant and useful to the organization
   (b) the disseminator role where the manager transmits information from the outside to members in the organization
   (c) the spokesman role where he/she transmits information from inside the organization to outsiders.

3 **Decisional category**
   (a) the entrepreneur role where the manager initiates controlled change in his/her organization to adapt to the changing environment
   (b) the disturbance handler role where the manager deals with unexpected changes
   (c) the resource allocator role where he/she makes decisions on the use of organizational resources
   (d) the negotiator role where the manager deals with other organizations and individuals.

Mintzberg found managers flitting from subject to subject; crisis to crisis; unable to concentrate for any length of time without the phone ringing or a colleague knocking at the door.

Revealed to be human after all, later analyses of managers' behavior have tended to highlight the softer side of management. It is much more than dictatorial supervision.

For example, over 700 managers – in a variety of organizations and at all levels of management – were surveyed at the Singapore Institute of Management at the beginning of the 1990s. From factor analysis five "mega-components" of management work were identified:

1 Goal setting and review

2 Creating a conducive working environment

3 Managing quality

4 Relating to and managing the external environment

5 Managing performance.[7]

Only the first of these components could be said to be consistent with machine age management. The others belong firmly in the new world.

The rule book is out of date. This is not to say that there is a need for a new rule book. "What's so wonderful about the Body Shop is that we still don't know the rules," says Anita Roddick.[8] Management by the rules is redundant when the rules are in a constant state of irrational flux.

Peter Drucker
The prophet of change

The man whose work spans both the machine age and the information age is **Peter Ferdinand Drucker** (born 1909), the twentieth century's most influential management thinker.

The bare bones of Drucker's career give little insight to the profound effect and influence he has had – and continues to have – on management thinking. Born in Austria, he became an investment banker in London in 1933. In 1937 he emigrated to the United States and worked in newspapers. In 1942 he became a Professor of Philosophy and Politics at Bennington College in Vermont and later a Professor of Management at New York University. During his career he has also been a consultant to many large organizations. Now, Drucker is the Clarke Professor of Social Science and Management at the Claremont Graduate School in Claremont, California (he also lectures on oriental art at the same institution).

Behind these scant details lies a career as a writer and thinker on virtually every aspect of management. Drucker's books are as diverse in content as they are numerous. His first book appeared in 1939, *The End of Economic Man*. A succession of others has followed. In the 1940s Drucker wrote *The Future of Industrial Man* and *The Concept of the Corporation*; in the 1950s his output included *The Practice of Management*; in the 1960s came *Managing for Results*, *The Effective Executive*, *The Age of Discontinuity*; the 1970s brought the encyclopedic, *Management: Tasks, Responsibilities, Practices*; the 1980s included *Managing in Turbulent Times* and *The Frontiers of Management*; and in the 1990s, *Managing the Nonprofit Organization* and *Managing for the Future*. By any stretch of the imagination, this is a phenomenal output. In addition, Drucker has written novels and the autobiographical *Adventures of a Bystander*.

Drucker has deliberately set himself apart from the mainstream of management education – not for nothing is the greatest management thinker of the century a professor at a relatively obscure institution. He has roundly condemned Harvard Business School and the business school system and, during his lengthy career, has studiously avoided becoming part of any one organization. The theorist has studiously retained an objective distance from organizational practice.

What is notable about Drucker's work is his uncanny ability to spot trends and describe them in an almost downbeat manner drawing wisdom from an array of sources (though Jane Austen and Trollope remain consistent inspirations to him). Later they are almost always picked up by others and become the height of managerial fashion. Often, their roots can be traced back to Drucker's work a decade previously. His 1969 book, *The Age of Discontinuity*, for example, is now much referred to as writers and managers attempt to come to terms with managing change. In this book he observed that America was "a knowledge economy" – a theme he later returned to in *Managing for the Future* (1992) in which he observed: "From now on the key is knowledge." Twenty five years on from his original observation, the concept of knowledge workers and knowledge-intensive organizations is gaining widespread attention (not least from Drucker himself).

> **What is notable about Drucker's work is his uncanny ability to spot trends and describe them in an almost downbeat manner drawing wisdom from an array of sources.**

PETER DRUCKER

Born Austria, 1909

American

Writer

Education: Doctorate in international and public law, Frankfurt University 1931.

Career: Journalist in Germany and the UK where he also advised banks; went to the US in 1937 to teach; 1939, *The End of Economic Man*, published; 1942, Professor of Philosophy and Politics at Bennington College, Vermont; Professor of Management at New York University; since 1971 Clarke Professor of Social Science and Management at the Claremont Graduate School in Claremont, California.

Books: *Concept of the Corporation*, John Day, New York, 1946; *The New Society*, Heinemann, London, 1951; *The Practice of Management*, Harper & Row, New York, 1954; *Managing for Results*, Heinemann, London, 1964; *The Age of Discontinuity*, Heinemann, London, 1969; *Management: Tasks, Responsibilities, Practices*, Heinemann, London, 1974; *Innovation and Entrepreneurship*, Heinemann, London, 1985; *The New Realities*, Heinemann, London, 1989; *Managing the Nonprofit Organization*, HarperCollins, New York, 1990; *Managing for the Future*, Dutton, New York, 1992; *Post-Capitalist Society*, Harper, New York, 1993; *Managing in Times of Great Change*, Butterworth Heinemann, Oxford, 1995; *Adventures of a Bystander*, originally published in 1978 but republished by John Wiley, New York, 1998.

Other of Drucker's works have ignited interest long after their publication. In the 1973 book, *People and Performance*, he discussed the broader social responsibilities of managers and organizations – once again, this is something organizations are slowly coming to terms with. Drucker called for less hierarchical structures and leaner organizations in the 1960s and again in the 1980s before they became fashionable in the 1990s.

Drucker predicted what is now labelled post-industrialism and examined how this would impact on managerial best practice. Indeed, his recent writings have re-affirmed the radical challenges facing managers: "The single greatest challenge facing managers in the developed countries of the world is to raise the productivity of knowledge and service workers. This challenge, which will dominate the management agenda for the next several decades, will ultimately determine the competitive performance of companies. Even more important, it will determine the very fabric of society and the quality of life in every industrialized nation."[9]

Perhaps his greatest achievements are *The Practice of Management* (1954) and *Management: Tasks, Responsibilities, Practices* (1973). In the latter, a massive work, he identifies five "basic operations in the work of the manager." These are:

1 Setting objectives

2 Organizing

3 Motivating and communicating

4 Measuring

5 Developing people (including him or herself).

The length of his career and his level of book production has enabled him to extol a company's virtues and then, later, to point out how and when its virtues became liabilities. Most famously, his book *Concept of the Corporation* analyzed and celebrated GM's divisional structure – in 1991 he recognized that what had once made the company successful, its long-established management practices, was now holding it back.

Undoubtedly, Drucker's ideas have evolved – his fascination with corporations, for example, has given way to an interest in small firms and non-profit organizations. His broad brush brings in history, sociology and anthropology and, by its very nature, courts disappointment and failure. *The Economist* observed that Drucker has "a burning sense of the importance of management. He believes that poor management helped to plunge the Europe of his youth into disaster, and he fears that the scope for poor management is growing larger, as organizations become ever more complicated and interdependent."[10]

Despite such concerns, Drucker is encouraged that the emphasis is now on changing organizations to become more efficient – rather than on dragging every ounce of energy out of tired managers and employees. He also believes that globalization will produce managers who are more in tune with the needs of the global environment than politicians. Only then will managers be able to take what Drucker regards as their rightful place as the driving forces behind the great economies.

Knowledge management

The traditional basics of management were once summed up by the unspeakable acronym, POSDCORB, which stands for:

- Planning
- Organizing
- Staffing
- Directing
- Co-ordinating
- Reporting
- Budgeting.

Many, if not all, of these activities remain central to many managerial jobs. But, in addition, new managers are expected to:

- manage on an international scale
- manage cultural diversity
- respond to multiple sources of authority
- combine a variety of leadership and team roles
- act strategically
- utilize technology
- communicate internally
- communicate externally
- establish, reinforce and develop values
- act responsibly
- distill complex flows of information
- manage across functions
- manage their own careers and personal and professional development.

Mobilizing every ounce of intelligence is now the key function of management – and, perhaps, it always should have been. In the new world the skills required of managers are diverse and continuously expanding.

Holding these multifarious activities together are the concepts of **intellectual capital** and **knowledge management**. Studying how companies manage knowledge has become the height of corporate fashion. Hardly a day goes by without a conference or the publication of a book on the implications of the growth of knowledge work and its significance for managers and organizations.

> *Mobilizing every ounce of intelligence is now the key function of management – and, perhaps, it always should have been. In the new world the skills required of managers are diverse and continuously expanding.*

The rise in interest is understandable. "If Hewlett-Packard knew what it knows we'd be three times more productive," reflects H-P chief, Lew Platt.[11] In the year 2000, it is calculated, the UK will have 10 million people who could be termed knowledge workers and seven million manual workers. In the US, despite the downsizing epidemic, the numbers of managerial and professional workers has *increased* by 37 per cent since the beginning of the 1980s.

Knowledge has been codified as part of corporate life. The Swedish company, Skandia, has a "director of intellectual capital" and other companies are following suit. (Skandia's Leif Edvinsson is one of the thought leaders in this field – he has developed a model for reporting on intellectual capital based around customers, processes, renewal and development, human factors and finance.) And with the fashion come the usual demanding questions – If knowledge is the vital corporate resource, how can it be valued, measured, utilized, understood and harnessed? Also, and more disturbing, if knowledge is the vital corporate resource what happens when it is the wrong sort of knowledge or outdated knowledge? Turning bland statements about knowledge and intellectual capital into reality is a substantial challenge. Knowledge is good, but how do you create knowledge?

"Enabling knowledge will to a large extent be dependent on the energy, commitment and durability put into knowledge creation," say the academics Georg Von Krogh, Ikujiro Nonaka and Kazuo Ichijo.[12] Essential in making this happen, they argue, is the role of the "knowledge activist." This they define as "someone, some group or department that takes on particular responsibility for energizing and co-ordinating knowledge creation efforts throughout the corporation."

The activist has three roles. First, the activist is a "catalyst of knowledge creation." This involves moving around the organization prompting people, asking questions and linking people and processes together. More theoretically, the catalytic role requires the activist to "create a space, or context" for knowledge creation.

The second role of the activist is as a connector of knowledge creation initiatives. This involves seeking to replace the fragmentation of knowledge with the sharing of knowledge. Finally, the activist is a "merchant of foresight." This is a more strategic role and involves giving "overall direction to the knowledge creation happening in various micro-communities."

To some extent, the message is a very simple one: belief in the importance of knowledge creation has to be matched by concerted action to nurture and enable knowledge at every level of the organization.

Such is the corporate fashion for knowledge management and intellectual capital that the downside has been largely overlooked. Research by Booz-Allen & Hamilton consultants Charles Lucier and Janet Torsilieri concludes that most knowledge management (or equivalent) programs have limited results. Indeed they estimate that "about one-sixth of these programs achieve very significant impact within the first two years; half achieve small but important benefits; and the remaining third – the failures – have little business impact."[13]

All is not lost. Lucier and Torsilieri say that their experience suggests that the less successful programs tend to be afflicted with four common problems which can be resolved. First, there are those who board the bandwagon caring little about its destination. They have "general aspirations like share best practices or stimulate collaboration" but no real aim. The second problem is that of "incomplete program architecture" – this means applying principles piecemeal and not taking advantage of links between different parts of the organization. The third pitfall is "insufficient focus upon one or two strategic priorities" and, finally, comes the all too frequent lament that top managers back the idea but don't actually involve themselves in making it happen. Clearly, if knowledge management is to make the leap into more general practice, greater understanding of its broad implications is required.

Key books

Edvinsson, Leif, and Malone, Michael, *Intellectual Capital*, Harper Business, New York, 1997

Klein, David A (editor), *The Strategic Management of Intellectual Capital*, Butterworth-Heinemann, Oxford, 1997

Roos, Johan (editor), *Intellectual Capital*, New York University Press, New York, 1998

Stewart, Thomas A, *Intellectual Capital*, Doubleday, New York, 1997

Decision theory

New world of management or not, on one aspect all are agreed: decision making is a vital part of managerial work no matter what you do or where you are.

Little wonder, therefore, that an entire academic discipline, decision science, is devoted to understanding management decision making. Much of it is built on the foundations set down by early business thinkers who believed that under a given set of circumstances human behavior was logical and therefore predictable. The fundamental belief of the likes of Frederick Taylor and computer pioneer, Charles Babbage, was that the decision process (and many other things) could be rationalized and systematized. Based on this premise, models emerged to explain the workings of commerce which, it was thought, could be extended to cover the way in which decisions were made.

The belief in "Decision Theory" persists. Indeed, most management books and ideas are inextricably linked to helping managers make better decisions. There is now a profusion of models, software packages and analytical tools which seek to distill decision making into a formula. Decision-making models assume that the distilled mass of experience will enable people to make accurate decisions. They enable you to learn from other peoples' experiences. Many promise the world. Feed in your particular circumstances and out will pop an answer. The danger is in concluding that the solution provided by a software package is *the* answer.

Whether in a software package or buried in a textbook, decision theorizing suggests that effective decision making involves a number of logical stages. This is referred to as the "rational model of decision making" or the "synoptic model." The latter involves a series of steps – identifying the problem; clarifying the problem; prioritizing goals; generating options; evaluating options (using appropriate analysis); comparing predicted outcomes of each option with the goals; and choosing the option which best matches the goals.

Such models rely on a number of assumptions about the way in which people will behave when confronted with a set of circumstances. These assumptions allow mathematicians to derive formulae based on probability theory. These decision-making tools include such things as cost/benefit analysis which aims to help managers evaluate different options.

Alluring though they are, the trouble with such theories is that reality is often more confused and messy than a neat model can allow for. Underpinning the mathematical approach are a number of flawed assumptions – such as that decision making is consistent; based on accurate information; free from emotion or prejudice; and rational. Another obvious drawback to any decision-making model is that identifying what you need to make a decision about is often more important than the actual decision itself. If a decision seeks to solve a problem, it may be the right decision but the wrong problem.

The reality is that managers make decisions based on a combination of intuition, experience and analysis. As intuition and experience are impossible to measure in any sensible way, the temptation is to focus on the analytical side of decision making, the science rather than the mysterious art. (The entire management consultancy industry is based on reaching decisions through analysis.) Of course, the manager in the real world does not care whether he or she is practising an art or science. What they do care about is solving problems and reaching reliable, well-informed decisions.

> *The reality is that managers make decisions based on a combination of intuition, experience and analysis. As intuition and experience are impossible to measure in any sensible way, the temptation is to focus on the analytical side of decision making, the science rather than the mysterious art.*

This does not mean that decision theory is redundant or that decision-making models should be cast to one side. Indeed, a number of factors mean that decision making is becoming ever more demanding. The growth in complexity means that companies no longer encounter simple problems. And that complex decisions are now not simply the preserve of the most senior managers but the responsibility of many others in organizations. In addition, managers are having to deal with a flood of information – a 1996 survey by Reuters of 1200 managers worldwide found that 43 per cent thought that important decisions were delayed and their ability to make decisions affected as a result of having too much information.

These factors suggest that any techniques, models or analytical techniques which enable managers to make more informed decisions more quickly will be in increasing demand. In the past models were the domain of economists and strategists. Now, there is increasing use of decision support systems. Some show the best types of decisions for a given situation. Typically, these involve how best to use resources. An oil refinery, for example, may use a support system to determine on a daily basis what is the optimum product that it should produce. Airlines run similar programs to establish optimum pricing levels. Other systems aim to yield increasingly better decisions based on past results. These learning-based models allow companies to take the data they have collected and any analysis they have undertaken and gather it up in one place directly related to the decision.

There is little doubt that decision theory and the use of such models is reassuring. They lend legitimacy to decisions which may be based on prejudices or hunches. But the usefulness of decision-making models remains a leap of faith. None is foolproof as none is universally applicable. And none can yet cope with the wilful idiosyncrasies of human behavior.

Key books

Baron, Jonathan, *Thinking and Deciding*, Cambridge University Press, Cambridge, 1994 (2nd edition)

Dearlove, Des, *Key Management Decisions*, FT Pitman, London, 1997

French, Simon, *Decision Theory: An Introduction to the Mathematics of Rationality*, Ellis Horwood and John Wiley, New York, 1988

Keeney, Ralph L, *Value-Focused Thinking: A Path to Creative Decision Making*, Harvard University Press, Boston, 1992

Richards, Max D, and **Greenlaw, Paul S**, *Management Decision Making*, Richard D Irwin Inc., Homewood, Illinois, 1966

Yates, J Frank, *Judgement and Decision Making*, Prentice Hall, Englewood Cliffs, New Jersey, 1990

References: The new world of management

1 Lawler, Edward, "New logic is here to stay," *Financial Times*, 28 January 1994.

2 Hamel, Gary, *Foreword* to *Financial Times Handbook of Management*, FT/Pitman, London, 1995.

3 Drucker, Peter, "The new productivity challenge," *Harvard Business Review*, November–December 1991.

4 Allen, Louis A, *Professional Management: New Concepts and Proven Practices*, McGraw-Hill, Maidenhead, 1973.

5 Quoted in Caulkin, Simon, "The boy from Brazil," *The Observer*, 17 October 1993.

6 Mintzberg, Henry, *The Nature of Managerial Work*, Prentice Hall, New Jersey, 1973.

7 Tan, JH, "Management work in Singapore: developing a factor model," Henley Management College/Brunel University, 1994.

8 Quoted in *The Observer*, 6 November 1994.

9 Drucker, Peter F, "The new productivity challenge," *Harvard Business Review*, November–December 1991.

10 "Peter Drucker, salvationist," *The Economist*, 1 October 1994.

11 Dearlove, Des, "Backing the grey matter," *MBA*, March 1998.

12 Von Krogh, Georg, Nonaka, Ikujiro and Ichijo, Kazuo, "Develop knowledge activists!," *European Management Journal*, Vol. 15, No. 5, October 1997.

13 Lucier, Charles and Torsilieri, Janet, "Why knowledge programs fail," *Strategy & Business*, Fourth Quarter 1997.

The new world
of organizations

"*It is not necessary for any one department to know what any other department is doing. It is the business of those who plan the entire work to see that all of the departments are working... towards the same end.*"

Henry Ford

"*Any company that cannot imagine the future won't be around to enjoy it.*"

Gary Hamel and CK Prahalad

The rise and fall of the functional organization

Practical use of Taylor's "scientific management," built around specialization and the division of labor, reached a high point with the advent of the mass production line with workers performing repetitive tasks on a mammoth scale. Management followed similar structures with different functions – such as marketing, sales, R&D and production – being ruthlessly separated.

Mass production techniques reaped impressive early dividends. **Henry Ford** (1863–1947), the arch exponent of the art, generated a huge fortune built on the increased productivity brought by mass production. Ford believed that managers should work in isolation, unencumbered by the problems of their colleagues, simply concentrating on what they are employed to do.

While Ford is routinely lauded as the man who brought the world mass production lines, his idiosyncratic career (from boy racer to multi-millionaire anti-war campaigner), as well as his many barbed observations, tend to be forgotten. There was, however, more to Ford than flow lines, workers doing mindlessly repetitive tasks and the ubiquitous Model T.

Marketing guru, Ted Levitt has argued that Ford's genius actually lay in marketing, not manufacturing. Ford first decided that the world was ready for an affordable car; and then that mass production techniques were the only way of providing it. Instead of controlling costs to produce lower prices, Ford set the price and challenged the organization to ensure costs were low enough to meet the figure.

Ford's masterly piece of marketing lay in his intuitive realization that the middle-class car market existed – it just remained for him to provide the products the market wanted. In management jargon, Ford stuck to the knitting. Model Ts were black, straightforward and affordable. "I have no use for a motor car which has more spark plugs than a cow has teats," said Ford. The trouble was that, when other manufacturers added extras, Ford kept it simple and dramatically lost ground. The man with a genius for marketing lost touch with the aspirations of customers.

Even now, Ford's achievements remain impressive. He built his first car in 1896; started his own company in 1903; and between 1908 and 1927 produced 15 million Model Ts. In 1920 Ford was making a car a minute.

Compare this with the approach of Ford's predecessors. The first car makers, such as France's Panhard et Levassor, employed a small number of skilled craftsmen. The cars they produced were unique – almost prototypes – with parts being filed and cut to make them fit. As the parts were of varying sizes, craftsmanship was required.

Ford brought in uniform and interchangeable parts. Skill departed and, instead, production was based round strict functional divides – demarcations. Ford believed in people getting on with their jobs and not raising their heads above functional parapets. He didn't want engineers talking to salespeople, or people making decisions without his say so. Management and managers he dismissed as largely unnecessary.

Ford believed in people getting on with their jobs and not raising their heads above functional parapets. He didn't want engineers talking to salespeople, or people making decisions without his say so. Management and managers he dismissed as largely unnecessary.

At the center of Ford's thinking was the aim of standardization – something continually emphasized by the car makers of today though they talk in terms of quality, and Ford in quantity.

While Ford will never be celebrated for his people management skills, he had an international perspective which was ahead of his time. His plant at Highland Park, Detroit, produced and the world – not just the US – bought. In addition, Ford introduced the $5 daily wage and was acutely aware that time was an important competitive weapon – "Time waste differs from material waste in that there can be no salvage," he observed.

"In some respects Ford remains a good role model," says Ray Wild, principal of Henley Management College. "He was an improviser and innovator, he borrowed ideas and then adapted and synthesized them. He developed flow lines that involved people; now, we have flow lines without people, but no one questions their relevance or importance. Though he is seen as having de-humanized work, it shouldn't be forgotten that he provided a level of wealth for workers and products for consumers which weren't previously available."[1]

Practitioner

HENRY FORD

1863–1947

American

Car maker

Career: Started his own company in 1903; the Model T was launched in 1908; in 1919 he resigned as company President with Edsel Ford taking over.

Books: *My Life and Work*, Doubleday Page & Co, New York, 1923.

Down the functional tunnel

The "science" of mass production – ruthlessly satirized by Charlie Chaplin in *Modern Times* – brought with it worker alienation, a lack of coordination between different functions and a complete absence of flexibility. Any sense of individual responsibility was sucked away by the system. Imaginations were never stretched; intelligence was not developed. But it made a lot of cars at affordable prices and provided the foundations for the emergence of a new corporate world.

It was – ironically enough – Adam Smith who identified the potential problem of mass production. "A man who spends his life carrying out a small number of very simple operations with perhaps the same effects has no room to develop his intelligence or to stretch his imagination so as to look for ways of overcoming difficulties which never occur. He thereby loses quite naturally the habit of using these faculties and, in general, he becomes as stupid and ignorant as it is possible for a human being to become."

Though the production line model of Henry Ford is disappearing and arguments over demarcation no longer fill the headlines, its legacy persists. Even in fashionably downsized, lean and flat organizations, there is likely to be an unhealthy quota of controllers, overseers and supervisors. Middle managers, planners and accountants have established themselves as middle men between technology and implementation. Technology, brought in to reduce complexity, has more often than not brought with it teams of managers each intent on finding or creating their own place in the corporate order.

Over the last 20 years great strides have been made in eradicating Taylorism from the factory floor. Management demarcations have, however, usually emerged unscathed.

Skeptics may argue that the functional organization works. Undoubtedly, it does. Companies have been organized along functional lines throughout the twentieth century. They have not failed, but they have worked inefficiently.

Skeptics may argue that the functional organization works. Undoubtedly, it does. Companies have been organized along functional lines throughout the twentieth century. They have not failed, but they have worked inefficiently.

The central problems of functional organizations are as follows:

1 **Goal setting** – functional organizations set goals that are functional rather than business oriented. This means that groups of people in different functions have their own alternative targets and *raison d'être*. There may be overall corporate strategies and objectives, but they are effectively relegated in importance. A manager working in a functional organization first and foremost requires that his or her function succeeds. Performance bonuses are usually related to divisional performance and managers are well aware that functions which succeed attract resources and the most talented people. The end result is that the performance of different functions within the same organization is often desperately uneven.

2 **Senior to junior process steps** – a business process often passes from one hierarchical level to another as it moves from one function to another. Frequently, a junior person needs input from

a senior manager – perhaps a signature or some other task – and in most of these cases the senior manager fails to take the work seriously. They may delay the work in preference to other work, even if the customer needs it urgently, or may make errors which the junior person has to correct.

3 **Narrow job definitions** – harnessed by the restraints of their particular function, staff are overly specialized. The language used in one function may be unfamiliar or obscure to another. Usually the concepts they hold dear are at odds with the pragmatic demands of customers. Because of this they are unable to react to increasingly diverse customer needs. Instead of maximizing the potential of people, a functional organization denies it. As a result, people become bored and frustrated, which leads to a higher staff turnover. Job definitions strongly reflect the functional nature of the organization. There are few jobs – apart from chief executive – which bridge the gap between different functions (and the chief executive may well have a specialized functional background). Job titles are unlikely to include the word "customer." Those that do are vested with little in the way of power or seniority.

4 **Avoiding responsibility** – in functional organizations customer service is not usually the responsibility of any one person. Any problems or customer queries spanning more than one department are passed on and on. Alternatively, problems are identified in purely functional terms – there is a problem with sales or an accounting problem. Identified in functional isolation they are solved in a similar style. Within one particular organization some salesmen personally looked after several hundred customers and an engineer typically handled around 100. Responsibility was effectively diluted until very little existed.

5 **Complex communication** – the functional organization is often characterized by Byzantine communication chains. Paper passes back and forth between departments. Delays are inevitable as in-trays become more full and customers more irate. The entire process is time consuming and inflexible.

6 **Corporate Bermuda Triangles** – in the Pacific Ocean there may well be no such thing as the Bermuda Triangle. In corporate *terra firma* its existence is more easily established. Functional

organizations often have stages of the process where no one has been assigned responsibility. Because processes tend to move to and fro between functions they remain unmanaged.

One chief executive said that an important part of his job was identifying who has responsibility for what in his organization. He found that managers were in the habit of passing things on to him when they were unsure of whose domain they belonged to. By abdicating responsibility the managers believed they had solved the problem. The chief executive then had to decide who should take responsibility for the particular issue. In effect he found himself in charge of the Bermuda Triangle.

While the functional organization appears to offer clarity of responsibility, in practice it often overlooks the grey areas between different functions where no one takes responsibility.

7 **Self-perpetuation** – as new functions and divisions are added to the basic functional structure, the old ones are never replaced. A company may have functional divisions as well as product divisions and, quite possibly, geographic, national, strategic and market-driven splits between different activities.

There is nothing new in revealing the inadequacies and limitations of vertical and functional structures. They have been recognized for a number of years, but attempts at breaking them down have tended to be isolated and short term. Companies have turned to temporary project teams, task forces and various alternative matrices at times of crisis or to tackle specific localized problems. Once the problem was solved, they resorted to their old ways, continuing to gloss over the fundamental problem.

Functional organizations inevitably produce functional solutions to their problems. Functional organizations produce functional managers. Managers become hidebound by managing things rather than getting them done.

In his book *Administrative Behavior,* Herbert Simon summed up this process and coined a phrase for it: "satisficing" – settling for adequate instead of optimal solutions.[2] This is an in-built characteristic of the conventional functional organization. Past strategy is fused with current organizational culture, so that people begin to believe that they know how things are done and stop questioning the assumptions behind their thoughts and actions. The recipe for success takes over and doubts about the company's ability to actually deliver success are automatically repressed. Success once bred success. Now, corporations are increasingly aware that success can breed complacency and then failure.

Alfred P Sloan
Antidotes to functional failure

While the deficiencies of the functional approach were soon apparent, solutions to the problems it raised have proved perennially elusive. The first concerted attempt at creating an antidote to straight functionalism was carried out by **Alfred P Sloan** (1875–1966) at General Motors. Sloan took what Ford had achieved on the factory floor and sought to apply it to managers and the organization as a whole.

Sloan's sole contribution to management literature is *My Years at General Motors*. Published in 1963, it is a one-paced, intricate account of how Sloan managed GM. Today, it appears dated – GM employees, for example, are generally conspicuous by their absence. Sloan was not an up-tempo evangelist with a pithy catch-phrase and a store of witty anecdotes and yet, the book is among the most important in management and Sloan one of the most influential managers of the century.

"His book is one thing, what he did at GM is quite another," says London Business School's Sumantra Ghoshal. "Sloan created a new organizational form – the multi-divisional form – which became a doctrine of management. Today, it is not ascribed to him, but Sloan was its instigator."[3]

Sloan became president of GM in 1923, chairman in 1946 and honorary chairman from 1956 until his death. When he took over, GM was struggling to hold its own as Ford, with its Model T, swept all aside. He set about revitalizing and reorganizing GM along "federal" lines, the very antithesis of the way Ford organized itself. He replaced GM's messy, bureaucratic, centralized system with one based on divisions, each with its own clearly delineated responsibilities. Over 30 divisions, further divided into groups, emerged. Instead of fighting for dominance, separate functions were treated as equals. In the marketplace, GM's products – including

Chevrolet and Cadillac – competed as separate divisions coming up with rapid model changes and added extras.

Practitioner

ALFRED P SLOAN

1875–1966

American

Car company executive

Career: General manager Hyatt Roller Bearing Co.; director, vice president, chief executive and honorary chairman, General Motors 1917–66.

Books: *My Years with General Motors*, Doubleday, New York, 1963.

Much of the current debate about being both local and global can be traced back to Sloan's delicate balancing act between the twin forces of decentralization and centralization. Sloan's triumph was in achieving a balance over so many years.

> *Much of the current debate about being both local and global can be traced back to Sloan's delicate balancing act between the twin forces of decentralization and centralization. Sloan's triumph was in achieving a balance over so many years.*

The decentralized structure proved the making of GM. By the late 1970s its US market share was over 45 per cent, compared to a relatively meager 12 per cent when Sloan took over in the 1920s. The federal structure meant that instead of concerning themselves with the nitty-gritty of production, executives could turn their energies to ensuring that divisions met their performance targets and to providing overall direction. GM's fortunes revived and Sloan began to meet his aim of providing a car for "every purse and every purpose."

Sloan believed senior managers had three functions: to decide on the company's strategy; to design its structure and select its control systems.

The new GM became venerated as a model of management. Its admirers included Peter Drucker and the economic historian, **Alfred Chandler** (born 1918). Chandler's important book, *Strategy and Structure* (1962) studied major US corporations between 1850 and 1920. At that time strategy was generally neglected – indeed, Chandler sparked interest in the subject. He argued that strategy came first and then organizations had to determine the most appropriate structure to deliver the strategy.

M Form

The organization of companies along multi-divisional lines seeking to combine the best of centralization and decentralization. This creates the need for strategic skills among managers at the center.

In practice, troubles emerged with the multi-divisional system. It was built around a vast web of committees and groups which became bogged down in their own power struggles and bureaucracy. Stringent targets and narrow measures of success stultified initiative. Also, by the 1960s the delicate balance was lost – finance emerged as the dominant function – and GM became paralyzed by what had once made it great.

Sloan's approach is now regarded as too inflexible and cumbersome to work effectively. "It was right for the 1970s, a growing handicap in the 1980s and it would have been a ticket to the bone-yard in the 1990s," caustically observed GE chairman Jack Welch.[4]

But that does not mean that Sloan's approach is dead. His legacy lives on – the multi-divisional organization remains dominant. In the 1980s it was estimated that 85 per cent of large corporations had adopted the multi-divisional structure.

Key books

Chandler, Alfred D, *Strategy and Structure*, MIT Press, Boston, 1962

Chandler, Alfred D, *The Visible Hand: The Managerial Revolution in American Business*, Harvard University Press, Cambridge, 1977

Chandler, Alfred D, and **Deams, H** (editors), *Managerial Hierarchies*, Harvard University Press, Cambridge, 1980

The life and death of organizations

While their approaches fundamentally differed, Ford and Sloan helped cement the predominant role of the corporation in society. The big company became the bastion of capitalism. "Economy, stability, and absence of friction are striking characteristics of large corporations," concluded King Gillette. Big corporations inspired confidence. What was good for General Motors really was believed to be good for the United States. The Fortune 500, the prestigious ranking of companies, became the corporate benchmark.

Study after study has sought to understand what it is that makes companies successful. Tom Peters and Robert Waterman's *In Search of Excellence* (1982) concluded that "excellent" companies:

- had a bias for action
- were close to the customer
- had autonomy and entrepreneurship
- believed in productivity through people
- were hands-on and value driven
- stuck to the knitting
- had a simple form and a lean staff
- had simultaneous loose-tight properties.

Other examinations of corporate success and longevity have followed. Perhaps the most convincing are Jerry Porras and James Collins' *Built to Last* (1995), Jeffrey Pfeffer's *The Human Equation* (1998) and Arie de Geus' *The Living Company* (1997).

"Built to last"[5]

Stanford's Jerry Porras and James Collins argue that companies with vision are the ones which achieve the much sought after longevity. The most successful companies are industry leaders; admired by business people; with long-serving CEOs who manage succession. The companies identified by Porras and Collins are largely predictable: including IBM, Merck, Motorola, Disney, Hewlett-Packard and 3M. Success stories are compared to those who failed to stand the tests of time so well – Columbia Pictures vs Disney; McDonnell-Douglas vs Boeing; Zenith vs Motorola.

> **Collins and Porras argue that a charismatic leader is not an essential ingredient in creating a visionary company. Indeed, some of the corporate leaders are plain boring.**

Porras and Collins' companies have outperformed the general stock market by over 15 times since 1926. Along the way, the companies have flown in the face of managerial mythology. First, Collins and Porras argue that a charismatic leader is not an essential ingredient in creating a visionary company. Indeed, some of the corporate leaders are plain boring. A charismatic figurehead can, they say, actually count against long-term success.

The second myth is that of hiring talent from outside. The companies featured in *Built to Last* repeatedly recruit their leaders from inside the organization. Spending your entire career with one company is unfashionable, but the best companies make it worthwhile to do so. When Jack Welch, homegrown at GE, replaced Reg Jones as company CEO in 1981, there were many doubters. The move paid off, and is typical of the faith visionary companies have in their own talent.

The third myth attacked by Porras and Collins is that of visionary companies being innately conservative. Instead, they say that visionary companies are driven by "Big Hairy Audacious Goals." They think big and are highly ambitious. They are also more attuned to risk taking than many suspect. Experimentation and trial and error are commonplace.

Perhaps the most important myths exploded by Porras and Collins are these:

- long-term successful companies are not totally driven by profits. Their *raison d'être* is not purely financial;

- visionary companies have strong values but they don't all have the same strong values. There is no universal set of values which can be put in place to ensure success;

- success does not emerge from one great idea. Many begin with a setback. The great idea theory of corporate success is a mirage.

"The Human Equation"[6]

To some, the answer is simple: companies succeed because of their people. Therefore, how they nurture and manage those people is the secret to corporate longevity. The most recent proponent of this argument is Jeffrey Pfeffer. Pfeffer's research suggests that success is not necessarily related to the industry you are in or whether it is a fast growing industry. Similarly, Pfeffer's research suggests that size is not the dominant factor. Even getting the right strategy is not that important. "Finding the answer is relatively easy; doing the answer is frequently impossible," notes one executive. Downsizing is also not the answer – "Downsizing will do only one thing: make the organization smaller."[7]

Instead, Pfeffer (also from Stanford) proposes that people and leadership are key. In particular, there are "three basic principles that leaders use to transform their organizations to a high-commitment model of management." First, they build trust. "You cannot build trust without treating people with respect and dignity," he says. Trust also demands that organizational values are meaningful and adhered to.

The second requirement is that leaders must encourage change. To do so, they must pay homage to and learn from companies such as Southwest Airlines which have enshrined change in all of their activities. Leaders must break habits by changing the way the company is organized – even changing office layouts promotes a climate of change.

The final ingredient is that leaders must measure what matters. "Most financial reporting systems provide tremendous detail about what has happened, but much less information about the organization's present condition or the reasons for its performance," notes Pfeffer. Measuring personal performance against the number of hours spent in training or accurately measuring job applications provides useful insights. (Southwest Airlines processes a massive 120 000 job applications a year – it wants to recruit the best possible workforce.)

> *"Leaders build systems – systems that build distinctive competence and capability and that, because of their internal coherence, are robust even as the competitive landscape and the macroeconomic environment change," Pfeffer writes.*

Success demands that leaders take on new roles. "Leaders build systems – systems that build distinctive competence and capability and that, because of their internal coherence, are robust even as the competitive landscape and the macroeconomic environment change," Pfeffer writes.

"The Living Company"[8]

For Arie de Geus, the corporation is a vital institution. The ultimate corporate man, de Geus spent 38 years with Royal Dutch/Shell. Such loyalty runs in the family – de Geus' father also worked for the company for 26 years.

The more de Geus examined the body corporate, the more he became concerned about its life expectancy. Companies may be legal entities, but they are disturbingly mortal. "The natural average lifespan of a corporation should be as long as two or three centuries," writes de Geus, noting a few prospering relics such as the Sumitomo Group and the Scandinavian company, Stora. But the reality is that companies do not head off into the Florida sunset to play bingo. They usually die young.

De Geus quotes a Dutch survey of corporate life expectancy in Japan and Europe which came up with 12.5 years as the average life expectancy of all firms. "The average life expectancy of a multinational corporation – Fortune 500 or its equivalent – is between 40 and 50 years," says de Geus, noting that one third of 1970s' Fortune 500 had disappeared by 1983. Such endemic failure is attributed by de Geus to the focus of managers on profits and the bottom line rather than the human community which makes up their organization.

In an attempt to get to the bottom of this mystery, de Geus and a number of his Shell colleagues carried out some research to identify the characteristics of corporate longevity. As you would expect, the onus is on keeping excitement to a minimum. More Ronald Reagan than James Dean. The average human centurion advocates a life of abstinence, caution and moderation, and so it is with companies. The Royal Dutch/Shell team identified four key characteristics. The long-lived were "sensitive to their environment"; "cohesive, with a strong sense of identity"; "tolerant"; and "conservative in financing."

Key to de Geus' entire argument is that there is more to companies – and to longevity – than mere money making. "The dichotomy between profits and longevity is false," he says. His logic is impeccably straightforward. Capital is no longer king; the skills, capabilities and knowledge of people are. The corollary from this is that "a successful company is one that can learn effectively." Learning is tomorrow's capital. In de Geus' eyes, learning means being prepared to accept continuous change.

Here, de Geus provides the new deal: contemporary corporate man or woman must understand that the corporation will, and must, change and it can only change if its community of people changes also. Individuals must change and the way they change is through learning. As a result, de Geus believes that senior executives must dedicate a great deal of time nurturing their people. He recalls spending around a quarter of his time on the development and placement of people.

> *de Geus believes that senior executives must dedicate a great deal of time nurturing their people. He recalls spending around a quarter of his time on the development and placement of people.*

According to de Geus, all corporate activities are grounded in two hypotheses: "the company is a living being" and "the decisions for action made by this living being result from a learning process."

The Living Company proposes that the wisdom of the past be appreciated and utilized rather than cast out in some cultural revolution. Contrast this with reengineering which (as practised, if not necessarily preached) sought to dismiss the past so that the future could be begun anew with a fresh piece of paper. De Geus suggests that the piece of paper already exists and notes are constantly being scrawled in the margins as new insights are added.

While de Geus and Porras and Collins have produced eloquent testimonies to what allows companies to achieve long-term prosperity, the basis of some of their arguments is open to increasing debate on a number of fronts.

First, is corporate longevity automatically a good thing? De Geus' arguments are probably at their weakest when he contemplates why it is that companies deserve to live long lives. After all, the average entrepreneur would probably accept a life expectancy of 12.5 years. "Like all organisms, the living company exists primarily for its own survival and improvement: to fulfil its potential and to become as great as it can be," writes de Geus. But life is littered with failed stars. Some fall by the wayside. We can't all be great. We can't all be Shell.

De Geus admits to surprise when asked "Why is it so important that Shell should survive?" De Geus' response is telling: "To me it was so natural that companies should seek their own survival. I had seen nothing else in my life. Companies struggle to keep going and to grow, for as long as possible." He rightly describes the human implications of a company's death and says that "People do, in fact, mourn when a company dies." The question must be what it is that they are mourning? Is it the salary; the security of work; the camaraderie; the power; or the work itself?

Andrew Campell of the Ashridge Strategic Management Center provides a characteristically robust riposte. He suggests that we have become preoccupied with creating immortal organizations rather than ones which work in the present. "Why do we want organizations to thrive for ever?" he asks. "On average organizations survive for less time than the working life of an individual. They become dysfunctional and, at that point, they should be killed off. What is encouraging is that, first through management buy-outs and now through demergers, we are becoming more adept at bringing an end to corporate lives which have run their course and creating new organizations in their place."[9] Or, as Peter Drucker has put it: "The Fortune 500 is over."

The new organizational model

The organization is changing. In a *Harvard Business Review* article, Larry Hirschhorn and Thomas Gilmore of the Wharton Center for Applied Research potently announced the new reality: "New technologies, fast-changing markets, and global competition are revolutionizing business relationships. As companies blur their traditional boundaries to respond to this more fluid business environment, the roles that people play at work and the tasks they perform become correspondingly blurred and ambiguous. However, just because work roles are no longer defined by the formal organizational structure doesn't mean that differences in authority, skill, talent and perspective simply disappear."[10]

Contemporary business organizations are shaped by the new facts of corporate life. First, hierarchies have spawned greater costs rather than improved productivity or higher quality products and services. The vast numbers of middle and junior managers are recognized by a growing number of organizations as a costly indulgence.

The most obvious side effect of the burdensome hierarchy is the slow speed of decision making. If every decision has to be filtered through ten lines of hierarchy, no decision is likely to be quick. In the past this was not a significant impediment to commercial success. In the 1960s and 1970s companies did not have to move quickly – markets were there, usually national in nature, and evolving at a slow pace. Now, with emphasis on the speed of product development and delivery, it is crucial that decisions are immediate. For example, 3M requires that 30 per cent of each of its unit's sales must be generated by products introduced in the last four years.

The obvious conclusion, drawn by companies throughout the world, is that layers of management need to be eradicated. Instead of pyramids of middle managers rarely communicating with one another, the onus is on project teams and cross-functional working.

IT enables managers to communicate more effectively than ever before.

Behind this is the inescapable impact of Information Technology (IT). IT enables managers to communicate more effectively than ever before. It is not constrained by hierarchical structures. Instead, it allows managers to cut through hierarchy to communicate with the people they need to communicate with, no matter where they are positioned in the organization – geographically or hierarchically. As many middle management jobs had become ones of filtering and directing information, they are effectively redundant.

Times are changing. But that does not mean that managers are necessarily moving as quickly as the trends which engulf them.

Though these trends and events have brought things to a head, the new organizational model is not an overnight phenomenon. "Organizations are a system of co-operative activities – and their co-ordination requires something intangible and personal that is largely a matter of relationships," observed Chester Barnard in the 1930s.[11]

Indeed, in the early 1960s, the British sociologist **Tom Burns** was one of the earliest thinkers to produce a coherent argument against the commonly accepted practices of mass production and organizations based around self-perpetuating bureaucracy. His 1961 book, *The Management of Innovation* (written with the psychologist, GM Stalker), concluded that the Weber-inspired bureaucratic machine was severely limited by the fact that it simply could not cope with changes in the internal or external environment. Burns and Stalker propounded an **organic organization**. Though it retains a ring of the 1960s, their organizational model contains many of the characteristics of the new model organization of the late 1990s.

Organic organization

An organizational model, developed by Burns and Stalker, which emphasizes "networks," shared vision and values, team working which crosses functions and effective sharing of knowledge and expertise.

For all its farsighted merits, Burns and Stalker's book met with a general and resounding silence – though it has now been reissued. Its ideas are important and have, during the last decade, reemerged as the deficiencies of previous organizational models have become increasingly recognized.

There are a growing number of radical role models. From traditional "heavy" industry, two star performers are repeatedly celebrated for their organizational dexterity – see General Electric and ABB below.

General Electric

In the US the modern blueprint for the organizational revolution can be seen at General Electric (GE). When Jack Welch became chief executive in 1981, the company was cumbersome and under-performing. Welch has since succeeded in overhauling and realigning it in a way which few thought possible. Between 1981 and 1990, GE cut the average number of management layers between Welch and the very front line from nine to four. Its headquarters was slashed from 2100 people to fewer than 1000. The number of senior executives across the company was cut, first from 700 to 500, and between 1990 and 1994 by another 100. The overall workforce was almost halved, from 404 000 to 220 000. Yet GE's revenues more than doubled through this period, from $27 billion to $60 billion.

Welch has stripped hierarchies away. When he took on the top job an average of five or six people reported to each manager. By the late 1980s this average had doubled and is now at about 14 – with some units reaching 25 or more. With more people to manage, managers have to manage in a different way using new skills and, increasingly, enabling others to do jobs once the sole preserve of management.

ABB

While Jack Welch and GE have grabbed the attention in the United States, Europe's benchmark of the new organizational model is the Swedish-Swiss conglomerate, Asea Brown Boveri (ABB).

The genesis of ABB began in 1987 when Percy Barnevik, at the time chief executive of the Swedish engineering group, ASEA, announced what was then the world's largest cross-border merger between ASEA and the Swiss company, Brown Boveri. ABB went on to acquire over 70 more companies, assembling a corporate monster worth $30 billion.

Barnevik – and successor Goran Lindahl – rigorously rooted out and extinguished any vestiges of bureaucracy with a rule that 30 per cent of central staff could be spun off into separate and independent profit centers; another 30 per cent could be transferred to the operational companies as part of their overhead; another 30 per cent eliminated as superfluous to requirements and the remaining 10 per cent could be kept on as the minimum required. At ASEA, Barnevik reduced the number of employees at head office from 2000 to 200.

ABB's revolution was based round a number of simple precepts:

- **Identify the skills required of executives and identify a small number of key executives** – (250 in ABB's case) to carry changes through.
- **Emphasize and practice open communication** – the ABB values – meeting customer needs, decentralization, taking action, respecting an ethic, and cooperating – were reinforced through intensive in-house programs of executive education. The prime values were acknowledged as meeting customer needs and decentralization. ABB emphasized human contact – what Goran Lindahl has labelled "human engineering."
- **Eliminate head office bureaucracy** – Barnevik reduced ABB's head office to 150 people.
- **Develop a matrix structure** – with its 250 top managers, ABB split itself into a federation of 5000 profit centers with defined product segments. Alongside this was a Top Management Council (70 executives who meet three times a year) and the Konzernleitung (Lindahl and seven others).

The matrix sought to utilize the company's global presence with local knowledge and speed. It confronted one of the great paradoxes of contemporary business. "ABB is an organization with three internal contradictions. We want to be global and local, big and small, and radically decentralized with centralized reporting and control. If we resolve these contradictions we create real organizational advantage," said Barnevik.[12]

The final phrase – "organizational advantage" – sums up the aims of the emerging new model organization. Instead of regarding structure as a means to an end – increased production – how a corporation organizes itself can have an impact on all aspects of its performance and its values. Interpreted in such a way, it becomes an infinitely more dynamic process than a pyramid-shaped chart on an office wall.

> *Instead of regarding structure as a means to an end – increased production – how a corporation organizes itself can have an impact on all aspects of its performance and its values.*

Seven habits of the new organization

1 **Flexible and free flowing** – "Tomorrow's effective organization will be conjured up anew each day," says Tom Peters in *Liberation Management*.[13]

2 **Non-hierarchical** – hierarchies have not disappeared and, indeed, they are unlikely to ever do so. But they have been reduced and organizations have become leaner and fitter. They will have to continue this process if they are to compete in the future.

3 **Based on participation** – managers don't have all the best ideas. The new organization recognizes this – and has managers who recognize it. It seeks out ideas and feedback from everyone – inside and outside the organization.

4 **Creative and entrepreneurial** – "The entrepreneurial process drives the opportunity seeking, externally focused ability of the organization to create new businesses," say Sumantra Ghoshal and Christopher Bartlett, authors of *The Individualized Corporation*.

5 **Based round networks** – Andy Grove, chief executive of Intel, has compared his business "to the theater business in New York, which has an itinerant workforce of actors, directors, writers and technicians as well as experienced financial backers... By tapping into this network, you can quickly put a production together. It might be a smash hit... or it might be panned by the critics. Inevitably the number of long-running plays is small, but new creative ideas keep bubbling up."

6 **Driven by corporate goals** – rather than narrowly defined functional ones.

7 **Utilize technology as a key resource** – the new organization brings technology into the mainstream rather than regarding it as the preserve of commercially naive geeks.

Key books

Ghoshal, Sumantra and **Bartlett, Christopher**, *The Individualized Corporation*, Harvard Business School Press, Boston, 1997

March, James G and **Simon, Herbert A**, *Organizations*, John Wiley, New York, 1958

Pugh, DS (editor), *Organization Theory, Selected Readings*, Penguin, London, 1990

Waterman, Robert, *The Frontiers of Excellence*, Nicholas Brealey, London, 1994

Weber, Max, *The Theory of Social and Economic Organization*, Oxford University Press, New York, 1947

Charles Handy
Shaping the future

Among the thinkers shaping the new organization is Charles Handy, one of the few European management thinkers to have been elevated to the heady status of guru. The publication of *The Age of Unreason* (1989), *The Empty Raincoat* (1994) and *The Hungry Spirit* (1997), have cemented his reputation, gaining worldwide attention. His work is increasingly philosophical rather than restricted to the confines of management or organizational behaviour. It is marked by a humane disaffection with how organizations are run and managed. Handy argues that the very nature of organizations and of managerial work needs to be radically altered if organizations and people are to prosper and develop in the future.

Handy's reputation has grown throughout a career which has taken him from Shell International to London Business School and now as a freelance luminary, writing and thinking. "Most of the things I have learnt were not learned formally but through accidents and failure. I learned from small catastrophes," he says. Unlike other leading business and management thinkers, he is not a consultant. "A consultant solves other people's problems," he says, "I could never do that. I want to help other people solve their own problems."[14]

After leaving university, Handy became an oil executive for Shell International based in Malaysia. Returning to London he became disillusioned with corporate bureaucracy and, after a time working for Anglo-American, joined MIT's Sloan Management Program.

Here, he came into contact with leading management thinkers such as Warren Bennis, Chris Argyris and Ed Schein. This proved to be the turning point in Handy's career. He returned to the UK to play a leading role in the early days of the London Business School and the creation of its Sloan Program.

Handy's first book was *Understanding Organizations* (1976), a densely packed potboiler which has become required reading for many managers. Perhaps the most idiosyncratic of Handy's books is his second, *Gods of Management* (1979), which explores corporate culture through an elaborate analogy. The four gods of the title are: Zeus (power and patriarchy); Apollo (order, reason and bureaucracy); Athena (expertise and meritocracy); and Dionysus (individualism). This creative approach signalled the beginning of a process of rigorous questioning which marks Handy's more recent work which has become progressively more personal.

CHARLES HANDY

Born Ireland, 1932

British

Educator and writer

Education: Oxford University (studied "Greats" a combination of classics, history and philosophy); Massachusetts Institute of Technology.

Career: Joined Shell International and became the company's South-East Asia economist; worked for a short time for the Anglo-American Corporation; MIT Sloan School of Management (graduated 1967); helped launch and then directed London Business School's Sloan Program; Professor at LBS; Warden of St George's House, Windsor Castle (a study center for ethics and social policy) 1977–1981; now Fellow of London Business School.

Books: *Understanding Organizations*, Penguin, London, 1976; *The Future of Work*, Basil Blackwell, Oxford, 1984; *Gods of Management*, Business Books, London, 1986; *The Making of Managers*, with John Constable, Longman, London, 1988; *The Age of Unreason*, Business Books, London, 1989; *Inside Organizations: 21 Ideas for Managers*, BBC Books, London, 1990; *The Empty Raincoat*, Hutchinson, London, 1994; *Beyond Certainty*, Century, London, 1995; *The Hungry Spirit*, Hutchinson, London, 1997.

The cornerstones of Handy's thinking are laid out most powerfully in *The Age of Unreason* and *The Empty Raincoat*. (The latter is entitled *The Age of Paradox* in the US.) In both he argues that fundamental and revolutionary changes are required in our perceptions of organizations and managers within them. "The way we are doing things is not the best way," argues Handy, calling on organizations to recognize that their single most important asset is their people. "The micro-division of labor has fostered a basic distrust of human beings. People weren't allowed to put the whole puzzle together. Instead they were given small parts because companies feared what people would do if they knew and saw the whole puzzle," says Handy. "Human assets shouldn't be misused. Brains are becoming the core of organizations – other activities can be contracted out." He points to Singapore which has largely exported its manufacturing activities elsewhere, but retains managerial control. Such approaches are necessary, he argues, if organizations are to achieve the objectives summed up by one chief executive as half as many people being paid twice as much to do three times as much work.

Behind the changes in the way we work and perceive work is the emergence of what Handy labels "the shamrock organization." There is, he admits, nothing revolutionary in this concept. Indeed, many organizations and businesses have used the shamrock organization for many decades.

Shamrock organization

Term invented by Charles Handy to describe "a form of organization based around a core of essential executives and workers supported by outside contractors and part-time help."

The shamrock has three leaves. The first represents **the core workers** of an organization. These, in Handy's analogy, are likely to be highly trained professionals. They are the high achieving executives who demand impressive salaries and work every hour of the day. Comparisons can be drawn with the people at the heart of advertising companies or management consultancies.

The second leaf of the shamrock is made up of **the contractual fringe**. These may be individuals or organizations. Often they are people who once worked for the organization but now provide it with a service. They are self-employed with their own shamrocks.

The third leaf includes the **flexible labor force**. This, Handy makes clear, is not a band of casual cheap workers. They, too, are vital to the success of the organization they work for, even if they carry out relatively menial tasks on a part-time basis or irregularly. If they are treated as entirely peripheral they will have no motivation to provide ideas, develop or carry out their work to a high standard. It is here that the shamrock analogy confronts its hardest challenge. The flexible labor force can too easily be treated as hired hands with no vested interest in anything other than a wage packet. "If the flexible labor force is seen to be a valuable part of the organization then the organization will be prepared to invest in them, to provide training, even training leading to qualifications, to give them some status and some privileges (including paid holidays and sick leave entitlement). Then and only then, will the organization get the temporary or part-time help that it needs to the standard it requires."

As a continuation of the shamrock, Handy also points out that customers have effectively become subcontractors in a growing number of businesses. Customers do many of the jobs which were once carried out for them by organizations. Customers fill in forms and take their own money out of the bank, they fill their cars up with petrol, and walk round supermarkets filling their trolleys. Compare this

> *Customers do many of the jobs which were once carried out for them by organizations.*

with the recent past when banks employed people in large numbers to carry out tasks now undertaken by computers, petrol stations employed people to fill our cars, and shops got what we wanted from the shelves and filled our baskets. We are now part of the shamrock and are generally pleased to be so.

The shamrock organization is not the only organizational model identified by Handy. He also believes there is growing use and awareness of "the federal organization." "Federalism implies a variety of individual groups allied together under a common flag with some shared identity. Federalism seeks to make it big by keeping it small, or at least independent, by combining autonomy with co-operation." It is, Handy admits, "the best of both worlds." And, when all the talk is of being global and local, a practical – though paradoxical – business solution.

The role of the center is increasingly discussed – in most depth in *Corporate-Level Strategy* by Andrew Campbell, Michael Goold and Marcus Alexander – and it is vital to the success or otherwise of the federal organization. Handy believes that federalism only works if there is **subsidiarity** – if the center truly surrenders power to its units. This demands a level of trust which is often little in evidence in organizations. If true power is granted to subsidiaries, then it follows that managers in the central function must surrender some of their own power.

To practise federalism demands a new generation of managers who regard the giving of power as more important than the acquisition of power; and of a new generation of business leaders.

> *To practise federalism demands a new generation of managers who regard the giving of power as more important than the acquisition of power; and of a new generation of business leaders.*

"Managers must think like leaders," Handy says. This involves changing attitudes to their career development. For example, they will need to become used to **horizontal tracking**. Instead of concentrating their sights on progressing up the corporate hierarchy, managers will have to learn to regard sideways moves as an essential part of their development, rather than a disappointing alternative to promotion. Sideways moves present fresh opportunities for learning and expose managers to new environments, new people and new business situations.

This final model brings together the three Is of **Intelligence, Information** and **Ideas**. Handy provides the equation $I^3 = AV$, with AV standing for Added Value. The three Is should be at the heart of the organization. Without its elements, any corporation is unlikely to thrive.

The three Is are fuelled by increased emphasis on quality and the growing application of IT. These trends encourage, says Handy, the effective utilization of the three Is. But, to work, the three Is demand intelligent people who are treated fairly and honestly by their employers. Herein lies a paradox. The organization must do its utmost to recruit and retain the best possible people to run its business. But it must do so at a time when the best people are increasingly unwilling to commit themselves to the organization. If employees regard the organization simply as a stepping stone why should the organization invest in them?

The solution – if it can be so called – is a combination of individual initiative and corporate support. Only by providing executives with the challenges and the development opportunities they require and expect will organizations retain them. The bottom line is that intelligent people prefer to agree rather than to obey.

References: The new world of organizations

1 Author interview.
2 Simon, Herbert, *Administrative Behavior*, Macmillan, New York, 1947.
3 Author interview.
4 Quoted in "The changing nature of leadership," *The Economist*, 10 June 1995.
5 Porras, Jerry and Collins, James, *Built to Last*, Harper Business, New York, 1995.
6 Pfeffer, Jeffrey, *The Human Equation*, Harvard Business School Press, Boston, 1998.
7 Pfeffer, Jeffrey, "The real keys to high performance," *Leader to Leader*, Spring 1998.
8 de Geus, Arie, *The Living Company*, Harvard Business School Press, Boston, 1997.
9 Author interview.
10 Hirschhorn, Larry and Gilmore, Thomas, "The new boundaries of the boundaryless company," *Harvard Business Review*, May–June, 1992.
11 Barnard, Chester, *Functions of the Executive*, Harvard University Press, Cambridge, Mass., 1938.
12 Taylor, William, "The logic of global business: an interview with Percy Barnevik," *Harvard Business Review*, March–April 1991.
13 Peters, Tom, *Liberation Management*, Knopf, New York, 1992.
14 Author interview.

The challenge
of technology

"The nerds have won!"

Tom Peters

"The business value of a computer is its management. The productivity of management is the decisive element that marks the difference of whether a computer hurts or helps."

Paul Strassmann

IT and the new organization

The corporate resource which has the largest role to play in creating the new organization is IT. On the surface this is not a surprising claim. Yet, IT has often failed to yield the productivity and performance benefits anticipated by managers and organizations.

The reasons for this are many and varied. One central reason is that managers often have only a limited understanding of what IT can do for their organization. They have a broad sympathy with investing in high technology, but have a restricted view of its practical power and business advantage. For example, a survey by Henley Management College of more than 200 chief executives, directors and other senior managers found that many top managers just did not understand the strategic importance of IT.

It is likely that, if asked, a great many managers would identify the benefits of IT in simple cost terms. IT reduces an organization's staff count, therefore it saves money. As Harvard's Shoshana Zuboff points out in her book, *In the Age of the Smart Machine*, companies have regarded IT as a means of reducing staff numbers through the automation of their jobs. The trouble is that the jobs which have been automated out of existence are often those which involve direct contact with customers. Zuboff argues that instead of automating tasks, IT's job should be to "informate" people – an ungainly, but apposite, word combining inform and educate. By regarding IT as a numbers and cost-cutting mechanism, organizations are failing to optimize its full potential which goes far beyond cost reduction.

> By regarding IT as a numbers and cost-cutting mechanism, organizations are failing to optimize its full potential which goes far beyond cost reduction.

While managers are comfortable with the concept of cost control and reduction, they find it difficult to come to terms with other implications of IT. With limited knowledge, managers find that they are unable to bring the same reporting and measuring disciplines to bear when some new IT product is introduced. A large investment in a new machine on the production line inevitably means that every effort is made by the company to measure and monitor the performance and productivity increases which the machine brings. The machine's *raison d'être* is simple and well understood. If, however, managers invest in a costly new IT system not only is it likely that they cannot use it – even though it could help them in their work – but they often have little idea how, or inclination, to accurately measure its productivity benefits. They may calculate direct cost savings but, in many cases, the more widespread advantages are assumed, with productivity gains neither monitored nor measured.

When it comes to IT, managers appear to suspend their disbelief and allow IT experts to get on with it. Managers also tend to have limited expertise in managing the obsessive enthusiasts who hone in on computer departments. It is not, perhaps, surprising that managers struggle to come to terms with IT – IT often unsettles their ways of working. IT may provide managers with information they have previously been starved of and sometimes never knew existed. Suddenly there is a deluge of statistical data and making a decision becomes ever more complex. As a result, there is the strong temptation to nod knowingly when the data falls onto your desk and carry on using the parameters and measurements you have always used as the basis for your decision making. Managers remain fearful of falling into the trap described by Gertrude Stein: "Everybody gets so much information all day long that they lose their commonsense."

A second factor in the failure of IT to boost productivity as significantly as it should, is the fact that it is often used for the wrong jobs. Quality programs, for example, have often exacerbated this situation to the extent that IT becomes marginalized. Instead of being regarded as a core tool by which quality and improved productivity can be achieved, IT has been treated simply as a means of collecting data and ensuring that quality processes are backed by sound statistics.

IT is a highly effective data-gathering device, but it is also much more. Unquestionably, IT is the best possible tool for organizations to gather a huge range of data about their business and its performance. The crunch comes when data is turned into information – this requires that companies have the systems, processes and people in place to ask the right questions. Data remains data until you ask a question. Information is the answer to the question.

While IT has been used as a means of data gathering, the emphasis of its practical use has also been on managing the links between different divisions, functions and activities rather than with customers. IT has traditionally looked at what departments do and then provided them with information. It has made an organization's internal life and systems easier to handle rather than providing improved service to customers.

Often IT is backed by an individual department or function which identifies ways by which IT can make its work more efficient. These do not, however, necessarily apply across the entire organization. The end result is that a number of different systems emerge with little in the way of linkages between them or any overall strategy. Any IT strategy must embrace all the aims of the company rather than taking a parochial view. The conventional approach to IT fails to see it in broader strategic terms. IT is regarded as a means of doing existing jobs faster. The obvious corollary of this is that organizations often make the same mistakes at twice the speed.

In many organizations IT has become yet another function when it should be a prime resource.

Key questions

- How does IT link your organization to customers?
- How do you measure the productivity gains brought by IT?
- Is IT managed and controlled by a single function?
- Has IT provided you with data or information?
- How has IT helped you provide customers with better service?

The virtual organization

New organizations no longer fit into strict hierarchical pyramids, rising to a pinnacle where the all-knowing, all-seeing chief executive surveys the corporate domain. Instead, new shapes and images are emerging to describe the organization. The new organization is described in the terminology of the new science of chaos theory. An article in the *California Management Review* describes the organization of the future as one which is "dynamically stable," "capable of serving the widest range of customers and changing product demands (dynamic) while building on long-term process capabilities and the collective knowledge of the organization (stable)."[1] From the traditional images of machinery, the organization has become an elusive ever-changing amoeba.

Describing the organization of the future, American writers William Davidow and Michael Malone say: "To the outside observer, it will appear almost edgeless, with permeable and continuously changing interfaces among company, supplier and customers. From inside the firm, the view will be no less amorphous with traditional offices, departments and operating divisions constantly re-forming according to need."[2]

The end result is what is now known as the **virtual organization**.

The theory is immaculate. Technology enables companies to dismantle their cumbersome headquarters buildings, the costly bricks and mortar of the conventional business. Employees can work at home or occasionally in satellite offices when required. Linked by networks of computers, communicating by e-mail and modems, people become more productive freed from the burdens of commuting and the regularity of office life. With no expensive tower blocks to support, organizations make massive cuts in operating costs. The virtual organization is life and profit enhancing. Virtuality creates a virtuous circle. QED.

> *Virtual organizations are, as yet, notable by their absence.*

But the remorseless logic of the argument cannot fail to disguise the fact that virtual organizations are, as yet, notable by their absence. There are organizations which appear virtual to customers, but are not truly virtual in reality. They still have their conventional headquarters building. Companies may relocate to cheaper alternatives, but they are still choosing to invest in reassuring concrete. If the arguments for the virtual organization are so persuasive, why are so few decision makers persuaded?

"People think that the virtual organization is the sole preserve of high-tech companies in California or fashionable ad agencies. This could not be further from the truth," says Eddie Obeng, founder of Pentacle – The Virtual Business School located not in Palo Alto, but in Beaconsfield, England. "The entire idea is nothing new. Auditors, accountants and many other professionals have been working in a virtual way for many years. It is not simply about cost or asset reduction, but about utilizing technology to mold a flexible organization which meets the needs of customers."[3]

Obeng believes that the leap from idea to practice has proved difficult for four reasons. First, managers and organizations are unable to change their old ways of thinking. The virtual organization requires a quantum leap rather than steady evolution. Second, the virtual organization creates a highly complex and continuously changing structure which has to be managed and understood if it is to work. Third, the virtual organization uses IT as a resource while most organizations continue to regard it as a function and often simply don't have the will or the ability to fully utilize IT. The final barrier is at an individual level. In the virtual organization managers find that their old tactics and power games no longer work. They have to change the habits of a lifetime.

> *"Few are going to be eager advocates of virtuality when it really means that work is what you do, not where you go" – Charles Handy.*

This list could be supplemented by the crucial fact that people, and managers in particular, remain wedded to their offices. "Few are going to be eager advocates of virtuality when it really means that work is what you do, not where you go," Charles Handy has observed.[4] Homeworking may be on the increase, but it has never made the anticipated in-roads simply because people do not find the idea attractive. "With its social rituals, human interest and politics, office life retains a strong attraction," says psychologist Robert Sharrock of consultants YSC. "Social instincts are one of the prime work drivers. In addition, there is ease of communication – people still believe in the primacy of face-to-face communication; and control – managers feel more in control if they can see the people they manage. Also, managers like the movement and activity of office life. They believe that things are happening, even if they are not."[5]

One means of making virtuality work is to employ **virtual teams**. The term is used to describe groups of people who are accountable for the achievement of transient or short-term objectives. The groups may be temporary – specially assembled to complete a certain task or project – or permanent. The idea is that virtual teams enable a flexible and continuously evolving fit between skills, resources and immediate needs.

One of the attractions of such a pragmatic approach is that executives do not have to travel the world, flitting from one jet-lagged meeting to another. Instead, technology provides constant links, whether through e-mail or computer noticeboards. This clearly places a premium on the communication and information platforms and groupware (software for groups on networks) selected.

Key books

Grenier, Raymond and **Metes, George**, *Going Virtual*, Prentice Hall Computer Books, 1995

Lipnack, Jessica and **Stamps, Jeffrey**, *The Age of the Network*, John Wiley, New York, 1996

Savage, Charles, *Fifth Generation Management*, Butterworth-Heinemann, Oxford, 1996 (revised edition)

The E company

Advances in technology provide better means to capture and utilize information about customer needs and behaviors – balancing customization with complexity. They also offer new ways to manage the physical flow of goods, such as vendor-managed inventories, resulting in greater availability at less cost. And, through electronic methods, they lower the cost and improve the functionality of supplier/channel interactions, such as ordering, invoicing, and payments.

Dr Walter S Baer, a senior policy analyst in RAND's Science and Technology division, has charted the history of electronic commerce over the past 20 years.[6] Baer points out that the technologies for electronic home services have actually been around much longer than most people realize. Television was developed in the 1920s, and video-phones were on display at the New York World Fair in 1939. But it wasn't until the 1970s that the growth of cable TV in the US provoked real interest in the concept of the "wired nation."

In the 1970s, videotex (Viewdata) and teletext (Ceefax) started up in the UK. In the 1980s, the French government invested heavily in the Minitel service. More recently, US companies have once again pushed the idea of interactive home services including the Full Network – a service that could offer two-way video, audio and data into the home.

Throughout its largely unprofitable history, however, Baer says that the sorts of service that have been offered electronically have remained surprisingly similar. Typically these are:

- news and sports information
- feature information (travel, recipes, etc.)
- interactive education
- home shopping
- banking and financial services
- ticket ordering (entertainment and travel)
- interactive games

- video-on-demand and pay-per-view
- electronic mail and chat services.

If the list looks familiar it is because these are the areas that are now being touted as the Internet services of the future. The Internet itself has been around for more than two decades. It existed for 20 years for government and military uses, and then academic

> *The Internet itself has been around for more than two decades.*

research. Expansion into the commercial market did not start until well into the 1990s.

As Baer confirms: "Despite obvious over-hyping, there are several reasons for viewing today's developments around the Internet as different:

- more households are buying personal computers;
- Internet growth to date has astounded almost everyone: as with all communication products, success breeds success;
- electronic mail usage is broadening;
- the World Wide Web is also becoming more popular and easier to use;
- Web advertising is expanding rapidly;
- electronic commerce."

In reality, achieving critical mass may well be the factor that finally allows electronic commerce to take off. Estimates from Nielsen Media Research suggest that as many as one in four American adults – 50 million people – is now an Internet user. The growth rate in Internet users has been 100 per cent per annum for the past five years. This would suggest that between 18 and 20 per cent of US adults now have some access to the Internet. One prediction estimates that the number of people on-line will expand from 57 million in 1997 to 377 million in 2000; another calculates that 2.5 million people have already bought products or services on the Web; and a market research company predicts that Internet-based sales in the US will jump from $518 million in 1997 to $6.6 billion by 2000.

Clearly, the Internet, the World Wide Web, and other related phenomena offer potent new channels for businesses. Yet, as with all unexplored territory, there are no hard and fast rules about the best way to use it. Shikhar Ghosh, chairman and co-founder of Open Market, an Internet-commerce software company, sums up the situation: "The Internet is fast becoming an important new channel for commerce in a range of businesses – much faster than anyone would have predicted two years ago. But determining how to take advantage of the opportunities this new channel is creating will not be easy for most executives, especially those in large, well-established companies."[7]

New players have everything to gain and nothing to lose from electronic commerce. Many are already building their business models around the new channel. Traditional businesses, on the other hand, may feel they have little to gain and everything to lose. The problem for established businesses is that most are wedded to their old – successful – channels and find it difficult to position themselves to take advantage of the new opportunities presented by electronic channels. For them, the Internet may appear to be more of a threat than an opportunity.

> *New players have everything to gain and nothing to lose from electronic commerce. Many are already building their business models around the new channel. Traditional businesses, on the other hand, may feel they have little to gain and everything to lose.*

For established businesses, the worrying thing about the Internet is that it threatens to disturb the old order. The traditional wisdom of big companies was that they needed critical mass to be serious players. In earlier decades, large companies used economic muscle to establish their brands and services in distribution channels to ensure they reached the end-user. In many cases, the cost of entry was prohibitive for all but the largest companies.

As Ghosh explains: "Three years after emerging into the spotlight, the Internet poses a difficult challenge for established businesses. The opportunities presented by the channel seem to be readily apparent: by allowing for direct, ubiquitous links to anyone anywhere, the Internet lets companies build interactive relationships with customers and suppliers, and deliver new products and services at very low cost. But the companies that seem to have taken advantage of these opportunities are start-ups like Yahoo! and Amazon.com.

"Established businesses that over decades have carefully built brands and physical distribution relationships risk damaging all they have created when they pursue commerce in cyberspace. What's more, Internet commerce is such a new phenomenon – and so much about it is uncertain – that it is difficult for executives at most companies, new or old, to decide the best way to use the channel. And it is even more difficult for them to estimate accurately the returns on any Internet investment they make." In many cases, creating an effective electronic channel requires both patience and deep pockets. As Rupert Murdoch demonstrated with satellite TV in the UK, a huge investment can pay off handsomely in the long run, but can eat up enormous amounts of cash in the meantime.

The old rules of the game were about competition for access to a limited number of channels. The evolution of the Internet, however, could change all that. In theory it allows someone in New York, London, or Tokyo to sell goods and services anywhere in the world. It enables a cottage industry in Alaska, Outer Mongolia or Timbuktu to do the same.

For this reason, many commentators and business people see the development of electronic commerce as the dawn of a new business era – a paradigm shift. When the rules of the game change, however, it is often new players who benefit at the expense of the old players. Electronic commerce is already redrawing the corporate map. It has spawned business models that simply could not have existed even a few years ago.

One of the best known is bookseller Amazon.com. The first books ordered through Amazon were dispatched in the Fall of 1994 (personally packed by founder, Jeff Bezoz, and his wife); in 1997 Amazon sold its one millionth book. In 1997, sales approached $148 million, an eight-fold increase year on year.

Already, it is proving difficult to predict where this exciting new channel will take business. For example, the original model for Amazon.com was to provide the world's largest bookshop with 2.5 million volumes available. But it quickly found that it was actually selling information as much as books. Today, for example, Amazon will send customers an e-mail every time a new book comes out on a subject in which they have registered an interest. That information also helps the company better understand its customers and target its marketing.

The site also encourages "chat" among its users as part of its service. To encourage discussion, it not only posts book reviews from leading newspapers, it also encourages customers to send in their own reviews which are published on the Amazon site. This, say McKinsey consultants John Hagel and Arthur Armstrong in their book *Net Gain*, is a powerful form of "community building" – a new trick for electronic channels – something that adds value to web transactions.[8]

Despite its popularity with consumers, business journalists and academics, Amazon.com has yet to make a profit. When it does, it may well have to face up to "me too" imitators replicating a successful channel. Other pioneers that have invested heavily in Internet services could face similar problems further down the road.

Yet, despite the risks involved with heavy investment in electronic channels, Shikhar Ghosh says companies simply cannot afford to ignore the Internet altogether. At the very least, he says, managers "need to understand the opportunities available to them and recognize how their companies may be vulnerable if rivals seize those opportunities first."

In his view, the Internet presents four distinct types of opportunities:

1 The Internet allows companies to establish direct links to customers (or to others, such as suppliers or distributors, with whom they have important relationships) to complete transactions or exchange information more easily.

2 The technology enables companies to bypass others in the value chain. For example, a book publisher could use the Net to bypass book retailers by selling directly to consumers.

3 Companies can use the Internet to develop and deliver new products and services for new customers.

4 A company could, theoretically at least, use the Internet to become the dominant player in the electronic channel of a specific industry or segment, effectively controlling access to customers and setting new business rules.

The future impact of the Internet – and electronic commerce in general – will depend on the ability of firms to create business models which take advantage of the special characteristics of on-line delivery; and also provide transaction security for customers. The experience of earlier IT applications suggests the prospects are extremely good.

> *The future impact of the Internet – and electronic commerce in general – will depend on the ability of firms to create business models which take advantage of the special characteristics of on-line delivery; and also provide transaction security for customers.*

Research carried out at London Business School suggests that, by the year 2007, in North America and Europe the following percentages of total sales will be on-line in some fashion:

- 10 per cent for retail, banks, travel agents, airlines and mail order clothing firms
- 30 per cent for music, books and newspapers
- 15 per cent for groceries
- 10 per cent for cars and white goods.[9]

All may not be plain sailing. The commercial possibilities of the Internet remain, for most businesses, tantalizing rather than real. "People looking back five or ten years from now may well wonder why so few companies took the on-line plunge," reflects multimedia expert Mark Hodges.[10]

The reasons for this are many and varied, but security and privacy remain central issues for both customers and companies. Fears about privacy mean that customers can be unwilling to divulge financial details over the Internet. There is also confusion on the other side. Around 20 companies have software packages offering payment or security solutions. Hodges notes "the lack of compatibility between methods of processing Web transactions." As a result, it can be difficult for companies and customers to agree on a method of payment or to confirm each other's identity. "We're well down the path to digital anarchy," says one industry spokesman calling for "a universal protocol between any wallet and any merchant." Until this is achieved, bandwagon boarders beware.

Key books

Collin, Simon, *Doing Business on the Internet,* Kogan Page, London, 1997

Cronin, Mary J, *Doing More Business on the Internet,* John Wiley, New York, 1997

Levinson, Jay Conrad and **Rubin, Charles,** *Guerilla Marketing Online,* Houghton Mifflin, Boston, 1997

Schwartz, Evan I, *Webonomics,* Broadway Books, New York, 1997

References: The challenge of technology

1 *California Management Review,* Vol. 35, No. 2, Winter 1993.
2 Davidow, William and Malone, Michael, *The Virtual Corporation,* Harper Business, New York, 1992.
3 Author interview.
4 Handy, Charles, *Beyond Certainty,* Hutchinson, London, 1995.
5 Author interview.
6 *Business Strategy Review,* Vol. 9, Issue 1, Spring 1998.
7 Ghosh, Shikhar, *Harvard Business Review,* March–April 1998.
8 Hagel, John and Armstrong, Arthur, *Net Gain,* Harvard Business School Press, Boston, 1997.
9 London Business School, Future Media Project.
10 Hodges, Mark, "Is web business good business?," *Technology Review,* August/September 1997.

4

Creating and implementing strategy

"The strategist's method is very simply to challenge the prevailing assumptions with a single question: Why? and to put the same question relentlessly to those responsible for the current way of doing things until they are sick of it."

Kenichi Ohmae[1]

"Strategic management is a comprehensive procedure which starts with a strategic diagnosis and guides a firm through a series of additional steps which culminate in new products, markets and technologies, as well as new capabilities."

Igor Ansoff[2]

The holy grail of strategy

The word strategy derives from the Greek for generalship, *strategia*, and entered the English vocabulary in 1688 as *strategie*. According to James' 1810 *Military Dictionary*, it differs from tactics, which are immediate measures in the face of an enemy. Strategy concerns something "done out of sight of an enemy." Its origins can be traced back to Sun-Tzu's *The Art of War* from 500BC. Indeed, **Sun-Tzu** has made a surprising return to the bestseller lists in the last decade. His book is full of neat aphorisms which seem to shed light on the mysterious world of strategy. They are reassuring, if not always appropriate.

Contemporary views of business strategy have their origins in the early 1960s. While the world discovered love, hallucinogenics and Jimi Hendrix, managers discovered strategy as their new holy grail. They did so, not in San Francisco or at Woodstock, but in **Igor Ansoff's** *Corporate Strategy*, published in 1965. "This book represented a kind of crescendo in the development of strategic planning theory, offering a degree of elaboration seldom attempted since," Henry Mintzberg later observed.[3]

Unstintingly serious, analytical and complex, *Corporate Strategy* had a highly significant impact on the business world. It propelled consideration of strategy into a new dimension.

"The end product of strategic decisions is deceptively simple; a combination of products and markets is selected for the firm. This combination is arrived at by addition of new product-markets, divestment from some old ones, and expansion of the present position," writes Ansoff. While the end product was simple, the processes and decisions beforehand produced a labyrinth followed only by the most dedicated of managers. Ansoff's subtitle was "An Analytical Approach to Business Policy for Growth and Expansion." The book provided a highly complex "cascade of decisions." Analysis – and in particular **gap analysis** (the gap between where you are now and where you want to be) – was the key to unlocking strategy.

The book also brought the concept of **synergy** to a wide audience for the first time. Today, the word is overused and much abused. In Ansoff's original creation it was simply summed up as "the 2+2=5" effect. In his later books, Ansoff refined his definition of synergy to any "effect which can produce a combined return on the firm's resources greater than the sum of its parts."[4]

While *Corporate Strategy* was a notable book for its time, it produced what Ansoff himself labelled "paralysis by analysis": repeatedly making strategic plans which remained unimplemented.

"Strategic planning was a plausible invention, and received an enthusiastic reception from the business community. But subsequent experience with strategic planning led to mixed results. In a minority of firms, strategic planning restored their profitability and became an established part of the management process. However a substantial majority encountered a phenomenon, which was named 'paralysis by analysis': strategic plans were made but remained unimplemented, and profits/growth continued to stagnate," he recently wrote.[5]

Undaunted, Ansoff looked again at his entire theory. His logic was impressively simple – either strategic planning was a bad idea, or it was part of a broader concept which was not fully developed and needed to be enhanced in order to make strategic planning effective. Characteristically, he sought the answer in extensive research. He examined acquisitions by American companies between 1948 and 1968 and concluded that acquisitions which were based on an articulated strategy fared considerably better than those which were opportunistic decisions.

IGOR ANSOFF

Born Russia, 1918

American

Consultant and educator

Education: Stevens Institute of Technology, degree in engineering and MS in math and physics; PhD Brown University in applied mathematics; UCLA senior executive program.

Career: Rand Corporation; Lockheed; Carnegie-Mellon University; founding Dean School of Management, Vanderbilt University; Professor European Institute for Advanced Studies in Management, Brussels; now Distinguished Professor of Strategic Management, US International University, San Diego.

Books: *Corporate Strategy*, McGraw-Hill, New York, 1965; *Strategic Management*, Macmillan, London, 1979; *Implanting Strategic Management*, Prentice Hall, London, 2nd edition, 1990.

Reinforced by his conviction that strategy was a valid, if incomplete, concept, Ansoff followed up *Corporate Strategy* with *Strategic Management* (1979) and *Implanting Strategic Management* (1984). In each of which he sought a broader concept which would include strategic planning and would assure effective implementation of strategic plans.

Using the concept of strategic management, Ansoff formulated a **Strategic Success Paradigm** which specifies conditions which optimize a firm's profitability. This paradigm (the result of "fifteen years of sweat, tears and smiles and occasional flashes of creativity") has five key elements:

1 There is no universal success formula for all firms.

2 The driving variable which dictates the strategy required for success of a firm is the level of turbulence in its environment.

3 A firm's success cannot be optimized unless the aggressiveness of its strategy is aligned with the turbulence in its environment.

4 A firm's success cannot be optimized unless management capability is also aligned with the environment.

5 The key internal capability variables which jointly determine a firm's success, are: cognitive, psychological, sociological, political and anthropological.[6]

Being aware of the spotty record of strategic planning, Ansoff (with the assistance of his graduate students) devoted the next 11 years to empirical validation of the Success Paradigm. The paradigm was tested in over 500 firms in the US, Japan, Indonesia, Algeria, Abu Dhabi, Australia and Ethiopia. The statistical results gave strong support to the paradigm. Ansoff translated the paradigm into a diagnostic instrument, called "Strategic Readiness Diagnosis" and used it in his consulting practice.

Having identified behaviors by firms which optimize their profitability, Ansoff has refocussed his research on management behaviors which cause firms to behave optimally.

Strategic management

As first postulated by Igor Ansoff, strategic management was a combination of strategy planning, planning of organizational capability and effective management of resistance to change, typically caused by strategic planning. Ansoff described it as "a comprehensive procedure which starts with a strategic diagnosis and guides a firm through a series of additional steps which culminate in new products, markets and technologies, as well as new capabilities."[7]

The analytical strangehold

The fuel for the modern growth in interest in all things strategic has been analysis. While analysis has been the watchword, data has been the password. Managers have assumed that anything which could not be analyzed could not be managed. The last 30 years have seen a ceaseless quest for things, actions and decisions which can be analyzed. The belief in analysis is part of a search for a logical commercial regime, a system of management which will, under any circumstances, produce a successful result. But, as Ansoff found, effective analysis does not guarantee effective, or even appropriate, implementation.

Indeed, all the analysis in the world can lead to decisions which are plainly wrong. IBM had all the data about its markets, yet reached the wrong conclusions. It is a problem not restricted to business. British Prime Minister Harold Macmillan was once asked what was the most difficult thing about his job. "Events, my dear boy, events," he replied. For all its usefulness, analysis does not dictate events. Things may add up, but they don't necessarily work.

There are two basic problems with the reliance on analysis. First, it is all technique. Watching the implementation of a strategy which

> *Watching the implementation of a strategy which is solely based on analysis is like listening to a synthesiser recreate the sound of a Stradivarius.*

is solely based on analysis is like listening to a synthesiser recreate the sound of a Stradivarius. It is hollow and dehumanized. Even in the technological age, dehumanized management remains a contradiction in terms.

The second problem is more fundamental. Analysis produces a self-increasing loop. The belief is that more and more analysis will bring safer and safer decisions. If analysis is insufficient, the manager begins to feel guilty. How can they produce a strategy when the data is non-existent or insubstantial? To assuage the guilt they carry out some more analysis. The process continues, relentlessly delaying any decision making. In such cases, strategy is driven by guilt and fuelled by analysis. Eventually, enough data is bound to filter through and a strategy of sorts will emerge. The process is, however, time consuming and tortuous. Before the resulting strategy becomes action it is likely that the self-perpetuating combination of analysis and guilt will continue to interfere with and slow the process.

The traditional view is that strategy is concerned with making predictions based on analysis. Predictions, and the analysis which forms them, lead to security. The bottom line is not expansion, future growth or increased profitability – it is survival. The assumption is that growth and increased profits will naturally follow. If, by using strategy, we can increase our chances of predicting successful methods, then our successful methods will lead us to survival and perhaps even improvement. So, strategy is to do with getting it right or, as the more competitive would say, winning. Of course it is possible to win battles and lose wars and so strategy has also grown up in the context of linking together a series of actions with some longer-term goals or aims.

This was all very well in the 1960s and for much of the 1970s. Predictions and strategies were formed with confidence and optimism (though they were not necessarily implemented with such sureness). Security could be found. The business environment appeared to be reassuringly stable. Objectives could be set and strategies developed to meet them in the knowledge that the overriding objective would not change. This approach became known as Management By Objectives.

Management By Objectives (MBO)

Identifying a target and developing strategies to achieve it. Under MBO, strategy formulation is a conscious, rational process. The process is backed with hard data and analysis so that a single, right answer can be identified and a clear plan articulated.

In practice, MBO demanded too much data. It became overly complex and also relied too heavily on the past to predict the future. The entire system was ineffective at handling, encouraging or adapting to change. MBO simplified management to a question of reaching A from B using as direct a route as possible. Under MBO, the ends justified the means. The managerial equivalent of highways were developed in order to reach objectives quickly with the minimum hindrance from outside forces.

"The confusion of means and ends characterizes our age," Henry Mintzberg observes and, today, the highways are liable to be gridlocked. When the highways are blocked, managers are left to negotiate minor country roads to reach their objectives. And then comes the final confusion: the destination is likely to have changed during the journey. Equally, while MBO sought to narrow objectives and ignore all other forces, success (the objective) is now less easy to identify. Today's measurements of success can include everything from environmental performance to meeting equal opportunities targets. Success has expanded beyond the bottom line.

> *Success has expanded beyond the bottom line.*

Another fatal flaw in the conventional view of strategy is that it tended to separate the skills required to develop strategy in the first place (analytical) from those needed to achieve its objectives in reality (practical). The divide between analysis and practice is patently artificial. Strategy does not stop and start, it is a continuous process of redefinition and implementation.

In his book, *The Mind of the Strategist*, the Japanese strategic thinker **Kenichi Ohmae** says: "In strategic thinking, one first seeks a clear understanding of the particular character of each element of a situation and then makes the fullest possible use of human brain power to restructure the elements in the most advantageous way. Phenomena and events in the real world do not always fit a linear model. Hence the most reliable means of dissecting a situation into its constituent parts and reassembling them in the desired pattern is not a step-by-step methodology such as systems analysis. Rather, it is that ultimate non-linear thinking tool, the human brain. True strategic thinking thus contrasts sharply with the conventional mechanical systems approach based on linear thinking. But it also contrasts with the approach that stakes everything on intuition, reaching conclusions without any real breakdown or analysis."[8]

When the future could be expected to follow neat linear patterns, strategy had a clear place in the order of things. Now, the neatness is being upset, new perspectives are necessary. Even attitudes to time are being questioned. Western admiration of the Japanese economic miracle makes Eastern notions of time intriguing – the East tends to use a cyclical conception of time which is not driven by achievement or by short-term objectives. Instead, it is deterministic and fatalistic.

If time can be questioned – or, at least, our perception of time – nothing is sacred, and corporations must constantly wrestle with fundamental issues. While accepting that every company needs a strategy – either explicit or implicit – it is increasingly recognized that expressing a need for strategy does not help to determine what strategy actually is or entails.

The Boston Matrix

Until the 1960s, models were the impenetrable domain of economists. The man who can be largely credited with bringing business models into the mainstream was the Australian, **Bruce Henderson** (1915–92). Henderson was an engineer who worked as a strategic planner for General Electric. He was also dismissive of economists: "Darwin is probably a better guide to business competition than economists are," said Henderson. From GE, he joined the management consultancy, Arthur D Little. In 1963, Henderson announced that he was leaving to set up his own consultancy, the Boston Consulting Group (BCG).

At the time, management consulting was beginning to establish itself as a profession and BCG is regarded by some as the first pure strategy consultancy. While strategy drifts in and out of fashion, it is a cause which BCG still robustly champions. "Strategy leads to the continuous creation of real value. Real value requires sustained competitive advantage. Leaping at opportunities without strategy consistently produces failure," it says. BCG quickly became a great success. Within five years it was in the top group of consulting firms – where it has largely remained. It has been called "the most idea driven major consultancy in the world."[9]

The first model discovered – or rediscovered in this case – by Henderson was something of an antique. In the 1920s, an obscure company called Curtiss Aircraft came up with the concept of the "learning curve," which also became known as the "experience curve." This posited that unit costs declined as cumulative production increased because of the acquisition of experience. This had been applied solely to manufacturing. Henderson applied it to strategy rather than production and found that it still worked and provided a useful practical tool.

BCG went on to originate or develop concepts such as sustainable growth; time-based competition; Segment-of-One marketing; value-based strategy; total shareholder value; even disease management. However, the model for which Henderson and BCG are best known is the Boston Matrix which measures market growth and relative market share for all the businesses in a particular firm. The hypothesis of the Boston Matrix is that companies with higher market share in faster growing industries are more profitable. The further to the left a business is on the Boston Matrix, the stronger it should be.

As with most such models, refinements have been added along the way. On its original matrix, BCG superimposed a theory of cash management which included a hierarchy of uses of cash, numbered from one to four in their order of priority. This identified the top priority as cash cows, characterized by high market share and low growth. Investment in cash cows is easily justified as they are dull, safe and highly profitable. (BCG itself falls into this category – it has grown every year since its founding and in the past two decades its growth has averaged 20 per cent per annum.) Next in line are the stars (high growth; high market share) though their investment requirements are likely to be significant. More problematic is the third category, question marks (or wildcats in some versions) where there is high growth and low share. Any investment in them is risky. The final category is the aptly titled dogs, where low market share is allied to low growth. Dogs should not be approached.

Celebrated in the 1960s, the Boston Matrix proved a highly popular innovation. From a business point of view, the matrix had the characteristics of any great model: it was accessible, simple and useful. However, it was also limiting. Measuring corporate performance against two parameters is straightforward, but potentially dangerous if

> **Celebrated in the 1960s, the Boston Matrix proved a highly popular innovation.**

these are the only two parameters used. A creature of its time, the matrix offered a blinkered view of a world where growth and profitability were all.

The Boston Matrix encouraged a preoccupation with market share. This was not to the liking of all executives. In a 1974 speech, David Packard warned Hewlett-Packard staff: "If I hear anybody talking about how big their share of the market is or what they're trying to do to increase their share of the market, I'm going to personally see that a black mark gets put in their personnel folder."

Not surprisingly, other consulting firms were quick to respond with their own variations on the Boston Matrix. The most credible response came in the form of the General Electric and McKinsey matrix. This measured performance against two variables – industry attractiveness and business strength – and was effectively a dandified version of the original.

As a business tool, the Boston Matrix had a significant and long-term impact. It provides a useful way of looking at the world. Of equal significance was its influence on the management consulting business. It spawned a host of imitators. Now, no consultants report is complete without a matrix of some sort. More importantly, BCG effectively introduced off-the-shelf consulting (though it wouldn't see it that way). Companies required a big idea. They wanted to see how they fared on the matrix and how it could shape their strategies. The consulting firm product was born.

> *As well as problem solving, consultancy became concerned with passing on the latest ideas, the frameworks, models and matrices which were the height of fashion.*

Previously consultants had gone in to client companies to solve specific business problems. The success of the Boston Matrix marked a change in tack. As well as problem solving, consultancy became concerned with passing on the latest ideas, the frameworks, models and matrices which were the height of fashion. Problem solvers became peddlers of big ideas. This opened up huge new vistas for the management consultancy profession which it has been assiduously – and profitably – chasing ever since.

Making strategy work

In an era of constant and unpredictable change, the practical usefulness of strategy is increasingly – and loudly – questioned. The skeptics argue that it is all well and good to come up with a brilliantly formulated strategy, but quite another to implement it. By the time implementation begins, the business environment is liable to have changed and be in the process of changing even further.

During the early 1990s, the death knell for traditional approaches to strategy was being sounded. "The humane thing to do with most strategic planning processes is to kill them off," concluded a report by OC&C Strategy Consultants. Research by the American Planning Forum found that a mere 25 per cent of companies considered their planning processes to be effective. Similarly, in his book *The Rise and Fall of Strategic Planning*, Henry Mintzberg took on the full might of conventional planning orthodoxy. "Too much analysis gets in our way. The failure of strategic planning is the failure of formalization," said Mintzberg, identifying formalization as the fatal flaw of modern management.

Mintzberg argued the case for, what he labeled, **strategic programing**. His view was that strategy had for too long been housed in ivory towers built from corporate data and analysis. It had become distant from reality, when to have any viable commercial life strategy needs to become completely immersed in reality. "Strategies appear at predetermined times, popping out when expected, full blown, all ready for implementation. It is almost as if they are immaculately conceived," he caustically observed.

After a decent period of mourning, strategic planning is undergoing something of a rebirth. Bernard Taylor of Henley Management College, the British doyen of strategic planning, identifies a number of "separate but converging trends."[10] First, rather than being regarded as an annual ritual, strategy is now more commonly seen as a continuous process, a dialog rather than a monolog. Second, "strategy discussions are not focused on operational plans but around a few strategic issues." The next trend is the demise of weighty planning departments filled with bright minds producing great plans destined never to see the light of day.

The new emphasis is on strategy as part of the corporate development brief with small teams working on distinct projects calling on outside consultants when necessary. The role of the consultants principally lies in benchmarking corporate performance, monitoring and identifying external trends and helping develop a corporate vision. "The key strategic issues should emerge as management identify the gaps between the corporate vision and the strategies which are being suggested by the various businesses," writes Taylor. "Management then face the task of aligning the organization behind the strategy."

Perhaps the most eye-catching of the trends identified by Bernard Taylor is "the emergence of the profit-accountable organization." Senior managers now have targets and budgets they have to work to. It is startling, not to say worrying, that this should be identified – no doubt correctly – as a notable trend. That it is so notable is testament to the drawbacks of conventional strategic planning which was often self-perpetuatingly elitist. As Taylor makes clear, if the new

Strategy remains deeply bedded in confusion.

dawn of strategic planning is to occur, it must broaden its perspective and involve many more in its processes.

The truth is that, amid its constant rises and falls, strategy remains deeply bedded in confusion. Rarely has so much theorizing amounted to so little effective practice. The confusion over such a well-debated issue can be attributed to a number of factors:

1 **Confusion of what strategy actually is** – there is a confusion between what an organization is actually doing, what it says it is doing and what it should be doing. In practice, strategy tends to embrace all three. In *The Financial Times Guide to Management and Strategy*, Richard Koch provides two senses for strategy:

   (a) "a good strategy is the commercial logic of a business, that defines why a firm can have a competitive advantage and a place in the sun. To be complete, a strategy must include a definition of the domain – the lines of business, types of customer and geographical reach – in which the firm competes. It must also include a definition of the firm's distinctive competencies and the competitive advantage that gives the firm a special hold on the chosen business domain;

(b) "strategy also means what a company does, how it actually positions itself commercially and conducts the competitive battle. You can always attempt to describe a competitor's strategy, whether or not you think it sound. In this sense a strategy is what a firm does, not what it says it does, or what its strategy documents propound."[11]

2 **The sheer profusion of approaches** – in the faddish world of management thinking no single subject has generated so many bright ideas – from strategic intent to core competencies.

3 **Confusion with the actual processes of developing and then implementing strategy** – the process remains clouded by verbiage. Does an organization study its marketplace and competitive environment and then change itself to meet perceived opportunities? Indeed, Harvard's Michael Porter defines strategy as the positioning of the company relative to its industry environment. Or, does strategy begin with the organisation examining what it excels at and then aiming to make the most of those assets in the current environment?

4 **The shift from linear thinking to emergent chaos** – in the current business environment where the calls for change and transformation are constant, the traditional methods of formulating and implementing strategy are increasingly questioned. The conventional approach takes as its guiding light the acronym **MOST** (**Mission, Objectives, Strategy** and **Tactics**). This offers an orderly progression from creating a mission to making the strategy happen.

Life is no longer so simple. "In practice, the real process of strategy development and direction setting is much more messy, experimental, uncertain, iterative and driven from the bottom upwards," says Andrew Campbell of the Ashridge Strategic Management Centre. "There are five reasons for rejecting the MOST framework. First, the competitive economic system in which companies act provides constraints that are often interpreted as objectives. Second, strategy and objectives are intertwined, not linear. Third, it is useless to develop a separation between strategy, tactics and operations – insights about creating value come as often from operating details as from broad strategic concepts. Fourth, academics and consultants differ in their views about how insights can best be developed and captured. Fifth, there are also differences in view about how best to implement strategy in an uncertain world."

5 **The battle between analysis and intuition** – from this it would seem that the days of highly analytical, rational, strategy creation are past. But strategy can neither be purely rational nor purely intuitive. Indeed, one of the core skills of managers is to know when and how to use their intuitive judgment of a particular situation.

Confusion is endemic. But, argues London Business School's Costas Markides, it need not be. "The confusion surrounding strategy manifests itself in a variety of ways. But, in reality, the confusion is unfortunate – and unjustified. Strategy is a very simple thing – at its simplest it is five or six creative ideas that tell us how our company is to fight the competitive battle in its industry. It is not a plan; it is not a hundred-page report; it is not a budget; and it is not a goal. It is just five or six creative ideas. If your company cannot put down its strategy on one sheet of paper then it does not have a strategy."[12] The problem is that managers have been reared on an unhealthy diet of weighty reports.

Michael Porter
Strategy and competitive advantage

Michael Porter of Harvard Business School is probably the world's most successful academic. While other management thinkers have compromised their approach in search of popular appeal, Porter's work is unashamedly academic in tone and content. Seriousness and rationality is all pervasive. "His work is academic almost to a fault," observed *The Economist*. "Mr Porter is about as likely to produce a blockbuster full of anecdotes and boosterish catch-phrases as he is to deliver a lecture dressed in bra and stockings."[13]

His approach is based on surgical precision, the dissection of the vital organs of companies and industrial nations. Porter's books, not surprisingly, have been few in number, but high in their ambition and influence.

"Strategic thinking rarely occurs spontaneously. Without guidelines few managers knew what constituted strategic thinking,"[14] he lamented in a 1987 article. His work has set about constructing the guidelines. This has brought him into conflict with a number of other leading thinkers. Henry Mintzberg, the champion of spontaneity and intuition, has been critical of Porter's "enthusiasm for generic strategies and checklists of all kinds."[15]

MICHAEL PORTER

Born 1947

American

Educator and consultant

Education: Degree in aeronautical engineering at Princeton; doctorate in economics, Harvard.

Career: Joined Harvard faculty 1973; also now runs a highly successful consultancy business, Monitor.

Books: *Competitive Strategy*, Free Press, New York, 1980; *Competitive Advantage*, Free Press, New York, 1985; *The Competitive Advantage of Nations*, Macmillan, London, 1990.

Porter's first book was *Competitive Strategy* (1980) which instead of tiptoeing round the edges of management theory went straight to the strategic heart. Porter tackled the apparently imponderable question of how organizations can achieve long-term competitive advantage. He sought a middle ground between the two polarized approaches then accepted – on the one hand, that competitive advantage was achieved by organizations adapting to their particular circumstances; and, on the other, that competitive advantage was based on the simple principle that the more in tune and aware of a market a company is, the more competitive it can be (through lower prices and increased market share).

Porter managed to absorb both these concepts. From analysis of a number of companies, he developed **generic strategies**. This was not an instant template for competitive advantage – Porter insisted that though the "generic strategies" existed, it was up to each organization to carefully select which were most appropriate to them and at which particular time. The four "generic strategies" are backed by five **competitive forces** which are then applied to five "different kinds of industries" (fragmented, emerging, mature, declining and global).

The logic behind the five forces framework is that:

- If **customers** have bargaining power over a supplier (no matter what the reason), they will exercise that power and reduce the supplier's profit margins.

- If an organization's **suppliers** have bargaining power over it, they will exercise that power and sell their products at a higher price.

- If there are **substitutes** to an organization's product or service, they will limit the price the organization can charge and, again, limit profits.

- If there is intense **rivalry** in an industry, it will force organizations to engage in price, R&D and advertising wars, all of which are likely to reduce profits.

- Finally, if **new entrants** move into an industry, they bring with them resources and the desire to steal market share from existing companies. Rivalry accelerates and profits decline.

"Given the logic of these five forces, a strategist needs to decide what to do about them," says London Business School's Costas Markides. "Traditionally, most people assumed that the way to proceed was to assume these five industry forces as given and then try and position their firm towards these forces. This is fundamentally wrong and this is probably the most serious misconception about strategy that has developed in the 15 years since the five forces framework was developed.

"Instead, what the strategist ought to do is to creatively break the established rules of the game by actively changing these five forces in the company's favor. In other words, the essence of strategy formulation is coming up with creative ideas in response to the following five questions:

- How can I reduce the bargaining power of my customers?
- How can I reduce the bargaining power of my suppliers?
- How can I reduce substitutes to my product or service?
- How can I limit rivalry in my industry?

- How can I prevent new entrants from coming into my industry?"[16]

Even so, Porter's "generic strategies" framework is persuasive and highly attractive to managers. It is clear and the logic irrefutable. The trouble is that, while Porter suggests that the model should only be used to stimulate thinking, organizations often regard it as a direct route to competitive advantage. There is considerable irony in companies using the same model to differentiate themselves from each other.

While Porter suggests that the model should only be used to stimulate thinking, organizations often regard it as a direct route to competitive advantage.

In *Competitive Advantage* (1985) Porter contends that there are three ways by which companies can gain competitive advantage:

- by becoming the lowest cost producer in a given market;
- by being a differentiated producer (offering something extra or special to charge a premium price); or
- by being a focussed producer (achieving dominance in a niche market).

To examine an organization's internal competitiveness, Porter advocates the use of a **value chain** – analysis of a company's internal processes and the interactions between different elements of the organization to determine how and where value is added. Viewing everything a company does in terms of its overall competitiveness, argues Porter, is a crucial step to becoming more competitive.

"In a volume of over 500 pages it is easy to miss Porter's one reference to human resource management. It occupies only two paragraphs," observes the UK management writer and thinker, Philip Sadler, of *Competitive Advantage*.[17] The human element is not often to be found in Porter's work.

This is even truer of *The Competitive Advantage of Nations* (1990). Probably Porter's most ambitious project, it is a detailed study of the competitiveness of the world's top eight economies which emerged from Porter's work on the Presidential Commission on Industrial Competitiveness set up by Ronald Reagan. Interestingly, Porter produces a more pragmatic view of the world in this book. He is highly critical of general prescriptions and the worldwide application of management fads such as just-in-time. What works in one country, fails miserably in another, he warns. This runs counter to much of the prevailing wisdom of globalization. Indeed, instead of national differences and characteristics becoming less pronounced, Porter found them to be as important as ever.

"You can boil Porter's magisterial work down to just three words: 'vigorous domestic rivalry.' That is: Firms that engage in the most intensive competition in their home market tend to improve fastest," commented Tom Peters, cheerfully saluting Porter as "an unlikely prince of disorder."[18]

Again, Porter's research produced a tidy checklist. His **national diamond** framework identified four factors which influence the competitiveness of nations:

- resources
- related and supporting industries
- demanding home customers
- domestic rivalry.

While Porter has attracted some criticism for his willingness to boil his mass of theories and ideas down to all-embracing bullet points, without them it is unlikely that his complex ideas would either be accessible or understood. That they are so influential is a triumph for Porter's abilities of dissection and logic.

The route from ideas to action

Where are you?

"The starting point must be a solid understanding of where you are starting from and the dilemmas you face. If organizations are not in touch with the reality of their situation – however depressing this may seem – they have no hope of moving forward," says Howell Schroeder of Ashridge Management College.

Where do you want to be?

In the process of simplifying strategy, the starting point must be to determine an organization's overall goals or objectives. If you don't know where you want to be you are unlikely to get there.

In pursuit of this starting point, organizations throughout the world have developed **mission statements**. "Most companies do have a mission statement. About 99.9 per cent are useless," says Costas Markides. Mission statements are also, confusingly, known by a variety of other labels (strategic intent, core objectives, visions, etc.) but the end result is usually remarkably similar.

> *If you don't know where you want to be you are unlikely to get there.*

Mission statements are, or should be, a pithy explanation of why a company is in business, what it intends to achieve and by what methods. The exercise of distilling an organization's *raison d'être* into less than 100 words is often useful in itself. However, the results are often fatuous in the extreme. Mission statements have become meaningless PR exercises, pinned on noticeboards, printed on corporate keepsakes and generally ignored by the people they aim to influence. "Many managers misunderstand the nature and importance of mission, while others fail to comprehend it at all," concluded Andrew Campbell and his co-authors in *A Sense of Mission*.[19]

Though they might help to encapsulate an organization's goals, mission statements are not strategy. They are more accurately described as the potential end result of strategy, the objectives of the organization. Indeed, Henry Mintzberg defines strategy as the embodiment of a company's visions.

Mission statements should be bold, but achievable, goals. It sounds straightforward, but the means of identifying these objectives is clouded by controversy.

What do you want to achieve?

Any statement of intent relies on some knowledge of what it is you wish to achieve. Michael Porter argues that what every company should aim to achieve is competitive advantage. It must be better than its competitors in some way.

This has led to the myth of **sustainable competitive advantage**. In reality, any competitive advantage is short lived. If a company raises its quality standards and increases profits as a result, its competitors will follow. If a company says that it is reengineering, its competitors will claim to be reengineering more successfully. Businesses are quick to copy, mimic, pretend and, even steal.

> *This has led to the myth of* **sustainable competitive advantage**. *In reality, any competitive advantage is short-lived.*

The logical and distressing conclusion is that an organization has to be continuously developing new forms of competitive advantage. It must move on all the time. If it stands still, competitive advantage will evaporate before its very eyes and competitors will pass.

The danger of developing continuously is that this generates, and relies on, a climate of uncertainty. The company also runs the risk of fighting on too many fronts. This is often manifested in a huge number of improvement programs in various parts of the organization which give the impression of moving forward, but are often simply cosmetic.

Constantly evolving and developing strategy is labelled **strategic innovation**. The mistake is to assume that strategic innovation calls for radical and continual major surgery on all corporate arteries. Continuous small changes across an organization make a difference. "We did not seek to be 100 per cent better at anything. We seek to be one per cent better at 100 things," says ex-SAS chief, Jan Carlzon.

Even major surgery has its compromises. More realistic than most, Kenichi Ohmae says that a good business strategy "is one, by which a company can gain significant ground on its competitors at an acceptable cost to itself." He believes there are four principal ways of doing this:

1 **Focus on the key factors for success (KFSs)** – Ohmae argues that certain functional or operating areas within every business are more critical for success in that particular business environment than others. If you concentrate effort into these areas and your competitors do not, this is a source of competitive advantage. The problem, of course, is identifying what these key factors for success are.

2 **Build on relative superiority** – when all competitors are seeking to compete on the KFSs, a company can exploit any differences in competitive conditions. For example, it can make use of technology or sales networks not in direct competition with its rivals.

3 **Pursue aggressive initiatives** – frequently, the only way to win against a much larger, entrenched competitor is to upset the competitive environment, by undermining the value of its KFSs – changing the rules of the game by introducing new KFSs.

4 **Utilizing strategic degrees of freedom** – by this tautological phrase, Ohmae means that the company can focus on innovation in areas which are "untouched by competitors."

"In each of these four methods, the principal concern is to avoid doing the same thing, on the same battle-ground, as the competition," Ohmae explains.[20]

What are your core competencies?

The phrase core competencies has now entered the language of management. In layman's terms, core competencies are what a company excels at.

Core competencies

Gary Hamel and CK Prahalad, who made the term famous, define core competencies as "the skills that enable a firm to deliver a fundamental customer benefit."

Hamel and Prahalad argue that strategic planning is neither radical enough nor sufficiently long term in perspective. Instead its aim remains incremental improvement. In contrast, they advocate **crafting strategic architecture**. The phraseology is unwieldy, but means basically that organizations should concentrate on rewriting the rules of their industry and creating a new competitive industry.

Ian Turner of Henley Management College believes that the concept of core competencies has often simply produced a vague and far from authoritative list of what an organization considers to be its strengths. While there tends to be executive talk of setting world class standards, it is usually glib and entirely inappropriate for smaller businesses.

"After spending many hours in relentless pursuit of their company's core competencies, managers often concluded that the concept, whilst enormously appealing in the abstract, in practice merely gives rise to frustration and bewilderment," says Turner.[21] He traces the beginning of the corporate fascination with the idea to Hamel and Prahalad's work which regards a core competence as something which competitors cannot easily emulate and which can be applied in a variety of business units. There are, inevitably, a number of other definitions and approaches. Others, for example, regard a core competence as a combination of complementary skills and embedded organizational knowledge. Significantly, most find it easier to say what a core competence isn't rather than actually defining it.

Turner provides a number of home truths which have been overlooked as the bandwagon has powered on. First, core competencies are rare. They are not handed around like confetti. Second, evolution of core competencies has not generally come from an edict from the CEO, but from "a number of separate actions which in turn led to the acquisition of distinctive skills and capabilities." Third, measuring and testing a core competence is not necessarily an effective means of achieving and sustaining it in practice. (He goes on to look at the issues raised when knowledge is a core competence.)

A further unexpected side effect of core competencies is also examined by Turner: the reemergence of diversification as a corporate weapon. After the trials and tribulations of the sixties and seventies, competency-based diversification has given an old idea new legs. It is, he writes, too soon to write off some of the diversifications, but history provides a pessimistic precedent.

Finding the core

Business activities can be divided into four main categories:

Peripheral

Providing no source of competitive advantage; not essential to the core purpose of the business.

Supportive

An essential but not core activity – failure in this area would cause serious damage to the business.

Strategic

An actual or potential source of competitive advantage.

Core

The primary activity(ies) of the business.

How do core competencies and objectives fit with the overall environment?

Nothing in the corporate world exists in a vacuum. Formulating a mission or any set of objectives must involve a plethora of people, as well as consideration of the broader forces at work in and on the organization.

> **Nothing in the corporate world exists in a vacuum.**

This process was neatly summed up by Peter Drucker in a 1994 *Harvard Business Review* article. Drucker argues that every organization has a theory of business – the assumptions on which it has been built and is being run. To create a "valid theory of business" requires four elements:

- The assumptions about environment, mission and core competencies must fit reality.
- The assumptions in all three areas have to fit one another.
- The theory of the business must be known and understood throughout the organization.
- The theory of the business has to be tested constantly.[22]

Along similar lines, Kenichi Ohmae argues that an effective strategic plan takes account of three main players – the company, the customer and the competition – each exerting its own influence. The strategy that ignores competitive reaction is flawed; so is the strategy that does not take into account sufficiently how the customer will react; and so, of course, is the strategic plan that does not explore fully the organization's capacity to implement it.

How do you achieve your objectives?

Implementation is where most strategies fail. Success relies on matching an organization's resources, culture, structure and people to the strategies which emerge from consideration of an organization's core competencies and the environment it exists in.

How to succeed with strategy

If strategy is to make the leap from theory to effective implementation the people behind it must:

- accept uncertainty as a fact of business life
- continually look outside the organization to learn lessons and improve effectiveness
- learn from past mistakes and achievements
- use unconventional images to communicate strategic initiatives
- produce short, highly informative strategy documents
- regard strategy as a business tool
- not allow preconceived ideas to interfere with honest interpretation
- distrust immediate consensus
- put faith in strong feelings and take risks
- assume nothing
- break down barriers
- involve everyone
- look to the future.

Key books

Hamel, Gary and **Prahalad, CK**, *Competing for the Future*, Harvard Business School Press, Boston, 1994

Markides, Costas, *Diversification, Refocusing and Economic Performance*, MIT Press, Cambridge, Mass., 1995

Moore, JI, *Writers on Strategy and Strategic Management*, Penguin, London, 1992

Ohmae, Kenichi, *The Mind of the Strategist*, McGraw-Hill, New York, 1982

Henry Mintzberg
Strategy as craft

The work of Canadian Henry Mintzberg counters much of the detailed rationalism of other major thinkers of recent decades. From his first publication, *The Nature of Managerial Work* (1973), Mintzberg has challenged orthodoxy, arguing the case for a more intuitive and humane approach to strategy formulation and practice, as well as the structure of organizations. *The Nature of Managerial Work* exposed many of the myths surrounding senior managers, revealing them to be creatures of the moment rather than farsighted strategists carefully planning their next move.

Mintzberg has generated a unique reputation, as someone apart from the mainstream able to analyze basic assumptions about managerial behavior. His most recent work tackles head on the role and process of strategic planning. Mintzberg argues that intuition is "the soft underbelly of management" and that strategy has set out to provide uniformity and formality when none can be created.

Despite a series of highly important and influential books and appointments at two of the world's leading business schools (McGill in Canada and INSEAD in France) Henry Mintzberg remains something of an outsider in the world of management thinking.

While his books are scholarly rather than populist, he emphasizes the creative and spontaneous, the right side of the brain rather than the left side with its prediction for analysis and rationality. He is a wry humanist who carries out his work with academic rigor. "A well published waif" is how he jokingly describes himself; "perhaps the world's premier management thinker," says Tom Peters.[23]

There is a sizeable dose of cynicism in Mintzberg's world view. Though, when asked, he is quick to add the explanatory coda: "I am skeptical about everything except reality." To keep hold of reality, he eschews the management guru merry-go-round. "There is a lot of obnoxious hype about being a 'guru' to the extent that the medium can destroy the message," he says, "I'm in one of the most competitive fields around, but I've never felt competition for a moment. You can compete by competing head on or by not competing at all. I care about doing things well, not doing them better – that is a low standard."

Mintzberg's name was initially brought to a wider audience with his first book, *The Nature of Managerial Work*. An article in the *Harvard Business Review* ("The manager's job: folklore and fact")[24] brought Mintzberg's research further into the public eye. Its origins (and those of subsequent books) lie in Mintzberg's grand plan. "In 1968, I set out to write a text called *The Theory of Management Policy*, to draw together the research-based literature that helps to describe the processes of general management."

Mintzberg's plan has expanded – each of the three central chapters became books and an early section of the fourth chapter also developed into a book.

At the time of its publication, *The Nature of Managerial Work* was radically alternative and rapidly dispensed with much conventional wisdom. "I had a lot of difficulty getting my first book published," Mintzberg recalls. "One publisher said they were publishing a book just like it – 20 years later, I have yet to see the book." In his research, Mintzberg got close to managers actually managing rather than pontificating from afar. His research involved spending time with five organizations and analyzing

> *In his research, Mintzberg got close to managers actually managing rather than pontificating from afar.*

how their chief executives spent their time. While this tracking approach is now commonplace, in the early 1970s it was ambitious – previous research had concentrated on the people managed by managers and the structure of organizations rather than the day-to-day reality of managerial behavior and performance.

The Nature of Managerial Work revealed managers to be hostages to interruptions, flitting from subject to subject rarely giving undivided attention to anything. "The pressure of the managerial environment does not encourage the development of reflective planners, the classical literature not withstanding," Mintzberg observed. "The job breeds adaptive information-manipulators who prefer the live, concrete situation. The manager works in an environment of stimulus-response, and he develops in his work a clear preference for live action." Instead of being isolated figureheads analyzing and generating carefully thought-out strategy, managers were suddenly exposed as fallible and human. The corollary of Mintzberg's conclusions was that if we don't understand how managers spend their time and what they do, how can management be improved and the skills of managers appropriately developed?

Twenty years on, Mintzberg's style and approach has remained determinedly iconoclastic. "My books succeeded because they were different," he says. "If you think differently and execute it poorly you are dead."

His background in mechanical engineering might explain the root of Mintzberg's techniques and thinking. "Mechanical engineering is not concerned with image or status. It is about reality and requires a certain kind of thinking," he says, recalling a college assignment to design a pump. While all the other students went away and looked at the latest catalogs to copy a design, Mintzberg didn't look at anything and came up with a pump virtually identical to pumps when they were first invented. In his later research, Mintzberg also seeks to reinvent or establish first principles for himself.

"I am not an intellectual. I am a writer and researcher," he says. "I write primarily for myself, to find things out. I never write anything to boost my reputation or image – sometimes it is *appropriate* to publish something in the *Harvard Business Review*. When I am writing, the painful stage is getting an outline and then there is joy when things click and integrate."

After his initial success, Mintzberg's focus shifted to organizational structure. In *The Structure of Organizations* he identified five types of "ideal" organizational structure:

- simple structure
- machine bureaucracy

- professional bureaucracy
- divisionalized form
- adhocracy.

Even so, at the core of Mintzberg's work is a belief in the excitement and spontaneity of management and faith in people rather than organizations: "I don't like to be organized – I am a voyeur." He has little time for the formal dictates of the organization. "We have become prisoners of cerebral management. I'm sympathetic to the management process which is intuitive, based on immediate responses," he says. Instead of seeing strategy as the apotheosis of rationalism Mintzberg has famously coined the term "crafting strategy," whereby strategy is created as deliberately, delicately and dangerously as a potter making a pot. To Mintzberg strategy is more likely to "emerge," through a kind of organizational osmosis, than be produced by a group of strategists sitting round a table believing they can predict the future.

Mintzberg regards full-time MBA programs as perpetuating the obsession with "cerebral management." He no longer teaches on MBA programs and contentiously advises: "Regular MBA programs should be closed down. It's the wrong way to train people who weren't managers to become managers. MBA programs are confused between training leaders and specialists. At the moment, we train financial analysts and then expect them to become leaders. If accountants were forbidden to be chief executives it would probably be an enormous benefit."

HENRY MINTZBERG

Born 1939

Canadian

Educator

Education: McGill University; MIT.

Career: Worked for Canadian National Railways 1961–63; later he was visiting professor at a number of universities and business schools; President of Strategic Management Society 1988-91; consultant to a large number of organizations; visiting professor at INSEAD; director of the Center for Strategy Studies in Organizations at McGill University; professor at Montreal's McGill University since 1968.

Books: *The Nature of Managerial Work,* Harper & Row, New York, 1973; *The Structuring of Organizations,* Prentice Hall, New Jersey, 1979; *Structures In Fives: Designing Effective Organizations,* Prentice Hall, New Jersey, 1983 – an expurgated version of the 1979 book; *Power In and Around Organizations,* Prentice Hall, New Jersey, 1983; *Mintzberg on Management: Inside Our Strange World of Organizations,* Free Press, New York, 1989; *The Strategy Process: Concepts, Contexts, Cases,* with JB Quinn, Prentice Hall, New Jersey, 1991 (2nd edition); *The Rise and Fall of Strategic Planning,* Prentice Hall International, Hemel Hempstead, 1994.

Mintzberg's most recent work is probably his most controversial. "Strategy is not the consequence of planning but the opposite: its starting point,"[25] he says, countering the carefully wrought arguments of strategists, from Igor Ansoff in the 1960s to the Boston Consulting Group in the 1970s and Michael Porter in the 1980s. *The Rise and Fall of Strategic Planning* is a masterly and painstaking deconstruction of central pillars of management theory. Arguing that "strategy is not the consequence of planning but the opposite: its starting point," Mintzberg exposes the fallacies and failings at the root of planning. These include:

- **Processes** – a fascination with elaborate processes creates bureaucracy and strangles innovation.

- **Data** – Mintzberg argues that "hard" data, the lifeblood of the traditional strategist, is a source of information; "soft" data, however, provides the wisdom. "Hard information can be no better and is often at times far worse than soft information," he writes. In *The Nature of Managerial Work,* Mintzberg similarly observed that managers relied on "soft information" rather than exhaustive written reports.

- **Detachment** – Mintzberg refutes the notion of managers creating strategic plans from ivory towers. "Effective strategists are not people who abstract themselves from the daily detail but quite the opposite: they are the ones who *immerse* themselves in it, while being able to abstract the *strategic* messages from it".

Looking at the development of his work, Mintzberg observes: "My perception of what constitutes effective management is not so different as it was. But now there is a lot more ineffective management." In *The Rise and Fall of Strategic Planning*, he produces a typical paragraph (on the role of the effective strategist) which has the air of someone thinking aloud, but perhaps sums up Mintzberg's own approach: "Perceiving the forest from the trees is not the right metaphor at all... because opportunities tend to be hidden under the leaves. A better one may be to detect a diamond in the rough in a seam of ore. Or to mix the metaphors, no one ever found a diamond by flying over a forest. From the air, a forest looks like a simple carpet of green, not the complex living system it really is."

New perspectives on strategy

Value migration

Strip away the management speak and value migration is based on a stark fact of business life. Over any period the needs and expectations of customers change. If a company fails to keep pace, it will find itself left behind

The trick, therefore, lies in being able to identify the level of value migration and then in doing something about it. And, inevitably, it is here the problems begin. When you are in the throes of actually managing a business, any perception of value migration is likely to be clouded. Paradoxically, the more successful you are, the less likely you are to be able to view value migration with any clarity.

Value migration

Defined by Adrian Slywotzky, Richard Tedlow and Benson Shapiro as "the flow of economic and shareholder value away from obsolete business models to new, more effective designs."[26]

To gain an insight into value migration, the American academics and consultants Shapiro, Tedlow and Slywotzky suggest that companies ask themselves a number of questions. These begin with "List your most important product and customer service attributes for five years in the future, for today and for five years ago" and also cover market share, percentage of new product failures and ratio of profit from new products. Honest answers to the questions provide a sense of how your company is positioned in terms of value migration. Warning lights flash, for example, if your customers' business is shrinking, if the *quality* of your market share is declining or if your profits from new products are low.

In response to the flashing lights, a company can do a variety of things. It may examine the value migration process within its industry; look more intensely at trends in customer needs; or make comparisons with the structure of competitors. Moving early is essential. Instead of being reduced to a panic-stricken burst of downsizing, Shapiro, Tedlow and Slywotzky suggest that companies should gradually shift investment away from the old design; invest in new capabilities; and protect the new businesses.

The dividing line between success and failure is narrow. As they point out, IBM – the archetypal "good" company – made $6 billion in 1990 and lost $5 billion two years later. IBM failed to change with the market and only moved when value had well and truly migrated.

Strategy innovation

Gary Hamel contends that strategy innovation is central to the creation of new wealth. The trouble is that the actual job of creating strategy is shrouded in mystery. Strategy is lucky foresight as much as anything else. Hamel argues that it is only by giving greater consideration to the emergence of strategy that we will be able to create strategies which succeed.

> **Hamel argues that it is only by giving greater consideration to the emergence of strategy that we will be able to create strategies which succeed.**

Hamel maps out five preconditions for the emergence of strategy.[27] First, the entire organization needs to have a voice in creating strategy. It is not the sole preserve of management but "pluralistic and participative." Second, discussion concerning strategy must cut across industries and organizations so that knowledge can be combined in new ways. Third, Hamel believes that people will embrace change when they identify opportunities for rewards and growth. (This also explains the redundancy of downsizing as a policy.) Finally, companies must carry out some market experimentation to determine which new strategies work.

Hamel's London Business School colleague, Costas Markides defines "strategic innovation" as "a fundamental reconceptualization of what the business is all about which in turn leads to a dramatically different way of playing the game in our existing business."[28]

Markides argues that such innovation is achieved by a small number of organizations. Among those he cites are CNN, IKEA, Body Shop and First Direct. (It is astonishing how regularly these names come up in management literature.) The number of innovators is so small due to a combination of structural and cultural inertia. Companies generally have little appetite for true innovation, strategic or otherwise.

Strategic innovation occurs when a company identifies a gap in the way it is positioned in a market; moves to fill the gap and uncovers a new mass market. Markides describes "gaps" in three ways – as "new customer segments emerging; or existing customer segments which are, however, neglected by existing competitors"; "new customer needs emerging; or existing customer needs which are, however, not served well by existing competitors"; and "new ways of producing, delivering or distributing existing (or new) products/services to existing (or new) customer segments."

To move to strategic innovation, Markides suggests a number of techniques. First, companies have to be prepared to ask basic questions of the way they currently do business. Successful companies find this almost impossible – profits tend to blunt their willingness to confront potential future difficulties. Strategic innovators, however, are able to ask questions. This Markides attributes to two reasons. First, they "monitored not only their financial health but also their strategic health." Suggestions that their strategies were coming adrift were speedily picked up on. Second, "they artificially created a positive crisis to galvanize the organization into active thinking."

Strategic innovators were also more adept at challenging existing strategic planning processes. "Established companies are constantly preoccupied with how they need to compete in their business without ever questioning the who and the what of their business," Markides laments. Questions lead to tomorrow's strategic answers.

Musical interludes

Music is becoming something of a fashionable strategy metaphor. In his 1997 book, *Jamming*, John Kao of Harvard Business School linked the flexible demands of management to jazz improvisations.[29] Conductor Benjamin Zander operates a sideline as a motivational business speaker and violinists have been contributing to business school strategy programs.

Stanford's Kathleen Eisenhardt has looked at the significance of improvisation in the strategic decision-making process.[30] Eisenhardt argues that researchers into strategic decisions have tended to follow three basic approaches. First is what she labels "bounded rationality." This approach ignores the influence of elements such as intuition, preferring a narrow, logic-based perspective. The second approach is termed "power and politics." This regards strategy as emerging from conflict and machinations among senior managers. Once again the emotional element is played down. The final approach is the "garbage can." This suggests that "decision making occurs through the random meeting of choices looking for problems, decision makers looking for something to decide, problems looking for solutions, and so forth." Once again, this is only partly the case and is, practically, unhelpful.

Strategic decisions, Eisenhardt suggests, need a new and more dynamic model: improvisation. By improvisation she does not mean a spur of the moment free for all, but something altogether more structured. She says that true improvisation has two characteristics. The first is that it requires people to communicate intensely with each other. And such communication belongs to the moment. The second key characteristic is that "improvisation involves performers relying on a few, very specific rules. There are not many rules, but those that do exist are religiously followed."

Backed by research, improvisation is a convincing metaphor. The question must be, how helpful can the metaphor be in practice?

The balanced scorecard

Measurement has lain at the heart of twentieth-century management. Indeed, measurement has often appeared to be the central function of management. Scientific management, for example, involved measuring the performance of workers against predetermined optimum times. Throughout the twentieth century, managers have found different things to measure and more sophisticated means of measurement. And, as every manager knows, what gets measured

The perennial problem for strategy has been that there are no obvious or meaningful means of measuring something so multi-faceted and complex.

gets done. The perennial problem for strategy has been that there are no obvious or meaningful means of measuring something so multi-faceted and complex.

The most fruitful area for this mania for quantification has been finance. Managers once simply talked of sales and profits. But, over the years, a complex array of ratios, measures, analytical tools and software packages has evolved. Every penny a company spends or produces can be analyzed in an infinite number of ways. Such are their powers of persuasion, that entire companies can be driven by these financial measures. The most famous instance of this was ITT in the 1960s, under the control of Harold Geneen. Geneen took management by financial measurement to its limits, creating an elaborate system of financial reporting. When he left the company, the deck of cards collapsed.

The obvious conclusion to be drawn from Geneen's approach is that if you concentrate solely on financial measures, you can achieve short-term, even medium-term success, but such narrow constraining measures are unlikely to yield long-term prosperity. The trouble was that financial ratios and performance were the easiest things to measure. Other elements of corporate performance – such as customer loyalty or employee satisfaction – were more abstract and measurement appeared to pose more questions than answers.

At the same time as companies were considering how to measure "softer" elements of their performance, they became increasingly addicted to managerial fads and fashions.

So, in the 1980s and 1990s, organizations were often faced with the dilemmas of unwieldy financial measurement systems; few reliable means of measuring other elements of their performance; and a predilection for short-lived fads whose impact was rarely measured in any way whatsoever.

The answer to these imbalances was proposed by David Norton and Robert Kaplan as the **Balanced Scorecard** ("a strategic management and measurement system that links strategic objectives to comprehensive indicators"). Norton is co-founder of the consulting company, Renaissance Solutions, and Kaplan is Marvin Bower Professor of Leadership Development at Harvard Business School. The duo developed the Balanced Scorecard concept at the beginning of the 1990s in research sponsored by KPMG.

The result was an article in the *Harvard Business Review* ("The balanced scorecard," January/February 1993). This had a simple message for managers: what you measure is what you get. Kaplan and Norton compared running a company to flying a plane. The pilot who relies on a single dial is unlikely to be safe. Pilots must utilize all the information contained in their cockpit. "The complexity of managing an organization today requires that managers be able to view performance in several areas simultaneously," said Kaplan and Norton. "Moreover, by forcing senior managers to consider all the important operational measures together, the balanced scorecard can let them see whether improvement in one area may be achieved at the expense of another."

Kaplan and Norton suggested that four elements need to be balanced. First, the customer perspective. Companies must ask how they are perceived by customers. The second element is "internal perspective." Companies must ask what it is that they must excel at. Third, the "innovation and learning perspective." Companies must ask whether they can continue to improve and create value. Finally, the financial perspective. How does the company look to shareholders?

According to Kaplan and Norton, by focussing energies, attention and measures on all four of these dimensions, companies become driven by their mission rather than by short-term financial performance. Crucial to achieving this is applying measures to company strategy. Instead of being beyond measurement, the Balanced Scorecard argues that strategy must be central to any process of measurement – "A good Balanced Scorecard should tell the story of your strategy."

Identifying the essential measures for an organization is not straightforward. One company produced 500 measures on its first examination. This was distilled down to seven measures – 20 is par for the course. According to Kaplan and Norton, a "good" Balanced Scorecard contains three elements. First, it establishes "cause and effect relationships." Rather than being isolated figures, measures are related to each other and the network of relationships makes up the strategy. Second, a Balanced Scorecard should have a combination of lead and lag indicators. Lag indicators are measures, such as market share, which are common across an industry and, though important, offer no distinctive advantage. Lead indicators are measures which are company (and strategy) specific. Finally, an effective Balanced Scorecard is linked to financial measures. By this, Kaplan and Norton mean that initiatives such as reengineering or lean production need to be tied to financial measures rather than pursued indiscriminately.

In many ways, the concept of the Balanced Scorecard is brazen common sense. Balance is clearly preferable to imbalance. (The counter intuitive reality is that unbalanced companies, usually driven by a single dominant individual, have often proved short-term successes.) The Balanced Scorecard is now widely championed by a variety of companies. Indeed, it

In many ways, the concept of the Balanced Scorecard is brazen common sense.

has somewhat ironically become a management fad. Its argument that blind faith in a single measurement or a small range of measures is dangerous is a powerful one. However, effective measurement of elements, such as management competencies or intellectual capital, remains elusive.

Key books

Kaplan, Robert S and **Cooper, Robin**, *Cost and Effect: Using Integrated Cost Systems to drive Profitability and Performance*, Harvard Business School Press, 1998

Kaplan, Robert S and **Norton, David P**, *The Balanced Scorecard: Translating Strategy into Action*, Harvard Business School Press, 1996

References: Creating and implementing strategy

1 Ohmae, Kenichi, *The Mind of the Strategist*, McGraw-Hill, New York, 1982.

2 Ansoff, H Igor, "A contingent paradigm for success of complex organizations," in *Milestones in Management Volume 5*, Schaffer Poeschel, Switzerland, 1994.

3 Mintzberg, Henry, *The Rise and Fall of Strategic Planning*, Prentice Hall, Hemel Hempstead, 1994.

4 Ansoff, H Igor, *Strategic Management*, Macmillan, London, 1979.

5 Ansoff, H Igor, *Milestones in Management Volume 5*, Schaffer Poeschel, Switzerland, 1994.

6 Ansoff, H Igor, *Milestones in Management Volume 5*, Schaffer Poeschel, Switzerland, 1994.

7 Ansoff, H Igor, "A contingent paradigm for success of complex organizations," in *Milestones in Management Volume 5*, Schaffer Poeschel, Switzerland, 1994.

8 Ohmae, Kenichi, *The Mind of the Strategist*, McGraw-Hill, New York, 1982.

9 Boston Consulting Group website.

10 Taylor, Bernard, "The return of strategic planning – once more with feeling," *Long Range Planning*, Vol. 30, No. 3, 1997.

11 Koch, Richard, *The Financial Times Guide to Management and Strategy*, Financial Times Pitman Publishing, London, 1995.

12 Markides, Costas, "Strategic Management," in *The Financial Times Handbook of Management*, Financial Times Pitman Publishing, London, 1995.

13 "Professor Porter PhD," *The Economist*, 8 October 1994.

14 Porter, Michael, "Corporate strategy: the state of strategic thinking," *The Economist*, 23 May 1987.

15 Mintzberg, Henry, *The Rise and Fall of Strategic Planning*, Prentice Hall, Hemel Hempstead, 1994.

16 Markides, Costas, "Strategic management," in *Financial Times Handbook of Management*, Financial Times Pitman Publishing, London, 1995.

17 Sadler, Philip, "Gold collar workers – making the best of the best," *Directions*, December 1992.

18 Peters, Tom, *Liberation Management*, Alfred Knopf, New York, 1992.

19 Campbell, Andrew, Devine, Marion & Young, David, *A Sense of Mission*, Hutchison Business Books, London, 1990.

20 Ohmae, Kenichi, *The Mind of the Strategist*, McGraw-Hill, New York, 1982.

21 Turner, Ian, "The myth of the core competence," *Manager Update*, Vol. 8, No. 4, Summer 1997.

22 Drucker, Peter F, "The theory of business', *Harvard Business Review*, September–October 1994.

23 Peters, Tom, "Plans down the drain," *Independent on Sunday*, 24 April 1994.

24 Mintzberg, Henry, "The manager's job: folklore and fact," *Harvard Business Review*, July/August 1975.

25 Mintzberg, Henry, *The Rise and Fall of Strategic Planning*, Prentice Hall, Hemel Hempstead, 1994.

26 Shapiro, Benson, Slywotzky, Adrian J and Tedlow, Richard S, "How to stop bad things happening to good companies," *Strategy & Business*, Issue 6, Spring 1997.

27 Hamel, Gary, "Strategy innovation and the quest for value," *Sloan Management Review*, Winter 1998.

28 Markides, Costas, "Strategic innovation: the leaders' dilemma," *Sloan Management Review*, Spring 1998.

29 Kao, John, *Jamming*, Harvard Business School Press, Boston, 1997.

30 Eisenhardt, Kathleen, "Strategic decisions and all that jazz," *Business Strategy Review*, Autumn 1997.

5

New ways of managing people

"By empowering others, a leader does not decrease his power, instead he may increase it – especially if the whole organization performs better."

Rosabeth Moss Kanter[1]

"The desire to stand well with one's fellows, the so-called human instincts of association, easily outweighs the merely individual interest and the logic of reasoning upon which so many spurious principles of management are based."

Elton Mayo[2]

From personnel to human resources

In the world of scientific management, people were relegated to second place behind the efficiency and productivity of machinery. Their wants, aspirations and motivations were largely ignored or paid dismissive lip-service. There were lone voices arguing that the fulfilment of individuals was an important prerequisite of any responsible organization, but they remained isolated and unheeded.

The American political scientist **Mary Parker Follett** (1868–1933), for example, argued that in a democratic society the primary task of management is to create a situation where people readily contribute of their own accord. She repeatedly emphasized the need for managers to learn from their own experience by systematically observing experiences, recording them and relating these experiences to the total situation. She saw the manager as responsible for integrating the contributions of specialists such as marketing, production, cost accountants and industrial relations so that they contributed effectively for the benefit of all.

MARY PARKER FOLLET

1868–1933

American

Political scientist

Education: Thayer Academy; Society for the Collegiate Instruction of Women; Cambridge University.

Career: Mainly spent in social work. Follett spent the last years of her life mainly in London.

Books: *The New State: Group Organization*, Longman, London, 1918; *Creative Experience*, Longman, London, 1924; *Dynamic Administration*, Harper & Brothers, New York, 1941; *Freedom and Coordination*, Pitman, London, 1949.

Humane approaches to management, however, have in general been notable by their absence. Though companies have been proclaiming for generations that theirs is a people business, in reality this has been as insincere as it is meaningless. There are a few exceptions. In the UK, Marks & Spencer has set high standards in its dealings with its

> *Humane approaches to management have in general been notable by their absence.*

employees and customers. It has heeded the observation of one of its founders, Lord Sieff, that "ultimately, whatever the form of economic activity, it is people that count most."[3] In the US, Levi Strauss & Co. has set exceptionally high ethical standards, but there are very few names that can be uncritically added to the list.

Recognition of the human side of enterprise can be traced back to a number of influential thinkers. Though their individual impact on the way companies manage themselves is limited, the cumulative effect has proved significant.

The impetus began with the **Hawthorne Studies** into workers' attitudes and behavior conducted between 1927 and 1932 at the Western Electric Plant in Hawthorne, Chicago. The Studies produced the Hawthorne Effect. This has been much debated and questioned. It found that the output of the workers improved when people believed that management was concerned about their well-being. An alternative, but cynical, view is that their performance improved simply because the experiment was underway.

The Hawthorne Studies were important because they showed that views of how managers behaved were a vital aspect of motivation and improved performance. Also, the research revealed the importance of informal work groups.

The most passionate advocate of the Hawthorne Studies was the Australian **Elton Mayo** (1880–1949). Mayo argued that self-esteem was vital to effective performance and that management needs to gain the consensus of working groups as well as individuals. "So long as commerce specializes in business methods which take no account of human nature and social motives, so long may we expect strikes and sabotage to be the ordinary accompaniment of industry," he wrote. Mayo believed that the informal groups revealed by Hawthorne could either be utilized to the individual and corporate good or ignored to everyone's detriment. Following on from the conclusion of the Hawthorne Studies, Mayo championed the need for efficient and recognized communication channels between workers and management in order that individuals and groups could identify with corporate goals and objectives.

ELTON MAYO

1880–1949

Australian

Psychologist

Education: Medical training in London and Edinburgh.

Career: Worked in Africa; an Adelaide printing company; taught at Queensland University; went to the US in 1923 and worked at the University of Pennsylvania, then Harvard.

Books: *The Human Problems of an Industrial Civilization*, Macmillan, New York, 1933; *The Social Problems of an Industrial Civilization*, Harvard University Press, Cambridge, Mass., 1945.

The work at Hawthorne was not really capitalized on until the 1950s when a group of like-minded thinkers – later christened the **Human Relations School** – emerged in the United States. Its influence has been wide ranging with its central figures, Douglas Macgregor, Abraham Maslow and Frederick Herzberg coming into contact with and influencing a wide range of later thinkers including Ed Schein, Chris Argyris and Warren Bennis.

The social psychologist **Douglas Macgregor** (1906–64) produced one of the most long-lasting contributions with his **Theory X** and **Theory Y** which sought to provide a rational and accessible framework to motivational factors.

Theory X was based on traditional, and instantly recognizable, carrot and stick thinking. It contended that workers were inherently lazy, needed to be supervised and motivated and that, for them, work was a necessary evil to provide money. In the 1970s, Theory X spawned a humorous offspring in Theory W (W for Whiplash) which advocated generous use of the stick.

More optimistically, Macgregor's Theory Y argued that people wanted and needed work and what should be sought was the individual's commitment to the firm's objectives and then a means of liberating their abilities.

When Macgregor died in 1964 he was working on Theory Z which aimed to bring together the needs and aspirations of the corporation and the individual. The work was never completed but was picked up by William Ouchi who took it as the title of a book which sought to extract lessons from Japanese management. Ouchi's Theory Z organization is centered on lifetime employment, concern for employees including their social life, decisions made by consensus, slow promotion, excellent transmittal of information, commitment to the firm and intense concern for quality. If Macgregor had lived to complete Theory Z it may well have contained some similar elements.

DOUGLAS MACGREGOR

1906–64

American

Psychologist

Education: City College of Detroit, Harvard.

Career: Instructor and tutor at Harvard; Assistant Professor at MIT; in 1948 became President of Antioch College, Ohio; 1954 Professor of Management at MIT; 1962 Sloans Fellow of Industrial Management, MIT.

Books: *The Human Side of Enterprise*, McGraw-Hill, New York, 1960.

In parallel to Macgregor's work was that of **Abraham Maslow** (1908–70). Maslow developed a **hierarchy of needs**. This identified an ascending series of human needs – starting with warmth, shelter and food and ending with self-actualization – achievement of personal potential. The hierarchy was based on the idea that once the need is satisfied you are no longer motivated by it. This is a theory which fired debate but bore little relation to the avaricious nature of human kind.

"What Maslow did not see is that a want changes in the act of being satisfied," says Peter Drucker. "As a want approaches satiety, its capacity to reward, and with it its power as an incentive, diminishes fast. But its capacity to deter, to create dissatisfaction and to act as a disincentive, rapidly increases."

ABRAHAM MASLOW

1908–70

American

Psychologist

Education: University of Wisconsin.

Career: Columbia University and Brooklyn College; 1945–47 plant manager, Maslow Cooperage Corp, CA; 1951 Professor at Brandeis University.

Books: *Motivation and Personality*, Harper & Row, New York, 1954; *Towards a Psychology of Being*, Van Nostrand Reinhold, New York, 1982; *Maslow on Management*, John Wiley, New York, 1998.

Developing from Maslow came **Frederick Herzberg** (born 1923). His career – much influenced by wartime experiences – has been dominated by impassioned humanity. "Man has two sets of needs. His need as an animal to avoid pain and his need as a human to grow psychologically," he says in *Work and the Nature of Man*.[4]

Herzberg, a clinical psychologist, identified **hygiene factors** (also called maintenance factors) as the basic economic needs; contrasted with **motivation factors** meeting deeper aspirations. Good hygiene is necessary but not enough in itself to provide adequate motivation. His influence was significant – his 1968 *Harvard Business Review* article, "One more time: how do you motivate employees?" sold over one million copies. Herzberg later coined the term **job enrichment**.

FREDERICK HERZBERG

Born 1923

American

Psychologist

Education: University of Pittsburgh.

Career: Served in the Second World War; clinical psychologist with the US Public Health Service; Professor of Management, University of Utah.

Books: *The Motivation to Work* with Mausner and Snyderman, Wiley, New York, 1959.

The late twentieth century shook the world of human resources. Accepted practices were radically rethought as organizations sought to restructure themselves. Traditional practices have not only been questioned but, in many cases, have been overturned.

With hierarchies decreasing and the growing emphasis on becoming leaner and fitter, the onus is increasingly on corporations extracting the best possible performance from all employees. In (best) practice this means recruiting well-qualified and highly skilled people and developing the skills of everyone in the organization.

With increased acceptance of its importance, personnel management has become human resource management. The emerging role of human resource management is radically different from that of the past when it dealt with the bureaucracy of employing people and little else. From being a caring role, human resources is being realigned as a strategic role, focussed on the business needs and strategic plans of the corporation.

> *With increased acceptance of its importance, personnel management has become human resource management.*

Indeed, the nitty-gritty of wages, vacations and benefits is often outsourced. Jim LeTart, an HR marketing manager, argues that when the going gets administrative, HR professionals need to automate to become strategic. "HR departments that have introduced employee self-service and other automated systems have dramatically enhanced service levels by virtually eliminating paper-intensive, error-prone work," says LeTart.[5] He has identified five processes as prime candidates for automation: benefits enrolment – Boeing employees and pensioners enrol for benefits via the Internet; requests for forms; internal job advertising; training enrolment; and entry and updating of personal data. If these aspects of the HR function are automated, the results can be better customer service and more reliable data. "HR executives and managers can't afford to make the mistake of allowing administrative resources to be depleted through chores that don't add solid value," concludes LeTart. "Today's HR executives can claim the position of in-house strategic consultant only after they lead their departments out of the business of administrivia and into the business of customer service and business analysis."

In its new role, human resource professionals regard it as:

- **A facilitator of change** – to carry people through upheaval requires the true management of human resources.

- **An integrated approach to management** – rather than being an isolated function, HR is regarded as a core activity, one which shapes a company's values. In particular, this can have an impact on customer service.

- **A mediator** – establishing and balancing the new and emerging aspirations and requirements of the company and the individual.

Even so, there is the danger of becoming carried away. Reality often lags behind tidy theories. Tony Grundy of Cranfield School of Management suggests that the fashionable talk of human resources strategy may not be backed up by real improvements in performance. Grundy contends that "integrating corporate strategy and HR matters into an organization and people strategy may prove more successful" than putting faith entirely in HR strategy.[6] Organization and people strategy is regarded by him as the fourth stage in the evolution of HR management from traditional personnel management to HR management, HR strategy and, finally, organization and people strategy.

This fourth stage is characterized by a principal focus on being proactive and interactive with business strategy – previous stages focussed on stability and were reactive. It integrates HR programs with operational change and is championed by line managers, with HR specialists fulfilling the role of change catalysts.

The chief attraction of Grundy's argument is that it is realistic. Instead of regarding HR and corporate strategy as isolated functions, the two are seen as interdependent. The emphasis is on strategic thinking rather than traditional strategic planning. Organizational and people strategy might bring HR further into the mainstream of corporate activities. In the age of knowledge work and intellectual capital, it is astonishing that it has taken so long.

Key books

Beer, M, Spector, B, Lawrence, PR, Mills, DQ and **Walton, R**, *Managing Human Assets*, Free Press, New York, 1984

Blyton, P and **Turnbull, P**, *Reassessing Human Resource Management*, Sage, London, 1992

Storey, J (editor), *New Perspectives on Human Resource Management*, Routledge, 1989

Storey, J, *Developments in the Management of Human Resources*, Blackwell, Oxford, 1992

Tyson, S and **Fell, A**, *Evaluating the Personnel Function*, Hutchinson, 1986

Tom Peters
Evangelizing people

Strangely, in the liberating atmosphere of the 1960s, the human side of management experienced a lull. In the 1990s, however, people have been pushed to the center of the organizational and managerial stage. For this, one major contemporary thinker should be attributed with a considerable degree of credit. Tom Peters, undoubtedly the pre-eminent contemporary management guru, has proved a potent champion of the humanity of sound business. Peters' books sell in their millions, his seminars fill auditoriums and his syndicated newspaper column is avidly read throughout the world. His message is passionately expressed. Describing his presentational style, *The Economist* observed: "Striding urgently back and forth, bellowing and bantering, he nearly achieves the difficult feat of making management seem exciting."[7]

Unquestionably, management **is** exciting to Peters. Even the titles of his books are exhortations (they have been called "charismatic shockers") – *Liberation Management, A Passion for Excellence, Thriving on Chaos* and, most famously, *In Search of Excellence*. The latter book, co-written with Robert Waterman, is the best-selling management book of all time, having sold over five million copies across the world.

In Search of Excellence marked an important development in management publishing as well as management thinking. Its popularity has fuelled a massive increase in the management book market. Its influence on the practice of management, of course, remains immeasurable. Peters has always insisted that the book's massive popularity should not disguise the fact that very few of the buyers actually read the book – and fewer still converted its potpourri of best practice into managerial reality.

TOM PETERS

Born 1942

American

Consultant and writer

Education: Masters in civil engineering from Cornell; MBA at Stanford.

Career: Worked in the Pentagon; served in Vietnam; Office of Management and Budget in Washington; consultant with McKinsey & Co.; author and consultant with his own diverse company, the Tom Peters Group.

Books: *In Search of Excellence*, with Robert Waterman, Harper & Row, New York and London, 1982; *A Passion for Excellence*, with Nancy Austin, Collins, London, 1985; *Thriving on Chaos*, Macmillan, London, 1988; *Liberation Management*, Alfred Knopf, New York, 1992; *The Tom Peters Seminar*, Vintage Books, New York, 1994; *The Pursuit of Wow!*, Vintage Books, New York, 1994; *The Circle of Innovation*, Hodder & Stoughton, London, 1997.

Books about Peters: Stuart Crainer, *The Tom Peters Phenomenon: Corporate Man to Corporate Skunk*, Capstone, Oxford, 1997.

The book emerged from work carried out by Peters and Waterman with their then employer, the consultancy McKinsey. Their research identified 43 successful companies and went on to identify the characteristics which were common to their success. The selection was based on six financial measurement: 20-year averages of compound asset growth; compound equity growth; ratio of market value to book value; return on capital; return on equity; and return on sales.

There was nothing earth shattering in this technique. Indeed, the conclusion was largely that the excellent companies managed to exercise common sense, keeping an obsessive eye on the business basics. The book's success was secured by the fact that it accentuated the positive at a time of unmitigated gloom – it was published in 1982. As managers lurched from crisis to crisis, and one bright new management theory to another, Peters and Waterman drew out what made successful companies tick and they did so in an approachable way.

An important element in the book was the **Seven S framework**. Its roots lay in the summer of 1978 when, as part of the research, Waterman asked two academics, Richard Pascale and Anthony Athos, to help him out. Waterman and Peters were trying to make sense of the research they had done on the characteristics of successful companies, but were struggling to establish the crucial links.

It was agreed that the four would spend five days in a small room discovering what they knew and didn't know about organizations. The theory was neat and tidy, though Athos and Pascale had reservations about the human dynamics. Athos suggested that an agenda for the five days was essential otherwise the hyperactive Peters would hijack the proceedings. Athos, then based at Harvard Business School, recalled an approach used by one of his colleagues, Cyrus (Chuck) Gibson. He had a scheme – strategy, structure and systems – which he had developed for Harvard's Program for Management Development which Gibson and Athos ran. Athos suggested starting with strategy on Monday, then moving on to structure on Tuesday, and systems on Wednesday. He had a couple of his own themes to add – guiding concepts, which he renamed super-ordinate goals, and shared values. Pascale suggested style, and the duo walked in with five of what eventually became the Seven Ss.

The idea of creating an accessible model was hardly original. Peters and Waterman later acknowledged their debt to Harold Leavitt's "Diamond" model, which boiled the facts of managerial life down to task, structure, people, information, control and environment. Leavitt's model is obviously not a million miles away from what became the Seven S model.

The difference was that though management tools come and go with ever-increasing rapidity, this one worked – at least when the quartet were ensconced in their discussions. Athos and Pascale persuaded Peters and Waterman to use the alliterative labelling, arguing that its advantages outweighed its lack of sophistication. Peters suggested adding "skill" to the framework.

So, armed with six words beginning with S which appeared to make sense of something, Peters and Waterman acquainted interested parties in McKinsey with their developing model. A few weeks later, they introduced the six Ss at an internal meeting. In preparing for the meeting, Peters and Waterman, still aided by Athos and Pascale, labored over how to make their message more accessible and understandable. Not content with six variables, Peters and Pascale suggested another was needed, one that had to do with timing and implementation. Athos and Pascale proposed calling it "sequencing."

This version of the magnificent seven proved short lived. Julien Phillips, an associate in McKinsey's San Francisco office, then joined the team. He argued that sequencing should be replaced by staff. The other four quickly agreed as sequencing was proving troublesome to fit in. Peters had suggested "people" should be included and, in his teaching at Harvard, Athos was using the awkward and decidedly unalliterative "aggregates of people." Peters also weighed in with the possibility of adding "power" somewhere. This didn't happen. So, the group were left with seven: systems, strategy, structure, style, skills, shared values, and staff.

The seven agreed words were then passed on to McKinsey's graphics department which created an image of a molecule. The Seven S model was born. It was neatly alliterative, accessible, understandable and with its logo (later named "the happy atom") highly marketable.

The Seven S model first saw the light of day in published form in June 1980. Waterman, Peters and Phillips put together an article entitled "Structure is not organization." This was published in

Business Horizons, the journal of Indiana University's Graduate School of Business. The article was tentative, almost apologetic – "As yet the Seven S framework is admittedly no more than a rough conceptual tool for helping managers to understand the complexity of effective organization change – and to design change programs that are rich in concept and humble in expectations. The framework's virtues – realism and relative simplicity – are likely to have a good deal more appeal to practicing managers than the academic researchers."

Meanwhile, Pascale and Athos were working on what was to become *The Art of Japanese Management*, published in 1981. This introduced the Seven S framework to a mass audience. Peters and Waterman also featured the framework in *In Search of Excellence* when it was published a year later.

The attraction of the Seven Ss is that they are brilliantly memorable and simple. The framework is a model of how organizations achieve success. Inevitably a model which simplifies something as complex as organizational behavior is open to abuse, misinterpretation and criticism. The Seven S framework has suffered more than its fair share. (Contrast this with the generally positive response still reserved for Michael Porter's five forces model of competitiveness which simplifies something equally as complex but does so in a far more analytical and academic way.)

> **The framework is a model of how organizations achieve success.**

The Seven S framework

1 *Strategy* – plan or course of action leading to the allocation of a firm's scarce resources, over time, to reach identified goals.

2 *Structure* – salient features of the organization chart (i.e. functional, decentralized, etc.) and how the separate entities of an organization are tied together.

3 *Systems* – procedualized reports and routinized processes (such as meeting formats), etc.

4 *Staff* – "demographics" description of important personnel categories within the firm (i.e. engineers, entrepreneurs, MBAs, etc). "Staff" is not meant in line-staff terms.

▶

> 5 *Style* – characterization of how key managers behave in achieving the organization's goals; also the cultural style of the organization.
>
> 6 *Shared* values – the significant meanings or guiding concepts that an organization imbues in its members.
>
> 7 *Skills* – distinctive capabilities of key personnel and the firm as a whole.

The messages which emerged from *In Search of Excellence* have now largely entered into the language and practice of management. In one way or another, Peters and Waterman anticipated the future interest in empowerment, core businesses, customer focus, balancing centralization and decentralization, the lean organization and the dismantling of hierarchies.

Over the years since its publication, *In Search of Excellence's* reputation has taken a good deal of criticism. In particular, commentators quickly latched on to the fact that the 43 excellent companies did not necessarily remain so. Indeed, the fortunes of some of the chosen few plummeted dramatically – the airline People's Express was a notable casualty as was the computer company, Wang. IBM, an unquestioned choice at the time, has since experienced an unprecedented period of decline.

The failure of "excellent" companies to last the course encouraged Peters to address the problem of how organizations can sustain success and cope with increasingly competitive and chaotic markets. In *Thriving on Chaos* he begins with the line: "There are no excellent companies." It reiterates many of the central ideas of *In Search of Excellence*. It has five basic themes:

- obsession with responsiveness to customers
- constant innovation in all areas of the firm with risk and some failures encouraged
- partnership
- leadership which loves change and shares an inspiring vision
- control by means of simple support systems aimed at measuring the right things.

In *Thriving on Chaos*, Peters launched a crusade against management hierarchies. He contends that Drucker's suggestion in the 1950s that there should be a maximum of seven layers in an organization is now outdated. "I insist on five layers as the maximum," said Peters, pointing somewhat surprisingly to the Catholic church's structure as a good example. "In fact, even the five-layer limit should apply only to very complex organizations such as multi-division firms. Three layers – supervisor (with the job redefined to deal with a span of control no smaller than one supervisor for 25 to 75 people), department head and unit boss – should be tops for any single facility."

Thriving on Chaos proved a stepping stone to the more dramatic vision of Peters' *Liberation Management*. This is a huge sprawling book – "Mr Peters has not extended his passion for downsizing to his own prose," noted *The Economist*.[8] Undoubtedly it is rambling and lacking in focus but, behind its folksy stories of service excellence, it possesses a fervent purpose. It celebrates the death of middle management – "Middle Management, as we have known it since the railroads invented it right after the

> **Peters seeks to put people, creativity, technology and speed of thought and action at center stage.**

Civil War, is dead. Therefore, middle managers as we have known them are cooked geese." The phraseology is colorful, but eulogizes about the successes of people in a way few other management books have ever contemplated. Peters seeks to put people, creativity, technology and speed of thought and action at center stage.

While challenging for readers to negotiate, *Liberation Management* proved highly successful. Once again Peters' timing and ability to identify trends cannot be questioned. *In Search of Excellence* came out as US unemployment headed to 10 per cent; *Thriving on Chaos* came out on the day Wall Street fell by 20 per cent; *Liberation Management* emerged as the world was coming out of recession and organizations were becoming aware of the need to understand new ways of working which utilize technology more productively.

Liberation Management noted the trend towards what Peters labels as "fashion" – "The definition of every product and service is changing. Going soft, softer, softest. Going fickle, ephemeral, fashion. An explosion of new competitors, a rising standard of living in the developed world, and the ever-present... new technologies are leading the way. No corner of the world is exempt from the frenzy."

Amid the frenzy emerge the "excellent" organizations of the 1990s – companies like CNN, Body Shop, ABB and many others which espouse organizational liberalism through their commitment to speedy decisions, free-flowing organization and individual ability. Unlike its predecessors, *Liberation Management* does not provide a recipe for success. Instead, the recipe is an apparently random, unique stew of best practice. Peters' message is more pragmatic – if it is a good idea, make it work for you.

Skeptics – and there are many – suggest that Peters has a flair for marketing and self-publicity. This is undoubtedly true. Rather like a nineteenth-century travelling preacher, he has a plentiful supply of colorful slogans – "the nano-second nineties," "crazy times call for crazy organizations." But what is eye-catching about *Liberation Management* is Peters' intimate knowledge of some of the world's most advanced and innovative corporations. He has a knack of getting under organizational skins – he may interview the chief executive but is just as likely to focus on the chief executive's chauffeur. Among others, *Liberation Management* is dedicated to two workers in a heavy manufacturing company who have revolutionized the way they work. Peters' message is that corporate revolution is not simply about doing away with parking spaces for directors, but is real and touches everyone.

It is this willingness to grapple with human nature which goes some way to explaining Peters' popularity. He is interested in what motivates people and the reality of their day-to-day work. Paradoxically, this sort of down-to-earth realism is set against his evangelical idealism.

Peters' work is an antidote to the dry analysis of strategy or the focus on how companies are organized. Yes, he says, these things are important, but people are the driving force. In an effort to understand people, his reading and references are increasingly broad ranging – as likely to include Zen Buddhism as baseball. He wrote that he would like his epitaph to be: "He was curious to the end."[9]

Peters' work since *Liberation Management* has represented a falling off in his standards. *The Tom Peters Seminar, The Pursuit of Wow!* and *The Circle of Innovation* revisit many of the same ideas in an increasingly breathless and populist style.

While Peters has cut an eye-catching swathe, Waterman's career has continued at a more leisurely pace. "Where Peters is the Savonarola of his cause, Waterman is a gentler prophet," observes Robert Heller.[10] His books, *The Renewal Factor, Adhocracy: The Power to Change* and *The Frontiers of Excellence* have fared less well than Peters'. They are, nevertheless, as perceptive.

In *The Frontiers of Excellence*, Waterman argues that companies which succeed pay primary attention to employees and customers rather than shareholders. Waterman provides a four-point plan to sustaining excellence: small, fairly autonomous units; "downward" rather than "upward" organization; effective "adhocracy" (groups cutting across functional lines) as well as bureaucracy; "sheer staying power and the will to commit to long-term plans."

Empowerment

Delegation has always been recognized as a key ingredient of successful management and leadership. But, in the 1980s, delegation underwent a crisis of confidence – managers were intent on progressing as quickly as possible up the corporate ladder, working 12 hours a day to succeed rather than delegating so that others could share the glory. In the corporate cut and thrust, delegation appeared to be a sign of weakness.

The 1990s saw a shift in attitudes. No longer was delegation an occasional managerial indulgence. Instead, it became a necessity. This has continued to be the case. At Chrysler in the US, there are now 50 workers to every manager; against 20 to every manager a decade ago. The figure is set to increase to around 100.[11] "With organizations becoming flatter and hierarchies disappearing, managers now have a far wider span of control than ever before," says John Payne, consultant and author of *Letting Go Without Losing Control*. "In that situation, delegation is vital. The trouble is that delegation is like driving a car – no one admits to being a bad delegator."[12]

It is not only the fact that many managers consider themselves to be competent delegators that causes problems. Good delegation is hard work and requires substantial amounts of confidence and faith – managers, after all, are usually delegating tasks which they are accomplished at carrying out to less experienced people.

The trouble is that old habits die hard. Organizations may have shrunk, but managers often remain wedded to habits of a lifetime. Delegation is often a last resort, a worry to the manager doing the delegating and an unwanted extra burden to the person handed the task. But, Richard Phillips of Ashridge Management College argues, it need not be like that. He has carried out extensive research on managers who act as coaches. By doing so, he says, managers turn conventional wisdom about delegation on its head. "Instead of selecting someone who can already do the work being delegated, coaches deliberately select someone who cannot do it. In addition to setting the goals of the actual work to be done, they add learning goals. They coach the learner to give them the necessary skills and confidence to carry out the task."

The once simple act of delegation has also been hijacked by management writers. Instead of delegating, managers are currently "empowering," granting new areas of responsibility. Though this is now part of the language of management, genuine examples of empowerment are not always what they may seem. Instead of granting genuine power to their staff, managers remain as likely as ever to make the important decisions and only pass on relatively unimportant tasks to others. It is worth remembering that empowerment and delegation are not one and the same.

It is worth remembering that empowerment and delegation are not one and the same.

Delegation

Part of a manager's job which he or she then asks someone else to undertake.

Empowerment

The removal of constraints which prevent someone doing their job as effectively as possible.

The danger is that while empowerment attracts the management theorists and fad-following companies, delegation remains neglected, its full potential unrealized. A persuasive argument to sit up and take notice comes from Richard Phillips: "Managers should remember that when they perform a task which someone else could do, they prevent themself from doing a task which only they could do."

Differentiating delegation and empowerment is not easy. Harvard Business School's Quinn Mills provides one solution: "Empowerment describes a management style. The term is very close in meaning to delegation, but if it is strictly defined, empowerment means the authority of subordinates to decide and act. It implies a large degree of discretion and independence for those who are empowered. Generally, empowerment takes place within a context of limitations upon the discretion of those empowered."[13] The nature of these limitations will continue to be debated.

Practising empowerment

For proponents of empowerment there is hope. Hope, this time, is located in the outskirts of Sao Paulo, Brazil, and the base of the Brazilian company, Semco.

When Ricardo Semler took over Semco from his father he spent the first day firing 60 per cent of the company's top management. Semco became a unique success story. It managed to buck Brazilian commercial chaos, hyper-inflation and recession to increase productivity nearly seven-fold and profits five-fold.

Walking through the door, visiting executives immediately notice that there is no receptionist. Everyone at Semco is expected to meet their own visitors. There are no secretaries, nor are there any personal assistants. Managers do their own photocopying, send their own faxes and make their own coffee. Semco has no dress code, so some people wear jackets and ties, others jeans.

"A few years ago, when we wanted to relocate a factory, we closed down for a day and everyone piled into buses to inspect three possible sites," recalls Ricardo Semler. "Their choice hardly thrilled the managers, since it was next to a company that was frequently on strike. But we moved in anyway."[14]

Semco takes workplace democracy to previously unimagined frontiers. Everyone at the company has access to the books; managers set their own salaries; shopfloor workers set their own productivity targets and schedules; workers make decisions once the preserve of managers; even the distribution of the profit-sharing scheme is determined by employees.

"We've taken a company that was moribund and made it thrive, chiefly by refusing to squander our greatest resource, our people," says Ricardo Semler. Semler does not regard the transformation of Semco as a lesson to be emulated by other companies. Instead, he believes it simply points to the need for companies and organizations to reinvent themselves. "There **are** some companies which are prepared to change the way they work. They realize that nothing can be based on what used to be, that there is a better way. But, 99 per cent of companies are not ready, caught in an industrial Jurassic Park."

Traditionalists among the management fraternity find Semler's message unpalatable. Managers are constantly appraised by Semco workers rather than a coterie of fellow executives, and they have to become used to the idea of accepting that their decisions are not sacrosanct. Semler seems to be adept at biting his tongue when decisions don't go his way and admits "there are a lot of people at Semco whose styles I don't actually like. I wouldn't have recruited them but quite clearly they do their jobs effectively – otherwise people wouldn't support them."

As part of Semco's revolution, Semler has to a large extent become redundant. The chief executive's job rotates between five people. Diminished power is clearly not something which fills him with sadness – instead, it is confirmation that the Semco approach works. "I haven't hired or fired anyone for eight years or signed a company cheque. From an operational side I am no longer necessary, though I still draw a salary because there are many other ways of contributing to the company's success," he says. Indeed, Semler believes that what many consider the core activity of management – decision making – should not be their function at all. "It's only when bosses give up decision making and let their employees govern themselves that the possibility exists for a business jointly managed by workers and executives. That is true participative management."

Rosabeth Moss Kanter
Creating empowerment

In the perennial search to pigeon-hole management thinkers under a suitable title or specialism, Rosabeth Moss Kanter has proved determinedly elusive. She is not an evangelist in the Tom Peters mold, but nor is she an unworldly academic. She travels the world consulting and lecturing, but remains a Professor at Harvard Business School (and, from 1989 to 1992, editor of the *Harvard Business Review*). "Seminars are a performance. But I'm not on the circuit; I have a job," she insists. "I am interested in being a player, a participant, not just a bystander; perhaps a bystander close to power."[15] Her books are tightly and rigorously researched, yet have a clear populist element and appeal. Their subject matter evades neat classification, ranging increasingly widely, geographically and theoretically.

Her early work was concerned with Utopian communities, such as the Shakers. ("In the 1970s I compared IBM to a Utopian culture," she now admits.) This interest perhaps can be identified as the thread which runs through her central trilogy of publications – *Men and Women of the Corporation* (1977), *The Change Masters* (1983), and *When Giants Learn to Dance* (1989). "Kanter-the-guru still studies her subject with a sociologist's eye, treating the corporation not so much as a micro-economy, concerned with turning inputs into outputs, but as a mini-society, bent on shaping individuals to collective ends," observed *The Economist*.[16]

ROSABETH MOSS KANTER

Born 1943

American

Educator and consultant

Education: Bryn Mawr, PhD at the University of Michigan.

Career: Associate Professor of sociology, Brandeis University; joined Harvard 1973; 1977–1986 taught at Yale and MIT; returned to Harvard as Professor of Business Administration; editor of the *Harvard Business Review* 1989-92; runs her own consultancy company, Goodmeasure.

Books: *Men and Women of the Corporation*, Basic Books, 1977; *The Change Masters*, Allen & Unwin, London, 1984; *When Giants Learn to Dance*, Simon & Schuster, New York, 1989; *World Class*, Simon & Schuster, New York, 1995; *Rosabeth Moss Kanter on the Frontiers of Management*, Harvard Business School Press, Boston, 1997.

"I don't fit easily into different slots. I see myself as a thought leader, a developer of ideas," she says. "I am idealistic and it was the idealistic entrepreneurs of the 1960s and 1970s who changed things so that business became a great arena for experimentation. I am always interested in positive models and positive change. Business became increasingly interesting to me because it is so pivotal. It is the bedrock."

Kanter's idealism has also led her into politics. She was involved in Michael Dukakis' presidential bid – writing a book with him along the way. Dukakis' revival of Massachusetts' economic fortunes briefly appeared to offer an example of idealism, entrepreneurism and commercialism in partnership. "I learned a lot working with Dukakis," says Kanter. "He was interested in harnessing the entrepreneurial spirit."

Given this strain of idealism, it is ironic that Kanter's first major book, *Men and Women of the Corporation*, proved more likely to dash any idealism than to nurture it. It was an intense examination of a bureaucratic organization and, in effect, marked the demise of comfortable corporate America. Among its generally depressing findings was that the central characteristic expected of a manager was "dependability." Undaunted by her examination of the limitations and restrictions of the contemporary corporation, Kanter turned her mind to creating the new organizational models. The book which forged her reputation was *The Change Masters*.

This book sought out antidotes to the corporate malaise identified in *Men and Women of the Corporation*. It succeeded in propeling empowerment and greater employee involvement onto the corporate agenda. These issues are developed throughout Kanter's work – "By empowering others, a leader does not decrease his power, instead, he may increase it – especially if the whole organization performs better," she says.

Change Masters discovered the corporate world in an awkward state of flux – unwilling to disengage itself from the last vestiges of corporatism and unable or fearful of what to do next. Its vision remained solidly American. Its success, however, allowed Kanter's gaze to move further afield. "*Change Masters* opened doors for me, as a result I've globalized myself in the last decade," she says. "At the same time, however, a lot of the romance with Japanese companies went away. Instead, there emerged a belief that the source of much managerial wisdom emanates from the US."

The wisdom she encountered on her increasing travels was distilled into her next book, *When Giants Learn to Dance*. Describing the process she goes through in writing a book, Kanter says: "Ideas are, to start off, very vague but, gradually things develop. I say things and if people look blank, I continue. Then I become immersed. I am inductive, not deductive. I need data and experience in front of me. As the book progresses there is a lot of back and forth, checking, questioning and developing." She is keen to emphasize that her works are not simply potboilers full of unsubstantiated or unworkable ideas. "I reject the term *guru* because it is associated with pandering to the masses, providing inspiration without substance. There is a little bit of the shaman in a guru. I have scholarly standards. My books are dense and theoretical. They have footnotes."

When Giants Learn to Dance marks the corporate transformation from slumbering behemoth to nimble new creation, what Kanter labeled "the post-entrepreneurial firm." *When Giants Learn to Dance* predicts that as companies recognize and focus on their core capabilities, expansion will tend to occur through strategic alliances, and peripheral activities will be taken over by specialist service providers. The burgeoning of the service sector in the developed economies is evidence of the kind of structural changes which Kanter describes. On the other hand, global companies harnessing economies of scale will create the need for managers with the ability to manage across cultural boundaries.

"The post-entrepreneurial corporation represents a triumph of process over structure. That is, relationships and communication and the flexibility to temporarily combine resources are more important than the 'formal' channels and reporting relationships represented on an organizational chart," writes Kanter. "The post-entrepreneurial corporation is created by a three-part mix: by the context set at the top, the values and goals emanating from top management; by the channels, forums, programs and relationships designed in the middle to support those values and goals; and by the project ideas bubbling up from below – ideas for new ventures or technological innovations or better ways to serve customers."

> *Kanter's argument is that businesses need to be flexible but not freewheeling.*

Kanter's argument is that businesses need to be flexible but not freewheeling – she points to the fact that small businesses often suffer from too little organization while larger ones suffer from the reverse problem.

The origins of many of her ideas can be traced back to the work of Elton Mayo in the 1930s and Douglas Macgregor in the

1950s. They, too, tried to come to terms with the imponderables of motivation and the relationship between individuals and large corporations.

In *When Giants Learn to Dance*, Kanter identifies seven "skills and sensibilities" essential for managers if they are to become what she labels "business athletes." These are:

- learning to operate without the might of the hierarchy behind them
- knowing how to "compete" in a way that enhances rather than undercuts cooperation
- operating with the highest ethical standards
- having a dose of humility
- developing a process focus
- being multi-faceted and ambidextrous
- gaining satisfaction from results.

Kanter's work has highlighted people-related issues which were long ignored by the world's top businesses. "I am increasingly encouraged by the progress some organizations are making in areas like empowernment, but wish they were further along," she says. "The real emergent issue is what will people do with their time if they are not working? Job dislocation is now the coming problem."

> *Kanter's work has highlighted people-related issues which were long ignored by the world's top businesses.*

In an era of relentless cost cutting and downsizing, the human side of enterprise has been easily neglected. Indeed, Kanter's idealism is now pragmatic. "Consulting is a way to create. It is practical and I learn. My education comes from the application of my academic knowledge on the job.

"I hope that things might happen in organizations which I have helped to create. It is highly satisfying when chief executives use words or phrases, such as infrastructure for collaboration, which I introduced them to, sometimes I invented them," she says. "It is a question of continually broadening the context. There is a halo effect. For some audiences what I say has a great deal of credibility. This brings with it a sense of responsibility. But I am now doing it for myself rather than for a particular audience."

360 degree feedback

The traditional approach to appraisals had the advantage of simplicity. The annual appraisal was a bureaucratic chore to be completed as speedily as possible. Every year, at an appointed hour (and often for an hour) you sat in an office with your boss. Your performance over the previous year was then discussed and dissected. If you were feeling brave you complained about a colleague or asked for a pay rise. You emerged from the room, shook yourself down and headed back to your desk, until next year.

The traditional form of appraisal may linger on in some companies – though you have to look harder and harder to find examples. In a fast growing number, however, the annual ritual has been reinvented. The new model appraisal tends to be flexible, continuous, revolves around feedback, involves many more people than one manager and a boss, and seeks to minimize bureaucracy.

> **The traditional form of appraisal may linger on in some companies – though you have to look harder and harder to find examples.**

"The traditional model usually involved a form with boxes, a talk with a manager and a final rating which was then filed away in the personnel department," says Angela Baron, policy adviser at the Institute of Personnel and Development (IPD). "It became bureaucratic and didn't actually improve performance."[17]

As Angela Baron points out, an appraisal's *raison d'être* is straightforward: to improve an individual's – and, therefore, an organization's – performance. To do so, the appraisal has to be responsive to individual needs and be available to individuals throughout the organization. In keeping with this climate of flexibility, many companies now employ a variety of forms of appraisal. The range and scale of appraisals used by Mercer Management Consulting is increasingly typical. "We put a lot of effort and resources into the review process. But we have no qualms about that. Everything we do is about our staff's commitment and knowledge, and the change and value they deliver for our clients," says Matthew Isotta, vice president of Mercer's European Central Resource Group.[18]

Mercer's appraisal process is all-embracing. There are long-established downward reviews written by partners on people working on an assignment. "You have to sit down at the end of a project anyway," explains Isotta. "It is a formalized way of doing so which has become ingrained in our culture." In addition, every six months groups of partners spend a day analyzing their personal performance. All of the partners have an adviser who takes case reviews and discusses them with the individual and other managers. Then a one-page career review summary is produced outlining an individual's strengths, areas of growth and development objectives for the next six months. "The review day involves 20 to 25 partners and makes the entire appraisal process transparent. The discussion is completely open, but people don't get het up because so much effort is put into the entire process."

Finally, Mercer has an upward review process which is currently being refined. This involves an anonymous component and the company is moving towards a survey model where everyone fills in an evaluation of people they work with every six and 12 months. The danger, warns Mercer's Matthew Isotta, is that the entire system becomes merely paper generation. "This process has to have bite. There is the risk of it being ignored so we feed it through to the compensation of partners. We don't have hard and fast rules but compensation is driven by a number of factors and the upward review process is key." Others seek to distance appraisal from rewards arguing that appraisal should concentrate on development issues rather than becoming bogged down in pay negotiations.

Companies such as Mercer Management Consulting regard appraisal in the more broad ranging context of "performance management." This means that it must embrace issues such as personal development and career planning, in addition to simple analysis of how well an individual has performed over the last year. "Some organizations have almost abandoned formal appraisals," says the IPD's Angela Baron. "They want to escape from the form-filling mentality and, instead, want managers to talk continuously about their performance against agreed objectives, development needs and future roles."

To the uninitiated, such talk can suggest that appraisals are now mere wish lists of the skills an individual would like to acquire. In fact, where appraisal is working successfully the reverse is true. People should emerge with action plans – rather than vague congratulations about a job well done – which can cover everything from the next week to the rest of their life. The emphasis on creating something from the appraisal is part of a shift towards making appraisals forward looking rather than historic.

Such changes in the nature of appraisals have significant repercussions for the human resources function. Traditionally, appraisal was the domain of HR. Its new role is mapped out by the IPD's Angela Baron: "The HR or personnel department will be active in the design of appraisal processes. It will take responsibility for training appraisers, the kinds of questions being asked, how people are measured and what the processes are seeking to achieve. It will act in a supporting role but the emphasis will be on working in partnership. Appraisal will no longer be done *because* of personnel, it will be seen as a management tool which should be used by line managers." Brian Brooks, human resource director of advertising group, WPP, says that he and his team now act as consultants. "Human resources has an educational role in advising how the system should be used and in developing the system in the first place," he says.

The changing nature of appraisals is nowhere more evident than in the fashionable enthusiasm for 360 degree feedback. This involves a manager's peers, subordinates, bosses and even customers airing their views on the manager's performance – usually by way of a questionnaire. It is not a process designed for the fainthearted.

"The enthusiasm for 360 degree feedback can be attributed to a number of reasons. The need for greater flexibility and for less prescriptive job descriptions means that appraisal systems have to be more flexible and take into account changing organisational needs and circumstances. There is also much more openness and a greater desire for feedback from a variety of sources whether it be subordinates or customers," says Dr. Victor Dulewicz, director of assessment services at Henley Management College.

As methods of appraisal go, 360 degree feedback is undoubtedly robust and rigorous. It takes feedback to unprecedented levels – and for those who desire even more there is 540 degree feedback which brings even more people into the process.

> *As methods of appraisal go, 360 degree feedback is undoubtedly robust and rigorous.*

The attraction of 360 degree feedback is that it gives a more complete picture of an individual's performance. Different groups see an individual in a variety of circumstances and situations and can, as a result, give a broader perspective than that of a single boss. This, of course, relies on a high degree of openness and trust.

Inevitably, the truth can become clouded by prejudice and politics. "For all the five point scales, graphs and bar charts, genuine perceptions are what matter," says psychologist Robert Sharrock of YSC.[19] "People can be incredibly sycophantic or completely negative. Perceptions and the objectivity of the data can also be affected by prejudices and other influential factors. An additional danger is that if managers are being judged by subordinates their motivation will be to be liked. Good management isn't necessarily about being liked, so there is the risk of management by popularity." The paradox is that a process aimed at encouraging openness depends on anonymity. In practice this means that there are a profusion of consultants offering to help companies install 360 degree feedback programs.

Research at Ashridge Management College into the growth of 360 degree feedback (published as "360 degree feedback: unguided missile or powerful weapon?") suggests that success requires a number of factors: a clear strategic rationale; top management support and involvement; a culture geared towards behaviors and attitudes rather than simply performance; sensitivity; a genuine and wide-based willingness to achieve change; and willingness to discuss any issue.

The central message of such criteria is that appraisal needs to be a considered and far-reaching process rather than an automatic ritual. It must embrace the goals of the organization and those of the individual in the short and long term. And, above all, it must be managed effectively.

Key books

Edwards, Mark and **Ewen, Ann J**, *360 Degree Feedback*, AMACOM, New York, 1996

Grote, Richard C and **Grote, Dick**, *The Complete Guide to Performance Appraisal*, AMACOM, New York, 1996

Lepsinger, Richard and **Lucia, Antoinette D**, *The Art and Science of 360 Degree Feedback*, Jossey-Bass, San Francisco, 1997

Tornow, Walter (editor), *Maximizing the Value of 360 Degree Feedback*, Jossey-Bass, San Francisco, 1998

Managing talent

Managerial talent was once a peripheral subject of debate. It was assumed that talent would emerge. The best people would rise to the top. Chief executives did not spend time considering how to identify and nurture the next generation of executives. Times have changed. Harvard Business School's Linda Hill argues that "Developing new managers... is a critical strategic challenge for organizations that hope to prosper," and meeting the challenge begins at the top.[20]

Part of the problem is that employees often no longer express any interest in becoming managers. Who would want a job increasingly bedeviled by insecurity and long hours? As a result, there is intensive competition for those who take the plunge into management and excel. Recruiting and retaining talent is a corporate imperative.

> *Recruiting and retaining talent is a corporate imperative.*

Unfortunately, the career development patterns of managers are little understood. The transformation from managerial novice to CEO once simply occurred over time with little real insight into what actually happened along the way. Hill identifies the debut managerial job as a "pivotal development experience." If talent is to be retained and shaped this is where the process must begin.

The new manager has to learn what it means to be a manager (managing their team as well as the broader context of the business); develop interpersonal judgment ("establishing credibility rather than relying on formal authority, building subordinate commitment rather than seeking subordinate control, and leading the team rather than managing individuals"); cope with emotion and stress; and gain self-knowledge.

These attributes present sizeable – sometimes impossible – challenges. "Becoming a manager is not about becoming a boss. It's about becoming a hostage," comments one disenchanted manager. "Transforming star performers into effective managers has always been a difficult process, but in today's economy it is even more challenging," says Hill. "There are few shortcuts and no magic formulas."

Clearly, recruiting and retaining talented managers is closely related to knowledge management. "Twenty or thirty years ago companies talked of labor management. Later it was realized that knowledge and skills are important. Now it has gone a stage further," says Philip Sadler, co-author of *Managing Talent*. "Knowledge is hard to destroy; hard to protect; and hard to measure. But the true source of competitive advantage is not so much knowledge as talent, which is the only remaining scarce resource."[21]

It is not a matter of indulgence, argues Sadler, but one of commercial necessity. "Some, perhaps most, organizations are totally dependent on identifying, nurturing and retaining talented people in order to survive," he says. "The long-term success of the business in attracting, retaining, developing, motivating and utilizing the best talent in its field is likely to be the biggest single factor in determining its long-term commercial viability."

Ten keys to managing talent

Philip Sadler's research highlighted ten fundamentals for the successful management of talent:

- provide a clear sense of direction and purpose
- develop an appropriate organizational framework
- understand your culture
- identify future requirements for talent
- develop recruitment and selection strategies
- identify high potential
- retain your talent
- set clear objectives and ensure they are met
- motivate and develop your talent
- evaluate your talent.

Managing change

The list of skills and competencies now required of managers is daunting. It is made even more so by the fact that they must manage in an environment beset by radical change. It is a truism to observe that managing change is the great managerial challenge of our times. But, for all its repetition, it is nevertheless true.

Change is now endemic in the business world. "If you want to be content you should be a dog," acerbically advises one corporate executive. No organization is immune. It is not an American phenomenon. Change is a worldwide issue.

The changes now facing managers are more significant, broad ranging and apparently endless than ever before. The many manifestations of change affect:

> *The changes now facing managers are more significant, broad ranging and apparently endless than ever before.*

- **Technology** – the IT revolution continues to make jobs quicker and less labor intensive than they were even five years ago.

- **Organizations** – new organizational structures are emerging, emphasizing and enabling speed of response.

- **Individuals** – people have to learn new skills and adapt to an uncertain environment.

- **Society** – the role of employment and organizations in society is increasingly debated.

- **Consumers and markets** – are becoming more demanding and are changing more quickly.

Change, if it is to work, must involve and alter the perceptions and behavior of people. The lengthy catalog of failed change and quality programs is testament to the general neglect of the people side of such initiatives and, when it is identified, of the failure of organizations to come to terms with it.

Change has to carry people along with it. Less than wholehearted support will stop any change program in its tracks. A program which looks good in the boardroom can remain a theoretical ideal if people do not commit themselves to the change process.

A survey by KPMG Management Consulting of top executives in 250 UK companies found that only 31 per cent believed their change programs were "very effective."[22] "Identifying the need for change is relatively straightforward, what really causes problems is making change happen successfully," the KPMG survey reports.

The people-related issues are here to stay. Yet, most of the extensive theorizing and practice in the field of managing change pays scant attention to the concerns and fears of the people involved in making it happen. Talk of turbulence and the relentless progress of change through global business is easy. Talk of the effects of upheaval and change on individual managers and employees is less straightforward, fraught as it is with fears and disappointment.

Centuries ago, the challenge was described by **Niccolò Machiavelli** (a man increasingly referred to in these traumatic times): "It should be borne in mind that there is nothing more difficult to arrange, more doubtful of success and more dangerous to carry through than initiating changes in a state's constitution. The innovator makes enemies of all those who prospered under the old order and only lukewarm support is forthcoming from those who would prosper under the new."[23]

Responding to change

Managers clearly need to prepare themselves to provide satisfactory answers to wide-ranging and fundamental questions from people who work for them. Typically, these will include:

- Will my job description change?
- Will I lose my job?
- What is the project about?
- How long will it take?
- Who is in the project team?
- What exactly are you doing?
- Will it affect the way I do my job?
- Why are you doing it?
- Will it save the company money?

- What's in it for me?
- Who has asked for the project to be done?
- Why do we need all this documentation?
- Does this mean I am not doing my job correctly?
- Are you checking up on me?
- What do I have to do?
- How does the project fit in with the computer department?
- What is a business process?
- Does this mean I am going to end up with more work?

A more pertinent perspective comes from McKinsey's John Hagel: "There are many reasons why people avoid change. Change is threatening. It means doing things differently, perhaps in ways that an individual will not be able to master. Change is difficult. It is always easier to continue doing things the same comfortable way rather than trying something new. Change is risky. If the new methods don't work, or if people lose sight of immediate needs while trying to master them, near-term performance may suffer, perhaps disastrously. Change is often illusory. Too many organizations have grown cynical as senior management announces yet another change initiative that will fall by the wayside three or four months later when some new issue diverts attention elsewhere."[24]

There is an ongoing debate over whether behavioral and cultural change – through empowerment, team working etc. – is an inherent result of a change program, or whether it needs to be launched before the program begins. At the center of this discussion is the common belief that a changed organizational structure or more

> *Changing organizational cultures is a lengthy, time-consuming and delicate process.*

radical reorganization naturally leads to a change in corporate culture. Though this may be the case, changing organizational cultures is a lengthy, time-consuming and delicate process.

It is unlikely that successful cultural change can be made in a wholesale way. The past is not easily dismissed – nor should you want to totally dispense with some of the more positive and established ways of thinking and working. Marrying the old and new cultures is a formidable balancing act.

How do people view change?

While the bookshelves of managers may bulge with advice on how to manage change, there remains a refusal to accept its necessity among many managers. Instead of being proactive, change is often reactive, the last resort.

Companies tend to commit themselves to change because of market pressure, plummeting profitability, or even the prospect of imminent bankruptcy. In such circumstances, the directors are prepared to take drastic steps to turn the company around. The trouble is that many more companies need to take radical action earlier to prevent themselves reaching this situation.

Managers, it seems, are at heart conservative and cautious. They regard change as logical and short term, a small step rather than a quantum leap into the unknown.

Fear of change is understandable. It creates a new sense of ambiguity. People are uncertain about their roles and unsure what they should be doing and with whom. This ambiguity covers a number of areas:

Fear of change is understandable.

- **Job definitions** – changes in the scope and nature of job definitions are, for many, deeply unsettling and remove a prime reference point.

- **Responsibilities** – people are unsure what they are responsible for and to whom.

- **Expectations** – people are uncertain about what colleagues and the organization expects from them.

An obvious adjunct to the process of ambiguity is the disappearance of career ladders. Organizations shorn of their vertical hierarchy can appear to offer little opportunity for progression. Those who plan to join the upwardly mobile and still believe in neat and well-ordered career structures are increasingly likely to be disappointed.

Research repeatedly shows that it is managers who are the chief stumbling block to making change happen. Changing organizational structures and managerial thinking challenges and undercuts traditional power bases. The future is nightmarish, elusively intangible. Functions are broken apart, sometimes disappearing from the organization, subcontracted to external suppliers. For the manager reared on the old functional certainties, the new world organization is very difficult to manage. Indeed, the vast majority of managers are neither trained nor equipped to manage in such an environment. Nor can they attend a short course to be converted from a functional to a process manager. Changing the way you work and think about your work is a process which is more likely to take months and possibly years than weeks and months.

Managers often feel threatened by any change, a reaction that is reasonable given the fact that many initiatives involve management de-layering. Change programs can be regarded as euphemisms for redundancy.

Managers are caught between the twin nightmares of redundancy and of radically altering the way they work. There are no easy options. Research suggests that while companies have developed a wide range of supportive packages to help people who have been made redundant they – perhaps not surprisingly – often forget the worries and concerns of those who remain with the organization.

Seven skills to manage change

1 Managing conflict – Managers are unused to the rigorous and ceaseless questioning which true change brings. Often they are extremely uncomfortable with the idea of their work being analyzed in anything other than a superficial way. The potential for dissension and conflict is high. Richard Pascale estimates that 50 per cent of the time contentious issues are smoothed over and avoided. Around 30 per cent lead to non-productive fighting and no resolution, while only 20 per cent are truly confronted and resolved.[25]

2 Interpersonal skills – Managers change from supervisors to coaches. They are there to provide resources, answer questions and look out for the long-term career development of the individual. How they deal with people is key to their day-to-day success and to the progression of their career within the organization.

3 Project management skills – Many aspects of change can be managed as discrete projects. Project management is no longer the sole preserve of the construction industry.

4 Leadership and flexibility – In organizations where the emerging emphasis is on horizontal cross-functional and team-based management, managers need to coach employees and empower them to feel ownership of the various processes. This demands a flexible style of managing, with the manager sometimes giving firm directions in order to ensure that the process output conforms to customer expectations, while at other times stepping back and allowing team members to take decisions.

5 Managing processes – Functional orientation is now being replaced by process orientation. In the majority of process-based companies, managers are required to improve their business processes on an ongoing basis. They need to be able to use the tools of process simplification and redesign, which include benchmarking and process-mapping tools (such as systems dynamics, flowcharting and activity diagrams) and require understanding of the potential business benefits of IT applications.

6 Managing strategy – Process ownership is not solely concerned with the nitty-gritty of direct implementation. Managers also need to understand how their process aligns with strategic goals and performance measures.

7 Managing their own development – To meet a new challenge requires managers to think beyond position and develop comprehensive general skills which will allow them to respond flexibly to organizational needs. It is not surprising, therefore, that people at all levels in organizations are seeing the opportunities for personal development. Indeed, it is increasingly regarded as a major part of what was once called the remuneration package.

Leading change

Harvard Business School's John Kotter has identified eight steps in the process of leading change:

- a leader with a good track record is appointed;
- one with an outsider's openness to new ideas;
- who creates a sense of crisis;
- who creates and communicates a new vision and new strategies;
- who then behaves accordingly, acting as a role model; and
- thus involves others in key jobs in the drive for change;
- these others then use thousands of opportunities to influence behavior throughout the organization;
- producing tangible results within two years, thus reinforcing the drive to persevere without the change program.

Key books

Bennis, Warren, Benne KD and **Chin, R**, *The Planning of Change*, Holt, Rinehart & Winston, 1970 (2nd edition)

Cunningham, Ian, *The Wisdom of Strategic Learning*, McGraw-Hill, Maidenhead, 1994

Kanter, Rosabeth Moss, Stein, Barry and **Jick, Todd D**, *The Challenge of Organizational Change*, Free Press, New York, 1992

Vaill, Peter, *Managing as a Performing Art*, Jossey-Bass, San Francisco, 1990

Richard Pascale
From change to transformation

While recognizing that change is happening there is still a widespread temptation for organizations and managers to believe that it does not affect them or perhaps that it can be managed through small incremental improvements rather than major shifts in attitude and behavior. Leading the call for the latter approach is American thinker, **Richard Pascale**.

Pascale urges management to invest the intellectual energy necessary to make an informed choice between **change** (incremental

147

improvement) and **transformation** (discontinuous shifts in capability). He believes a mental muddle surrounds these choices with many change efforts masquerading as "transformation." An impassioned critic of management fads, Pascale advocates that organizations commit themselves to relentless self-questioning and reinvention.

Pascale has been described as the "scourge of the complacent and prodder of the timid".[26] Undoubtedly,

> *Pascale has been described as the "scourge of the complacent and prodder of the timid".*

his views and advice have made increasingly uncomfortable reading and listening for managers. He believes that gurus, writers, speakers and the ultimate consumers – managers – are caught up in a game of soundbites and simplistic remedies.

"It's like the practice of medicine in the Middle Ages," he states. "A leech under the armpit and one to the groin. With no understanding of bacteria, virus or how the body worked, there were lots of prescriptions by the physicians of the Middle Ages – but cures were largely the product of random chance. A parallel holds today. Lots of remedies but very few successful examples of authentic transformation. Organizations churn through one technique after another and at best get incremental improvement on top of business-as-usual. At worst, these efforts waste resources and evoke cynicism and resignation.

"What is needed is a much deeper inquiry into, first, a business's unfolding competitive situation and second, an understanding of the largely invisible patterns of thinking and behavior which define the 'box' inside which a company operates. Once revealed, it becomes clear whether the organization (improving at a predictable pace given past performance) can successfully meet the demands of competition. If not, there is a need for transformation. This is a difficult but manageable journey."

On a personal level he is a somewhat reluctant revolutionary. "I would describe my life as backing away from what didn't work toward a better fit with my gifts and capabilities," he says. But, Pascale – like other leading management thinkers – has pursued a single-minded path once the course became clear. "As I was finishing my MBA at Harvard, my colleagues were frantically searching for the 'perfect' job. I found myself troubled by the process and unable to engage in it with enthusiasm," he recalls. "Then, one day, I had an epiphany – what I really wanted to do was spend a quarter of my life teaching; a quarter consulting (to test the relevance of theory in practice); a quarter writing (something I enjoy – and when you put your ideas on paper you discover the holes in the logic); and, finally, a quarter of my life on holiday (to re-create). I have endeavored to achieve that balance ever since."[27]

For the first 25 per cent of his time, as a teacher, Pascale spent 20 years at Stanford's Graduate School of Business – his course on organizational survival was the most popular on the MBA program. As a consultant, his clients include many of the world's largest corporations.

"Over time, I have focused increasingly on the challenge of renewing large organizations," he observes. "I regard my clients as learning partners. Clearly, I am expected to add value and I endeavor to do so. But I am consistently learning from those I work with and confronted with how much further we have to go to enable corporations to revitalize themselves with a higher likelihood of success."

As a writer, Pascale's ideas first reached a mass audience through the 1981 book, *The Art of Japanese Management* (co-authored with Anthony Athos). The inspiration for the book was derived from Pascale's work with the National Commission on Productivity (a White House task force of Fortune 500 chief executives and national union leaders). "I had spent a year in Japan in the late 1960s," he states. "While deeply impressed, I doubted we could learn much from the Japanese as their culture is so different from ours. One night on a flight back from Washington DC, it hit me: why not study Japanese companies in the United States? How would they adapt their ideas to American managers and an American workforce? This became the cornerstone of the study."

The Art of Japanese Management was a bestseller, eventually published in 20 languages. It drew lessons from archetypal Japanese success stories – such as Honda in the US. Japanese successes, like their best-managed American counterparts, derived from a relentless commitment to learning and meticulous attention to the factors that motivate people, reinforce core values and fine-tune the

RICHARD PASCALE

Born 1938

American

Educator and consultant

Education: Harvard Business School.

Career: Member of the faculty, Stanford's Graduate School of Business; White House Fellow, Special Assistant to the Secretary of Labor, and Senior Staff of a White House Task Force reorganizing the President's executive office; consultant to many Fortune 500 companies including AT&T, General Electric, Intel, Shell, 3M, British Petroleum and Coca-Cola.

Books: *The Art of Japanese Management*, with Anthony Athos, Penguin, London, 1981; *Managing on the Edge*, Viking, London, 1990.

interconnected elements of an organization. Pascale and Athos were the first to coin the term **Managing by Walking About (MBWA)** and to call attention to the singular importance of **shared values**.

Another contribution of *The Art of Japanese Management* derives from the 1970s when Pascale worked with Tom Peters and Robert Waterman (then at the McKinsey consulting firm) and Anthony Athos (a professor at Harvard Business School). Pascale had a hand in developing the **Seven S framework**. "It's nothing more than seven important categories that managers use to make an organization work," he states.

Despite the book's success, Pascale was anxious not to become typecast as a Japan expert. "I don't define myself as a Japan scholar – what I am interested in is making Western organizations more productive." Under pressure to come up with a sequel, Pascale wrote a three-page outline on what he believed was the next horizon for improving competitiveness: the importance of constructive contention as the fuel of self-renewal in organizations. "I thought I could write the book in six months," he says. "But all the data and interviews I had in my files only skimmed the surface. People conceal their conflicts; organizations suppress it. The most important contention is often an undiscussable. Yet it is precisely these hidden tensions within an organization that can be a source of vitality if they are channeled effectively."

Managing on the Edge: How the Smartest Companies use Conflict to Stay Ahead further cemented Pascale's reputation. The book is densely packed with anecdotes and ideas. At their root is Pascale's observation that many of the "excellent" companies which Peters and Waterman had celebrated in *In Search of Excellence* had fallen from grace within the short span of a few years. At the heart of their vulnerability were the very qualities that historically had enabled them to excel. Paradoxically, internal coherence (an asset during stable times) rendered them ill-equipped to deal with radical shifts in the environment. "They couldn't get out of their own way," says Pascale, "like weight lifters with tremendous upper body strength suddenly asked to compete in the high hurdles."

Coincidentally, Pascale had also "stumbled" upon a law of cybernetics known as the Law of Requisite Variety. The law states that for any organism to adapt to its external environment, it must incorporate "variety." If you reduce "variety" internally you are less able to deal with it when it comes at you externally. "But how does variety show up in a social system?" asked Pascale. "It shows up as deviance from the norm – in other words, as conflict. The problem is that most companies are conflict averse. For many it is associated with wounded egos, harmed relationships and turf wars. Contention is often mistaken as an indicator of mismanagement. The trick is to learn to disagree without being disagreeable and channel this contention as a means of self-questioning and keeping an organization on its toes."

In practice, Pascale believes that when contention arises 50 per cent of the time it is smoothed over and avoided. Another 30 per cent of the time it leads to non-productive fighting and no resolution. Only in 20 per cent of the cases is contention truly confronted and resolved. "It's ironic," observes Pascale. "A threat that everyone perceives but no one talks about is far more debilitating than a threat that is clearly revealed and resources mobilized to address it. Companies, like people, tend to be as sick as their secrets," says Pascale – who prescribes revealing the "undiscussables" and who maintains that "breakdowns" be regarded as a source of learning.

His increasingly broad-ranging and holistic world view remains influenced by Japanese thinking. In particular, Pascale argues that Western managers need to become more attuned to the difference between **doing** and **being**. "My exposure to the Japanese language made me aware of two words, *Ki* and *Kokoro*, which refer to the core essence of a person (in other words, who they are). These terms are as commonplace to the Japanese language as 'me,' 'self,' 'I' and 'my' are to most Western languages. What this means is that a Japanese person, regardless of educational attainment, is constantly cued by his language to pay attention to who they are while in the process of doing something. (We see in this their seemingly ritualistic approach to the tea ceremony, flower arranging or sumo wrestling.)

Pascale argues that Western managers need to become more attuned to the difference between doing and being.

The way in which this comes to root in business is that it would not occur to the Japanese just to 'do' a management technique – such as Total Quality Management. Of course, they would also 'be' quality. By contrast, they view their Western counterparts as precocious children – always chasing after the latest management technique and striving to distil it down to a recipe for doing. Organizations that churn through a succession of 'doings' (such as TQM and reengineering) without altering their underlying being often end up older, maybe slimmer, but rarely wiser. Transformation entails a shift in being – at the personal and organizational level."

To transform itself an organization needs to tackle its very core – its context – the underlying assumptions and invisible premises on which its decisions and actions are based. This sounds arcane but is no more complicated than assembling a critical mass of key stakeholders (perhaps the 100 to 200 people who really make things happen in a company) and conducting an organizational audit that reveals the invisible box inside which the company operates. Once revealed, it is easy to have a straightforward discussion about whether the organization, operating at its current level (i.e. doing what is predictable), can respond to the unfolding competitive threats. If not, a dramatic shift in organizational capability (i.e. transformation) is required.

Pascale points to a number of leading US companies such as Motorola, General Electric and even the department store chain, Nordstrum, as examples of successful ongoing transformation (or reinvention). **Transformation** and **reinvention** are Pascale's coda for the future. "Many companies need to reinvent themselves," he says. "And reinvention is not changing what is, but creating what isn't. A butterfly is not more caterpillar or a better or improved caterpillar; a butterfly is a different creature. Reinvention entails a series of continuous metamorphoses of this magnitude over time."[28]

The problem with programs of change, Pascale has more recently argued, does not lie with the programs themselves.[29] Instead, their central limitation is that they are driven by and involve so few people. True transformation requires the involvement and commitment of all in the organization. Involving employees fully in the principal business challenges facing the company is the first "intervention" required if companies are to thrive. The second is to lead the organization in a way which sharpens and maintains incorporation and "constructive stress." Finally, Pascale advocates instilling mental disciplines that will make people behave differently and then help them sustain their new behavior.

Pascale plays down his reputation: "I don't think of myself as a guru or as a repository of ultimate knowledge. That's the kiss of death as far as your own continuous learning is concerned. You can witness the undesirable impact of celebrity that accompanies guru-hood. When you become a persona rather than a person, it consumes your energy at the expense of the underlying inquiry upon which your reputation was built in the first place."

References: New ways of managing people

1 Griffith, Victoria, "It's a people thing," *Financial Times*, 24 July 1997.
2 Mayo, Elton, *Human Problems of an Industrial Civilization*, Macmillan, New York, 1933.
3 Sieff, Lord, on Management: Marks & Spencer Way, Wiedenfeld & Nicolson, 1990.
4 Herzberg, Frederick, *Work and the Nature of Man*, World Publishing, 1966.
5 LeTart, Jim, "Technology frees HR's time for strategy," *HR Magazine*, December 1997.
6 Grundy, Tony, "How are corporate strategy and human resources strategy linked?," *Journal of General Management*, Vol. 23, No. 3, Spring 1998.

7 "Take me to your leader," *The Economist*, 25 December 1993–7 January 1994.

8 "Tom Peters, performance artist," *The Economist*, 24 September 1994.

9 Peters, Tom, Foreword to Bennis, Warren, *An Invented Life*, Addison-Wesley, Reading, Mass., 1993.

10 Heller, Robert, "In pursuit of paragons," *Management Today*, May 1994.

11 Griffith, Victoria, "Blue-collar team, white-collar wise," *Financial Times*, 11 May 1994.

12 Author interview.

13 Mills, D Quinn and Friesen, Bruce, "Empowerment" in *Financial Times Handbook of Management*, FT/Pitman, London, 1995.

14 Author interview.

15 Author interview.

16 "Moss Kanter, corporate sociologist," *The Economist*, 15 October 1994.

17 Author interview.

18 Author interview.

19 Author interview.

20 Hill, Linda A, "Developing the star performer," *Leader to Leader*, Spring 1998.

21 Sadler, Philip and Milmer, Keith, *Managing Talent*, FT/Pitman, London, 1993.

22 KPMG, *Change Management*, KPMG, 1993.

23 Machiavelli, Niccolo, *The Prince*, Penguin, London, 1967.

24 Hagel, J, "Keeping CPR on track," *McKinsey Quarterly*, May 1993.

25 Pascale, Richard, "The benefit of a clash of opinions," *Personnel Management*, October 1993.

26 Lorenz, Christopher, "Change is not enough," *Financial Times*, 12 January 1994.

27 Author interview.

28 Pascale, Richard, Athos, Anthony and Goss, Tracy, "The reinvention roller coaster," *Harvard Business Review*, November/December 1993.

29 Pascale, Richard, Millemann, Mark and Gioja, Linda, "Changing the way we change," *Harvard Business Review*, November–December 1997.

6

Careers and working life

"We are CEOs of our own companies: Me Inc. To be in business today, our most important job is to be head marketer for the brand called You."

Tom Peters[1]

"The economics of free agency relate to a basic psychological shift, a tremendous San Andreas Fault between employee and employer."

Stan Davis[2]

From corporate man to Generation X

What kind of manager did the systems championed by Taylor, Ford and Sloan produce? The answer is pithy: corporate man. Dedicated, loyal, unquestioning, hard working and clean-cut; corporate man was the paragon of rational management.

One of his first champions (corporate woman was yet to come) was **Chester Barnard** (1886–1961), an executive with AT&T and then president of New Jersey Bell. "The most important single contribution required of an executive, certainly the most universal qualification, is loyalty, domination by the organization personality," wrote Barnard in his impenetrable but important *The Functions of the Executive*.[3]

Despite such sentiments, Barnard recognized the role of the individual and saw the executive's role as creating shared values within the organization. "I rejected the concept of organization as compromising a rather definitive group of people whose behavior is coordinated with reference to some explicit goal or goals. In a community all acts of individuals and of organizations are directly or indirectly interconnected and interdependent," he said.

Practitioner

CHESTER BARNARD

1886–1961

American

Telecommunications executive

Education: Studied economics at Harvard but left without a degree.

Career: Joined AT&T as a statistician; special assistant to the Secretary of the Treasury during the Second World War; became President of New Jersey Bell in 1927; retired 1952.

Books: *The Functions of the Executive*, Harvard University Press, Cambridge, Mass., 1938; *Organization and Management*, Harvard University Press, Cambridge, Mass., 1948.

These relationships remained largely unacknowledged in the first 50 years of the twentieth century. The employee–corporation relationship was narrowly defined and even more stringently practised. Linking the two together in a more dynamic way has preoccupied a great many minds in recent decades.

One of the most successful creators of corporate man was (and, perhaps, is) IBM. Its growth was built on service excellence and clear company values, as well as products and manufacturing processes. Within companies like IBM, corporate culture and the individuality of managers became intertwined in a way never envisaged when the manager was a mere supervisor.

> *One of the most successful creators of corporate man was (and, perhaps, is) IBM.*

The person largely responsible for the IBM culture was **Thomas Watson Senior** (1874–1956). Few business people create companies in their own image which then thrive after their departure. Most plummet after the final farewell from the great leader, unable or unwilling to carry on as before. Thomas Watson is one of the rare exceptions. Under Watson, IBM became the stuff of corporate and stock market legend, continuing to dominate long after Watson's death.

Watson created a corporate culture which lasted. IBM – "Big Blue" – became the archetypal modern corporation and its managers the ultimate stereotype – with their regulation sombre suits, white shirts, plain ties, zeal for selling and company song. Beneath this, however, lay a belief in competing vigorously and providing quality service. Later, competitors complained that IBM's sheer size won it orders. This was only partly true. Its size masked a deeper commitment to managing customer accounts, providing service and building relationships. These elements were established by the demanding perfectionist, Watson. "He emphasized people and service – obsessively," noted Tom Peters in *Liberation Management*. "IBM was a service star in an era of malperforming machines."

IBM's origins lay in the semantically challenged Computing-Tabulating-Recording Company which Watson joined in 1914. Under Watson the company's revenues doubled from $4.2 million to

$8.3 million by 1917. Initially making everything from butcher's scales to meat slicers, its activities gradually concentrated on tabulating machines which processed information mechanically on punched cards. Watson boldly renamed the company International Business Machines. This was, at the time, overstating the company's credentials though IBM Japan was established before the Second World War.

IBM's development was helped by the 1937 Wages-Hours Act which required US companies to record hours worked and wages paid. The existing machines couldn't cope and Watson instigated work on a solution. In 1944 the Mark 1 was launched, followed by the Selective Sequence Electronic Calculator in 1947. By then, IBM's revenues were $119 million and it was set to make the great leap forward to become the world's largest computer company.

While Thomas Watson Senior created IBM's culture, his son, **Thomas Watson Junior** (1914–1994), moved it from being an outstanding performer to world dominance. Watson Jr. brought a vision of the future to the company which his father had lacked. Yet, the strength of the original culture remained intact. Indeed, Watson Jr. fleshed it out, creating a framework of theories round the intuitive and hard-nosed business acumen of his father.

Typically, Watson Sr. made sure his son served a brief apprenticeship – as an IBM salesman – and Watson Jr. remained driven by his father's lessons throughout his career. "The secret I learned early on from my father was to run scared and never think I had made it," he said. And, sure enough, when IBM thought it had made it the ground slipped beneath its previously sure feet.

In his book, *A Business and Its Beliefs* – an extended IBM mission statement – Watson Jr. tellingly observes: "'The beliefs that mold great organizations frequently grow out of the character, the experience and the convictions of a single person." In IBM's case that person was Thomas Watson Senior.

Corporate man existed confidently enough until the early 1980s. Indeed, his demise can be linked to the precipitous fall in IBM's own fortunes. The end of corporate man was – in media terms at least – brought about by the rise of the new breed of entrepreneurial, all-action, management heroes. In fiction they were embodied by Gordon Ghekko in Oliver Stone's film, *Wall Street*.

Eschewing corporate loyalty, individual initiative was back in fashion. If the corporation couldn't give you what you wanted, why belong to the corporation? Management was seen as exciting and intuitive, built round deals, instant decisions and hard work. Corporate man gave into his machismo and allowed it full rein.

With the reinvention of the traditional manager, organizations struggled to keep pace. The 1980s saw a host of books on how to set the individual free in organizations – managers were, for example, encouraged to become "intrapreneurs," entrepreneurial within the constraints of the organization.

The trouble with managers reinventing themselves was that organizations failed to keep pace. Fed on a steady stream of corporate men – and increasingly corporate women – the great corporations weren't about to do a U-turn and relish the possibilities of individual inspiration. They liked the way Gordon Ghekko made money, but they didn't like the way he did it or what he stood for.

Career management

When jobs were for life and the corporate apron strings were rarely abandoned, careers took care of themselves. The thought of actually managing your career never occurred to the vast majority of managers. "The way managers manage their careers is intrinsically linked to the way organizations behave, shape themselves and regard their managers. To ignore this basic truism is to risk misunderstanding the complex nature of career management," say career management experts Carole Pemberton and Peter Herriot.[4]

The psychological contract

An implicit agreement between an individual and an organization about the way they should be treated and the extent of their obligations to the organization. The phrase was coined by MIT's Ed Schein.

Career anchor

A term invented by Schein as a corollary to the psychological contract, describing the perceptions individuals have about themselves and their worth and role in an organization which encourage them to stay in it. It makes clear that the aspirations, motivations and goals of individuals differ considerably.

Schein's career anchors[5]

Technical/functional
- exercising particular skills
- reluctant to give up expertise
- management per se of little interest

Managerial
- being accountable for total results
- willing to abandon technical for generalist role
- integrating the efforts of others

Autonomy/independence
- freedom from organizational restrictions
- control of how, when and what to work on

Security/stability
- geographic, financial, organizational security
- performs well in certain types of organization only
- sees career management as the organization's responsibility

Service/dedication
- achieving something of personal value/concern
- would change organization to be able to do so
- would leave organization whose values were incompatible

Pure challenge
- the process of winning is central
- problems or opponents are there to be overcome
- search for novelty and variety

Lifestyle integration
- identity is tied to total life rather than to organization or occupation
- balance sought between home and work

Entrepreneurship
- building something new
- accepting risk.

The other highly influential model of career motivation comes from another American academic, **John Holland**. The logic behind Holland's identification of occupational interests is that at the beginning of their career, or at some time during it, people are drawn to a particular occupation because of some sort of interest in it.

The interests Holland identifies fall into six categories:

1 **Realistic** – a preference for activities that entail the explicit ordered or systematic manipulation of objects, tools, machines, animals; and an aversion to educational or therapeutic activities.

2 **Investigative** – a preference for activities that entail the observational, symbolic, systematic and creative investigation of physical, biological and cultural phenomena in order to understand and control such phenomena; and an aversion to persuasive, social and repetitive activities.

3 **Artistic** – a preference for ambiguous, free, unsystematized activities that entail the manipulation of physical, verbal or human materials to create art forms or products; and an aversion to explicit, systematic and ordered activities.

4 **Social** – a preference for activities that entail the manipulation of others to inform, train, develop, cure or enlighten; and an aversion to explicit, ordered, systematic activities involving materials, tools or machines.

5 **Enterprising** – a preference for activities that entail the manipulation of others to attain organizational goals or economic gain; and an aversion to observational, symbolic and systematic activities.

6 **Conventional** – a preference for activities that entail the explicit ordered systematic manipulation of data, such as keeping records, and an aversion to ambiguous, free, exploratory or unsystematized activities.[6]

Today, the very nature of this psychological contract is being questioned and reinvented. Managers are questioning why they should stay with corporations; what is in it for them in the short term and in relation to their long-term careers? The changing nature of the psychological contract takes a variety of forms, shown below:

> *Managers are questioning why they should stay with corporations.*

Table 7.1 The changing psychological contract between managers and the organization[7]

	Traditional	Future
Duration of tenure	Long-standing	Time-limited
Certainty of tenure	Safer	Less certain
Management development	Planned by the company via promotion	Opportunistic, self-determined via company changes
Motivational drivers	Loyalty	Enhancing future employability
Salaries	Lower, incremental, predictable	Higher, offset by risk, less predictable

The nature and pattern of careers has changed. Career management is an increasingly personal and powerful force – and it is the individual manager who is now doing the work. The corporate career model of slow progress up the hierarchy has ruled the roost for the best part of the twentieth century. Now, comes the post-corporate career which, say London Business School's Maury Peiperl and Yehuda Baruch, has a number of characteristics.[8]

First, the new form of career is outside of large organizations. Second, people often end up working as suppliers to their previous employer. The third characteristic is that these new careers "confer independence on individuals and provide them with the flexibility to respond quickly to demands and opportunities."

In the new career model people do not identify with a single company. Instead, they identify with an industry or a profession. The greater emphasis on customer service in smaller companies tends to highlight this change in emphasis.

> *In the new career model people do not identify with a single company. Instead, they identify with an industry or a profession.*

The final characteristic of the new career is that it creates a better balance between work and family life. And here the negative side begins. Working at home can mean that people find it impossible to relax or turn off from work. There is also the constant danger of isolation. (The worst scenario for this is a society in which inter-personal communication is negligible.) The route forward, therefore, must be to create networks through the development of new types of professional communities and through use of the latest technology. (Ironically, the anti-social Internet may be the antidote to becoming anti-social.) "Those who succeed will be those who can not only stand on their own, but can form and sustain links,' write Peiperl and Baruch. "Links that will take them beyond existing individual and organizational models, to entirely new kinds of careers."

But where does this leave corporations?

Bruce Pasternack, Shelley Keller and Albert Viscio of consultants Booz-Allen & Hamilton suggest there is a need for a "new people partnership" which marries personal and business needs. This must: continually improve performance and enhance value for shareholders; enable companies to attract and retain top talent;

motivate all employees to work to their fullest potential; develop the skills of white and blue collar workers; and balance the interests of all stakeholders, including shareholders, employees, unions, government and society.[9]

Key to achieving this is the creation of a dynamic internal job and education environment. Intel, for example, encourages employees to own their own careers through open communication, increased investment in training (6 per cent of its annual payroll) and through supporting the internal job market – rather than look elsewhere, employees are encouraged to look within the company for their next career move.

Perhaps the most innovative part of Intel's approach is its redeployment program which costs between $6 and $10 million every year. When employees are laid off, they enter a redeployment pool. They then have four to six months to: find another job within the company; train so they can find a new position; or take a temporary assignment. This offers security to employees – who can welcome redeployment – and flexibility to the company. Intel can effectively close down a plant and ensure that talented or potentially talented people stay. (Of course, this is not nirvana: poor performers don't reach the pool.)

More generally, the new people partnership is built on five principles: "both parties commit to employee well-being as a core value; open communication forms the foundation for the day-to-day relationship; employees manage their own careers; employees gain 'employable' security by building critical skills; and accountability for performance extends to all levels of the organization." This represents a sizeable challenge for most companies but, say the consultants, implementing some form of the partnership is a prerequisite for survival.

The role of the company is increasingly to **manage a core group of employees with key skills** (rather than managing large numbers of employees with multifarious specialist functional skills). As a result, the onus is on individual managers to ensure that their skills are the ones the organization requires.

Inevitably, examining the current status of your career and your aspirations is harder than it seems. Managing the future is secondary when managing the present is so demanding. But, managers have to make the time.

Taking control of your career involves two basic skills, says psychologist Robert Sharrock. "The first skill is insight. People have to have a realistic view of their own strengths and limitations. This is something managers are often particularly poor at – they don't know what their strengths are and where they would be best used," he says. "The second element is being proactive. Managers have to actively seek out opportunities and be prepared to take personal risks. In fact, talented managers have always taken their development seriously. They know their strengths and where they would be best utilized."[10]

Of course, coming to terms with your strengths also involves accepting gaps in your knowledge and experience. Managers need to develop humility. Self-awareness is key to successful career management. They need to realize that they have to learn. For many this means that they

> **Managers need to develop humility.**

have to learn how to learn. In addition, managers must become more efficient users of their networks. KPMG encourages managers to make a basic list of their network. Managers are expected to come up with over 100 names.

With managers seeking out their skills and mapping out their own careers, the cosy corporation of the past also has to find a new role. "Organizations need to commit themselves to the development of their people. Mobility will also need to be valued by the individual and the organization. For individuals it helps broaden experience and sharpen skills; from the organization's view it will enfuse new blood into the body corporate,' says Robert Sharrock.

The skeptical might suggest that this is an abdication of a company's responsibility. Companies can't simply abandon managers to plough their own furrow. Effectively managing your own career and development revolves round relationships with a wide range of people. The key relationship, however, must be with the organization.

To some extent, despite the all-pervasive atmosphere of change, the bottom line remains the same. Organizations need to find and keep the most talented managers. And the people most likely to succeed are managers who take the initiative and develop themselves and their careers in tandem with the direction of the organization. Long-term employability may be preferable to long-term employment.

13 tips for creative careers

Mitch McCrimmon, a consultant with PA Consulting Group, provides a list of action points for organizations adopting a more innovative approach to career management. McCrimmon says they should:

- Share employees with strategic partner organizations (customers or suppliers) in lieu of internal moves.

- Encourage independence: employees may go elsewhere for career development, possibly to return in a few years.

- Fund groups of employees to set up as suppliers outside the organization.

- Encourage employees to think of themselves as a business and of the organization's various departments as customers.

- Encourage employees to develop customers outside the organization.

- Help employees develop self-marketing, networking and consultancy skills to enable them to search out, recognize or create new opportunities for both themselves and the organization.

- Identify skilled individuals in other organizations who can contribute on a temporary/project basis or part-time.

- Regularly expose employees to new people and new ideas to stimulate innovation.

- Balance external recruitment at all levels against internal promotion to encourage open competition, "competitive tendering" for jobs to discourage seeing positions as someone's territory – which causes self-protective conformity.

- Foster more cross-functional teamwork for self-development.

- Eliminate the culture of valuing positions as career goals in favor of portraying a career as a succession of bigger projects, achievements and new skills learned. The concept of "position' is part of the outdated static concept of the organization. Positions are out. Processes and projects are in.

- Abandon top-down performance appraisal in favor of self-appraisal based on internal customer satisfaction surveys and assess people as you would suppliers.

- Replace top-down assessment processes with self-assessment techniques and measure performance in terms of results.[11]

Key books

Bridges, William, *Jobshift*, Nicholas Brealey, London, 1995
Toffler, Alvin, *The Third Wave*, Bantam, New York, 1984
Tulgan, Bruce, *Managing Generation X*, Capstone, Oxford, 1996
Zuboff, Shoshana, *In the Age of the Smart Machine*, Basic Books, New York, 1988

New ways of working

The eighties are perhaps best regarded as an immoral blip, a time of righteous extremism in politics as well as corporations. Crucially, however, they shifted the balance. Individuals began to look for more control over their working lives. This has continued – though in a more faltering and haphazard way than many commentators suggest – and is expected to grow in importance in the future. The world of work is moving into a new age.

Integral to this is a fundamental change in attitude towards corporate employers. Corporate man has given way to Generation X. It is easy to dismiss the entire notion of Generation X as journalistic invention, one of those neat phrases which are of little practical use or relevance. Reared on a diet of MTV and Nirvana albums, Generation Xers are cynical thirty somethings. But how can they be

Corporate man has given way to Generation X.

managed and how do they manage? Jay Conger of the Leadership Institute of the University of Southern California has examined the reality behind the mystique. "History shapes the attitudes and tastes of a generation," he notes, citing the preference of the older generation of Americans to still buy American-made cars.[12]

According to Conger, Generation Xers (born between 1965 and 1981) exhibit four important characteristics. First, they seek to achieve a balance between their working and private lives. They are far removed from the corporate beings of previous generations whose personal lives were subsumed by the body corporate. Their second characteristic is that they are fiercely independent. This is partly attributed by Conger to the impact of the right wing politics of the eighties which emphasized personal responsibility.

The third characteristic of Generation Xers is their appetite for technology. They are the witnesses to – and often the instigators of – the IT revolution. Finally, Xers prefer to see companies in terms of communities. Conger points out that the organizational model of companies such as Microsoft, Nike and Sun Microsystems is the college campus as much as the traditional organization.

Generation Xers aren't the dissolute hedonists they are made out to be. The reality is that, in the age of flexible employment, downsizing and career management, loyalty is increasingly elusive as managers flit from job to job, company to company. Linda Stroh and Anne Reilly, two American academics, have carried out research into loyalty since 1989. They conclude, hardly surprisingly, that loyalty is decreasing. More surprisingly, their research suggests that free agents, the managers who take control of and responsibility for their own careers, tend to be more loyal to their new employers than their previous employers. The logic behind this is that those who have remained with their employer since 1989 have usually seen a decrease in opportunities and their view of the company has probably suffered a buffeting. Those who left, therefore, tend to feel that their decision was the right one and feel more benevolently towards their current employer.[13]

Stroh and Reilly confirm many of the fashionable theories about managing your own career. First, they confirm that managers who are free agents are more successful in career terms than those who are not. Second, they conclude that women managers are particularly sensitive to a perceived supportive corporate climate. Third, maintaining a strong employer–manager relationship is essential.

While none of this is staggering it adds yet more weight to arguments in favor of career management and mobility, as well as confirming the need for companies to consider and cater for the career development needs of their employees.

Freewheeling flexibility is the order of the day. Charles Handy, for example, predicts that, with numbers of full-time workers decreasing, the onus will be on developing a **portfolio of work**. The skeptical might suggest that this is likely to be a portfolio of poorly paid part-time jobs. Handy, however, believes we have to embrace more positive possibilities. Portfolios of work could include work which can be divided into five main categories: wage work and fee work (which earn money); homework, gift work and study work (which do not).

To most people this sounds idealistic. Yet, it is simply a more flexible and better organized way of identifying the elements in many of our lives. It is the kind of flexibility that those who work for a large organization with its career progression, regular monthly salary and perks are ill-equipped to come to terms with. It does, however, fit in with the world of many self-employed people who are used to the pressure – and perhaps pleasure – of finding the means of earning money to pay for particular things. If they want a new computer, they know they have to find an imaginative way of making the money to pay for it; rather than simply ringing the IT department for one to be despatched The self-employed – as well as many in small businesses and professional partnerships – do not see bartering or selling their time and skills as unusual, but as facts of life. More full-time workers will have to embrace this approach if they are to develop their portfolios.

Handy's development of the concept of portfolios is a rejoinder to the idea of the leisure society. This, he argues, was simple idealism. Humankind is not made for a life of pure, unadulterated leisure. Instead, leisure needs to be seen as part of a balanced portfolio of interests and activities.

According to Daniel Pink, formerly Vice President Gore's chief speechwriter: there are 14 million self-employed Americans; there are 8.3 million "independent contractors'; and a further 2.3 million who work for temporary agencies. This adds up to around 25 million "free agents," "people who move from project to project and who work on their own, sometimes for months, sometimes for days."[14]

Many work at home in the supposed nirvana of homeworking and telecommuting. Strangely, homeworking continues to be distrusted by large corporations. American research found that most telecommuters (65 per cent) are employed by companies with less than 100 employees.[15] The reasons for adopting telecommuting were divided between boosting efficiency (45 per cent); saving money (35 per cent); and attracting qualified employees (33 per cent).

Self-managed development

When it came to management development, managers were once pawns in the hands of the organization. If the company thought a manager needed a particular skill they were speedily despatched on a suitable course. As their careers progressed, managers assembled an impressive list of courses they had attended – though what they actually learned was infrequently measured.

In some companies development is still regarded in these terms. The trouble is that the skills needed by managers in the 1990s are so broad ranging that picking off skills is no longer enough. Managers and their organizations have to be more selective and focussed when it comes to development.

As part of this growing trend, managers – and their companies – now realize that developing managerial skills and techniques is not simply the responsibility of the company. Managers, too, have a role to play in being proactive and identifying areas in which they need to develop. Today, instead of being pawns moved around by corporate might, managers are increasingly encouraged to examine their own strengths and weaknesses to develop the skills necessary for the future. Rather than having their development mapped out for them, managers are managing it for themselves.

> *Managers – and their companies – now realize that developing managerial skills and techniques is not simply the responsibility of the company.*

The growing awareness of the potential of self-managed development is, to some extent, prompted by companies committing themselves to ideas such as empowerment. There is also growing interest in the whole concept of management competencies – the skills which managers will require to manage successfully in the future.

Companies realize that they need to extract more and better work from less people. They are intent on investing responsibility – rather than simply money – in their managers. Major companies are already making significant strides in developing their managers through self-managed development.

"Even though many companies are now expressing an interest in self-managed development, the trouble is that the habits of a generation are hard to break. Managers fed on a diet of conscripted training are uneasy about having the burden of their own development thrust upon them," says Fiona Dent, co-author of *Signposts for Success*. "Being **sent** on a course is something you can complain about – sometimes with justification. It is completely different when you have to identify your own needs and the best methods of satisfying them."

There are other reasons why self-managed development is a difficult concept for many managers to come to terms with. Some point to a lack of motivation. Why, they say, should they develop themselves when their company offers little or nothing in the way of support or rewards? There is also a strong fear of failure. In some areas, training has traditionally been regarded as a last resort, an admission of inadequacy. Other managers are simply unsure of what to do. They don't know where or how to start the process and, even if they begin, don't know how to maintain momentum. Another disincentive from following self-managed development is simple lack of knowledge. Managers may be unable – or perhaps unwilling – to identify areas in which they need to develop and have little or no knowledge of the myriad techniques, approaches and activities at their disposal.

When they are actually given the time, resources and support to look at their own development, managers quickly become excited, realizing that there are opportunities rather than obstacles. For many it is an entirely new experience. Given two days on a training course to analyze their own development needs, it often takes more than a day for managers to really come to terms with what they are doing. It can be a revelation.

At an individual level, managers are usually prompted to think about their own development through changes in their job. It could be that taking on a new project motivates them to take a close look at the skills they require. A completely new job often encourages greater self-examination.

Perhaps the most widespread stimulus in the current climate is the disappearance of layers of management from major organizations. While once managers anticipated regular moves up the career ladder and the corporate hierarchy, they are now having to become used to the idea of horizontal rather than vertical moves. As the rungs upwards disappear, managers have to ensure that they make the right moves

> *Managers are now having to become used to the idea of horizontal rather than vertical moves.*

sideways which bring them into contact with important and useful new skills.

If it is to work, self-managed development involves and relies on the participation of the manager's organization. The company has a vital role to play, providing opportunities, support and resources. Fundamentally, however, it is the individual manager who has to take final responsibility and control.

They can't do this in isolation. Companies can't abandon their managers to plough their own furrow. Also, people need and want to share and test ideas with others. Self-managed development involves relationships with a wide range of people – from colleagues on courses to mentors and coaches; from the manager's boss to family and friends.

Many managers already have and use such networks. The trouble is they often don't realize that they exist or that they already do use them. If you ask a manager whether they have a mentor, many will quickly reply that they don't. Further questioning often reveals that a senior colleague is and has been instrumental in shaping their career and skills development – they have simply overlooked this or don't recognize it as mentoring.

In fact, self-managed development in many ways fully utilizes relationships and resources which already exist. When managers set out to gather information about a particular topic they often don't know where to start. Yet, given guidance, they can quickly uncover information and resources they have previously ignored or been unable to use.

It is also true that many managers have neatly compartmentalized their lives and refuse to acknowledge links between their home and working lives. Self-managed development can remove the barriers which prevent managers learning lessons in their private lives which might be useful in their business roles. It regards development as a continuous process taking in all aspects of a person's behavior and outlook rather than simply taking in one small aspect of it.

Self-managed development offers a degree of flexibility which traditional management training fails to provide. There is no set timescale or approved way of doing things – self-managed development revolves around managers thinking about how they learn and what they need to know. Traditional courses are based on the idea of moving a manager to a stated destination – knowing more about a particular subject or acquiring a new skill. Once the destination is reached, the process is regarded as complete. Self-managed development emphasizes the journey rather than the destination. After all, the skills and techniques you plan to acquire are constantly changing.

Fiona Dent believes self-managed development contains four fundamental stages:

1 **Analysis** – managers can use a variety of methods to help them to identify possible development issues. They might, for example, look at how performance reviews would help them and what form they could take.

2 **Review** – they might then move on to reviewing – thinking, in a structured way, about what the data is telling them about their learning needs.

3 **Planning** – how you intend to meet your development needs. This covers thinking through what course or other form of learning is most useful; where to go to do it and why it is necessary.

4 **Activity** – developing and taking part in the most appropriate vehicle for meeting the development need.

There is nothing cut and dried about these stages. Managers can join the process at the point they think is most appropriate for them. Flexibility, combined with responsibility, is the key.

Self-managed development is based on common sense principles. Put simply, it is a matter of recognizing what you can and can't do and then trying to improve your performance. Experience at many companies suggests that self-managed development is going to be an integral part of developing managers in the future and ensuring that companies retain their best people.

References: Careers and working life

1 Peters, Tom, "The brand called you," *Fast Company*, August–September 1997.
2 Pink, Daniel H, "Free agent nation," *Fast Company*, Issue 12.
3 Barnard, Chester, *The Functions of the Executive*, Harvard University Press, Cambridge, 1938.
4 Pemberton, Carole and Herriot, Peter, "Career management," in *Financial Times Handbook of Management*, FT/Pitman, London, 1995.
5 Schein, Edgar H, *Career Anchors: Discovering Your Real Values*, Pfeiffer, San Diego, 1990.
6 Holland, JL, *Making Vocational Choices*, Prentice Hall, Englewood Cliffs, New Jersey, 1985 (2nd edition).
7 Sharrock, Robert, "Developing top managers," in *Financial Times Handbook of Management*, FT/Pitman, London, 1995.
8 Peiperl, Maury and Baruch, Yehuda, "Back to square zero: the post-corporate career," *Organizational Dynamics*, Spring 1997.
9 Pasternack, Bruce, Keller, Shelley and Viscio, Albert, "The triumph of people power and the new economy," *Strategy & Business*, Second Quarter 1997.
10 Author interview.
11 McCrimmon, Mitch, "Goodbye to careers?," *Human Resources*, Spring 1994.
12 Conger, Jay A, "How Gen X managers manage," *Strategy & Business*, First Quarter 1998.
13 Stroh, Linda K and Reilly, Anne H, "Loyalty in the age of downsizing," *Sloan Management Review*, Summer 1997.
14 Pink, Daniel H, "Free agent nation," *Fast Company*, Issue 12.
15 McCune, Jenny, "Telecommuting revisited," *Management Review*, February 1998.

7

The quality revolution

"Good management techniques are enduring. Quality control, for instance, was treated as a fad here, but it's been part of the Japanese business philosophy for decades. That's why they laugh at us."

Peter Senge[1]

"Total Quality is a world movement. Regardless of country or industry, the laggards are at risk; conversely, the leaders acquire insulation against failure."

Richard Schonberger[2]

The discovery of quality

Following the Second World War Japan's industry was devastated. Not only was its industry in tatters, but the goods it produced were known for their indifferent quality. Indeed, this stereotype proved a lingering legacy – in the 1950s and 1960s Japanese cars were virtually impossible to sell in the United States or Europe.

Yet, within two decades Japan was the world's leading industrial powerhouse, renowned for the quality of its products and the long-sighted nature of its management. Japanese cars became the industry leaders, renowned for their quality and reliability. No one now laughs at a Mitsubishi or a Toyota. The turnaround was as dramatic as it was unexpected.

Ironically for the West, Japan's resurgence owed a great deal to Western thinking. In fact, the Japanese have repeatedly proved themselves masters at magpie-like taking of the best of Western ideas and reinterpreting them to fit their own culture and circumstances.

For example, the Japanese businessman Konosuke Matsushita – the founder of one of the world's largest electronics groups – was greatly influenced by the work of Henry Ford. His interpretation of Ford's work, however, marks one of the seminal differences between Western and Japanese management during the twentieth century.

When looking at Ford, Matsushita was inspired by the prospect of mass production and also took on board Ford's passion for using price reductions to generate more sales. Matsushita took as his creed the very Ford-like objective of producing "an inexhaustible supply of goods." But, to this he added "thus creating peace and prosperity throughout the land." The conjunction between these two inspirations is something managers in the West have little understanding of. Ford was obsessed with production and forgot the broader view (though he did take a brief stab at achieving world peace). Matsushita looked to the future and beyond the confines of the factory or the marketplace. He saw the company as having a role in society.

This broader view is manifested in many ways. Employees are important – not mere functionaries ensuring a steady stream of products are produced. And, so too, are customers and suppliers.

Matsushita was visiting the factories of his suppliers in the 1930s and giving them advice on how to produce their products more effectively. The logic is simple – one company's success is reliant on the support of others; if there is an effective partnership all sides win and society benefits from the prosperity generated. Such approaches are only now being contemplated in many Western organizations.

W Edwards Deming and Joseph Juran
The quality gospel

Matsushita was not alone. Other Japanese managers and their organizations seized the initiative. They were guided in the decades after the war by two Americans, **W Edwards Deming** (1900–1993) and **Joseph Juran** (born 1904).

Having earned a doctorate in mathematical physics in 1928 Deming, in the depressed America of the thirties, became interested in the pioneering work of Walter A Shewhart who was seeking to apply statistical methods to the control of variation in industrial production. With the impetus of the Second World War, Deming and Shewhart's innovative systems were introduced to American manufacturing in 1942. They resulted in marked improvements in performance in the organizations where they were instituted. However, following the Allied victory in 1945, American industry, which was suddenly enjoying booming markets, reverted to procedures based around product inspection.

The failure of American corporations to listen to Deming and Juran has often been commented on. In retrospect it appears to be one of the century's most profound errors. At the time, however, it was understandable. In terms of quality, American products were as good as European ones and far better than those produced in Japan. The American preoccupation was with lowering prices and the vehicle for achieving this was generally recognized to be lowering labor costs.

> *The failure of American corporations to listen to Deming and Juran appears to be one of the century's most profound errors.*

In a *Harvard Business Review* article, Juran also made much of the fact that his Japanese audiences in the early 1950s were the chief executives of major corporations, whereas his North American listeners were primarily engineers and quality inspectors. Juran's message was not, he admitted, new or revolutionary. Making things to a specific design and then inspecting them for defects was something the Egyptians had mastered 5000 years previously when building the pyramids. The American engineers weren't ready for history lessons.

Juran's influential *Quality Control Handbook* was published in 1951 and his work in Japan got underway in 1953. More original was Juran's insistence that measurement and testing need not simply be restricted to production. This idea had been originally inspired by Juran's own analysis in the mid-1920s of the large number of tiny circuit breakers routinely scrapped by his then employer Western Electric. By scrutinizing the manufacturing process rather than simply waiting at the end of a production line to count the defective products, Juran solved the problem and worked out how the company could substantially reduce the level of waste. His diagnosis was not, however, translated into practice – it was decided that quality was not Juran's problem. This proved Juran's point.

Juran developed a concept called **Company-Wide Quality Management (CWQM)** – the first of many quality-inspired acronyms. His aim was to create a systematic means of disseminating quality throughout an organization. Though his approach sounds dry, it was more humane than Deming's. Indeed, Juran's insistence on the responsibility of each and every employee for quality was a precursor of today's fashion for empowerment.

Deming was similarly well received in Japan and, in 1950, he told Japanese business people: "Don't just make it and try to sell it, but redesign it, and then again bring the process under control... with ever-increasing quality... The consumer is the most important part of the production line." In 1951, the first award ceremony for the now prestigious Deming Prize was held.

The timing of Juran and Deming was impeccable. But it was not only a question of arriving at a time when the Japanese were striving to rebuild their economy. Their ideas struck a chord in the East. Their emphasis on groups rather than individuals was attractive to the Japanese, while it simply failed to ignite a spark in the United States. The Western preoccupation with individual achievement meant that sublimating individual aspirations to group consciousness was a quantum leap rather than a logical progression.

Culture is key to understanding and implementing the lessons preached by both Deming and Juran. Deming appreciated that no matter how powerful the tool of mathematical statistics might be it would be ineffective unless used in the correct cultural context. This combination of culture and measurement eventually evolved into what is now labelled **Total Quality Management**.

> *Culture is key to understanding and implementing the lessons preached by both Deming and Juran.*

Commenting on Deming's work, management writer Robert Heller observed: "His work bridges the gap between science-based application and humanistic philosophy. Statistical quality control is as arid as it sounds. But results so spectacular as to be almost romantic flow from using these tools to improve processes in ways that minimize defects and eliminate the deadly trio of rejects, rework and recalls."[3]

The arid world of statistics is the coping stone of Deming's approach (and led to criticism from Juran). Every business generates overwhelming masses of numbers. But data is not information. Deming sought a means of providing a continuous supply of the data which drives decisions. Generating the right statistics and interpreting and acting on them were crucial elements in his philosophy. Unfortunately, this has in many cases generated a bureaucracy of quality which concentrates on measurement above all else.

Demings philosophy was distilled into 14 points.

Deming's 14 points

1   Create constancy of purpose toward improvement of product and service, with the aim to become competitive and to stay in business, and to provide jobs.

2   Adopt the new philosophy. We are in a new economic age, created by Japan. Transformation of Western management style is necessary to halt the continued decline of industry.

▶

3　Cease dependence on inspection to achieve quality. Eliminate the need for inspection on a mass basis by building quality into the product in the first place.

4　End the practice of awarding business on the basis of price tag. Purchasing must be combined with design of product, manufacturing, and sales to work with the chosen suppliers: the aim is to minimize total cost, not merely initial cost.

5　Improve constantly and forever every activity in the company, to improve quality and productivity and thus constantly decrease costs.

6　Institute training and education on the job, including management.

7　Institute supervision. The aim of supervision should be to help people and machines to do a better job.

8　Drive out fear, so that everyone may work effectively for the company.

9　Break down barriers between departments. People in research, design, sales and production must work as a team to tackle usage and production problems that may be encountered with the product or service.

10　Eliminate slogans, exhortations, and targets for the workforce asking for zero defects and new levels of productivity. Such exhortations only create adversarial relationships; the bulk of the causes of low quality and low productivity belong to the system and thus lie beyond the power of the workforce.

11　Eliminate work standards that prescribe numerical quotas for the day. Substitute aids and helpful supervision, using the methods to be described.

12a　Remove the barriers that rob the hourly worker of the right to pride of workmanship. The responsibility of supervisors must be changed from sheer numbers to quality.

12b　Remove the barriers that rob people in management and in engineering of their right to pride of workmanship. This means, inter alia, abolition of the annual or merit rating and of management by objective.

13　Institute a vigorous program of education and retraining. New skills are required for changes in techniques, materials and service.

14　Put everybody in the company to work in teams to accomplish the transformation.

While distilling his ideas down to the fourteen points, Deming insisted that effective implementation could only be achieved by a full understanding of the underlying theory. "Experience, without theory, teaches management nothing about what to do to improve quality and competitive position," he argued.

In practice, many organizations have claimed to have taken on Deming's philosophy. Often, however, their attempts at implementation come to an abrupt halt because of basic misinterpretations. The "fourteen points" should not be interpreted as tablets of stone, but require subtle interpretations. Quality is not, according to Deming, a matter of setting a standard of how many defects are acceptable. A manager once told Deming: "I need to know the minimum level of quality necessary to satisfy a customer." Deming commented: "So much misunderstanding was conveyed in a few words."

Also, Deming's philosophy revolves around fundamental changes in the way businesses deal with figures and statistics. Instead of setting aspirational profit targets, Deming argues the emphasis should be on providing quality products and services for customers. By working at constantly improving all processes within a business, customer satisfaction will increase and, inevitably, so too will profits.

Deming continued preaching his message until shortly before his death in 1993. Companies such as Ford, Rothmans and Bosch are among those which have adopted his philosophy. A prophet without honor in his own country for so long, Deming's last years were spent travelling the world. "I'm desperate. There's not enough time left," he is reported to have told a colleague. "For companies that haven't fully adopted the ideas and practices that Deming, as much as any man, made universal, those last five words will be their epitaph, not his," concluded Robert Heller.

W EDWARDS DEMING

1900–93

American

Statistician and consultant

Education: University of Wyoming; Yale (PhD in mathematical physics).

Career: Department of Agriculture; 1939 head statistician and mathematician for the US census; 1945 New York University as professor of statistics; later a consultant.

Books: *Quality, Productivity and Competitive Position*, MIT Center for Advanced Engineering Study, MIT, Mass., 1982; Out of the Crisis, Cambridge University Press, Cambridge, 1988.

Books about Deming: Aquayo, R, *Dr Deming: The Man Who Taught the Japanese About Quality*, Mercury, London, 1990; Price, Frank, *Right Every Time*, Gower, Aldershot, 1990.

Quality for the masses

It is staggering that Deming and Juran remained largely ignored in the West until as late as the 1980s, and then it took a TV program to bring their ideas and experiences to a wider Western audience. The television documentary, "If Japan can, why can't we?" examined the rapidly increasing performance of Japanese companies and the role of the quality gurus in making it happen.

Propelled into the consciousness of the world's managers, Deming and Juran's messages are now corporate truisms. Organizations routinely accept that inspection is not the route to improved quality; that functions should work together rather than in competition; and that improved processes and systems are more effective than exhortations.

The basics have become part of the everyday life of management. But that does not mean that quality is universally practised or has proved to be a universal panacea for corporate ills. Indeed, the very basic nature of quality leads to a host of misinterpretations and bastardized versions.

Quality is not revolutionary. In fact, it is anything but revolutionary. Quintessentially it is simple – "Quality is free" argues Philip Crosby, one of the host of gurus who emerged in the wake of Deming and Juran providing their own insight into how to achieve quality. The aphorisms are platitudinous. But they are true.

After the euphoria of the 1980s when quality was *discovered*, there has been a return to the disappointment of reality. Quality has failed to revolutionize the business world though it has revolutionized many individual businesses.

> **Quality has failed to revolutionize the business world though it has revolutionized many individual businesses.**

Many organizations across the world have brought in external experts to launch their own version of quality management. But, too often, quality initiatives have bitten the corporate dust or reaped isolated or negligible rewards. Juran now estimates that less than 50 of the top 500 US companies have "attained world class quality," a meager reward for so much investment.[4]

Commonly, quality initiatives lead to a single division or function recording a significant quality improvement. Rarely is this experienced throughout an organization. Similarly, the ideal of continuous improvement has proved to be fatally flawed. Indeed, the service economy and those service elements of industry which now dominate product costs have failed to respond to continuous improvement initiatives, evidenced by a reduction in pre-tax profits of 50 per cent over the last ten years.

Juran, still preaching his quality gospel, is dismissive of the attempts by the West to take on his quality philosophy. He believes there are a number of reasons for this failure. First, Juran argues that senior managers have often failed to fully understand what achieving quality involves. Instead of being regarded as important in itself, it was seen by many US corporations as a way of competing with imported products. If you can't beat them, copy them.

Juran's chief gripe is that quality is simply not regarded as important enough. Chief executives, as a result, fail to give personal leadership to quality initiatives and do not realize that you need "to manage and measure quality as seriously as one would for profitability."

In other respects the response has been half-hearted: benchmarking, for example, often sets unattainable goals or is calculated on financial measures. Reward systems fail to be related to quality and people are trained indiscriminately or inconsistently. While the importance of quality is widely accepted, Juran laments that its implementation remains as imprecise and unfocussed as ever.[5]

There are, of course, a myriad books and manifestos which promise instant quality. Most are worthless. Perhaps the most realistic and practical insight comes from pan-European research by consultant George Binney.[6] He identifies four key characteristics among companies which have gained some measure of success in becoming quality organizations:

1 **Forthright, listening leadership** – charismatic leadership, contrary to popular belief, is not one of the features of successful companies. Instead, the common factor is leadership which is both forthright and listening. It is very assertive about standards and objectives, making clear that quality is non-negotiable and that customer service is genuinely and consistently the number one priority. At the same time, the leadership not only encourages employees to give their views about how to improve quality, it actively listens to those views, acts on them and draws on the knowledge and experience of staff at all levels.

2 **Provoking, not imposing change** – the successful companies involve people at all levels at a very early stage in their quality initiatives. This real involvement ensures that those participating have a strong sense of ownership of the new ways of working. Some senior managers resist the temptation to impose ready-made solutions drawn from their previous experience, investing time instead in helping their staff to find their own solution. A clear and compelling vision is created and managers make every effort to ensure that their own behavior and decisions reinforce the vision.

3 **Integrating quality into the fabric of the business** – continuous improvement is part of the way the business is run. In these companies quality is the responsibility of everyone, not of a special department or team. Structures and processes support the drive for quality, they do not cut across it. Measurement systems use indicators that matter to customers. Appraisal procedures

emphasize customer satisfaction and development of self and of staff in addition to financial results. The selection criteria for recruitment stress attitudes to quality.

4 **Learning by doing** – In the successful companies, time and space are allowed – and respected – for learning and experimentation. There is an emphasis on action and results and on appreciation of the need for regular reviews in order to learn how to improve. Feedback is encouraged; people are able to try out new ideas without fear of pointless retribution or blame if things go wrong.

With the importance of quality now almost universally accepted, the debate has moved on. The emphasis is increasingly on involving the customer in the organization. Indeed, for all their eulogizing, Juran and Deming have a tendency to overlook the role of the customer.

> *The most notable and persuasive champion of customer service is Tom Peters.*

The most notable and persuasive champion of **customer service** is Tom Peters.

Others are now following suit, describing ways in which organizations can become customer friendly. In *The Only Thing That Matters*,[7] for example, American consultant Karl Albrecht argues that quality can only work if customers are brought into the center of the business. He describes what he calls "fifth dimension organizations," ones which have made service into an art form. They have moved beyond the stage of making a serious effort to improve quality. Their closeness to their customers has made them peak performers.

Albrecht believes "fifth dimension organizations" have seven key characteristics:

- leadership which is mentally and behaviorally flexible
- an understanding of and special insight into the needs of their customers
- the ability to redefine the playing field and deliver in ways that separate them from the competition
- commitment to changing themselves in directions that are consistent with evolving customer needs and expectations

- they recognize that human energy is the greatest untapped resource in an organization and that participation from customers, owners and employees is critical
- a caring and sharing culture
- a drive to be the best and a commitment to continuous improvement in all aspects of their organization.

Key books

Crosby, Philip, *Quality is Free*, McGraw-Hill, New York, 1979

Feigenbaum, AV, *Total Quality Control*, McGraw-Hill, New York, 1983

Juran, Joseph, *Managerial Breakthrough*, McGraw-Hill, New York, 1964

Juran, Joseph, *Juran on Planning for Quality*, Free Press, New York, 1988

Schonberger, Richard, *Building a Chain of Customers*, Free Press, New York, 1990

Reengineering

Research at the Massachusetts Institute of Technology suggests that management fads follow a regular life cycle. This starts with academic discovery. The new idea is then formulated into a technique and published in an academic publication. It is then more widely promoted as a means of increasing productivity, reducing costs or whatever is currently exercising managerial minds. Consultants then pick the idea up and treat it as the universal panacea. After practical attempts fail to deliver the impressive results promised, there is realization of how difficult it is to convert the bright idea into sustainable practice. Finally, there follows committed exploitation by a small number of companies.

Nothing better exemplifies this pattern than the rise to global prominence and inevitable fall of business process reengineering.

The idea of reengineering was brought to the fore by **James Champy,** co-founder of the consultancy company CSC Index, and **Michael Hammer,** an electrical engineer and former computer science professor at MIT. The roots of the idea lay in the research carried out by MIT from 1984 to 1989 on "Management in the 1990s."

Champy and Hammer's book, *Reengineering the Corporation*, was a bestseller which produced a plethora of reengineering programs; led to the creation of many consulting companies; and a deluge of books promoting alternative approaches to reengineering. (Thanks to the popularity of reengineering, CSC became one of the largest consultancy companies in the world with revenues in excess of $500 million and over 2000 consultants worldwide. Revenues prior to the success of the book were $70 million.)

The basic idea behind reengineering is that organizations need to identify their key processes and make them as lean and efficient as possible. Peripheral processes (and, therefore, peripheral people) need to be discarded. "Don't automate; obliterate," Hammer

> *The basic idea behind reengineering is that organizations need to identify their key processes and make them as lean and efficient as possible.*

189

proclaimed. Champy and Hammer defined reengineering as "the fundamental rethinking and radical redesign of business processes to achieve dramatic improvements in critical measures of performance such as cost, quality, service and speed."

As can be seen, the beauty of reengineering was that it embraced many of the fashionable business ideas of recent years and nudged them forward into a tidy philosophy. There were strains of total quality management, just-in-time manufacturing, customer service, time-based competition and lean manufacturing in the reengineering concept. Big name corporations jumped on the bandwagon and the book was endorsed, somewhat surprisingly, by no less a figure than Peter Drucker.

To Champy and Hammer, reengineering was more than dealing with mere processes. They eschewed the phrase "business process reengineering," regarding it as too limiting. In their view the scope and scale of reengineering went far beyond simply altering and refining processes. True reengineering was all-embracing, a recipe for a corporate revolution. Hammer proved himself highly quotable, proclaiming that he was intent on reversing the industrial revolution – "I think this is the work of angels. In a world where so many people are so deprived, it's a sin to be inefficient." Unfortunately, many reengineered companies found themselves to be sinners.

JAMES CHAMPY

Born 1942

American

Consultant

Career: Consultant with CSC Index; in August 1996 Champy left CSC to join Perot Systems to lead its management consulting activities.

Books: *Reengineering the Corporation*, with Michael Hammer, Harper Business, New York, 1993; *Reengineering Management*, Harper Business, New York, 1995.

To start the revolution, Champy and Hammer advocated that companies equip themselves with a blank piece of paper and map out their processes. Having come up with a neatly engineered map of how their business should operate, companies could then attempt to translate the paper theory into concrete reality.

The concept was simple. Indeed, it contained strong echoes of Frederick Taylor's Scientific Management with its concentration on processes and efficiency. While its relative simplicity made it alluring, actually turning reengineering into reality has proved immensely difficult. The revolution has largely been a damp squib.

The first problem was that the blank piece of paper ignored the years, often decades, of cultural evolution which led to an organization doing something in a certain way. Such preconceptions and often justifiable habits were not easily discarded.

The second problem was that reengineering appeared inhumane. In some cases, people were treated appallingly in the name of re-engineering. Reengineering, as the name suggests, owed more to visions of the corporation as a machine than a human, or humane, system. The human side of reengineering has proved its greatest stumbling block. To reengineering purists, people were objects who handle processes. Depersonalization was the route to efficiency. (Here, the echoes of Taylor's management by dictatorship are most obvious.)

Reengineering became a synonym for redundancy and down-sizing. For this Champy and Hammer could not be entirely blamed. Often, companies which claimed to be reengineering – and there were plenty – were simply engaging in cost cutting under the convenient guise of the fashionable theory. Downsizing appeared more publicly palatable if it was presented as implementing a leading edge concept.

The third obstacle was that corporations are neither natural nor willing revolutionaries. Instead of casting the reengineering net widely they tended to reengineer the most readily accessible process and then leave it at that. Related to this, and the subject of Champy's sequel, *Reengineering Management*, reengineering usually failed to impinge on management. Not surprisingly, managers were all too willing to impose the rigors of a process-based view of the business on others, but often unwilling to inflict it upon themselves. "Senior managers have been reengineering business processes with a passion, tearing down corporate structures that no longer can support the organization. Yet the practice of management has largely escaped demolition. If their jobs and styles are left largely intact, managers will eventually undermine the very structure of their rebuilt enterprises," Champy noted in 1994 at the height of reengineering's popularity. He suggested reengineering management should tackle three key areas: managerial roles; managerial styles; and managerial systems. In retrospect, the mistake of reengineering was not to tackle reengineering management first.

MICHAEL HAMMER

Born 1948

American

Educator and consultant

Education: Trained as an electrical engineer.

Career: Computer science professor, MIT; president of Hammer and Company, a management education and consulting firm.

Books: *Reengineering the Corporation* with James Champy, Harper Business, New York, 1993; *The Reengineering Revolution* with Steven Stanton, HarperCollins, New York, 1995.

Lean production

During the last 40 years, Western car makers have lurched from one crisis to another. They have always been a step behind. And the company they have been following is the Japanese giant, Toyota.

If you go into the Toyota headquarters building in Japan you will find three portraits. One is of the company's founder; the next of the company's current president; and the final one is a portrait of W Edwards Deming. While Western companies produced gas-guzzling cars with costly, large and unhappy workforces in the 1970s, Toyota was forging ahead with implementation of Deming's ideas. In the early eighties, Western companies finally woke up and began to implement Deming's quality gospel. By then it was too late. Toyota had moved on. (In fact, it didn't mind telling Western companies all about total quality management for this very reason.)

Toyota progressed to what became known as "lean production," or the "Toyota Production System." (The architect of this is usually acknowledged as being **Taichi Ohno** who wrote a short book on the Toyota approach and later became a consultant.) From Toyota's point of view, there was nothing revolutionary in lean production. In fact, lean production was an integral part of Toyota's commitment to quality and its roots can be traced back to the 1950s. In 1984, when Toyota opened up a joint venture with General Motors in California, the West began to wake up and the word began to spread.

And the word was based on three simple principles. The first was just-in-time production. There is no point in producing cars, or anything else, in blind anticipation of someone buying them. Waste ("muda") is bad. Production has to be closely tied to the market's requirements. Second, responsibility for quality rests with everyone and any quality defects need to be rectified as soon as they are identified. The third, more elusive, concept was the "value stream." Instead of seeing the company as a series of unrelated

> *There is no point in producing cars, or anything else, in blind anticipation of someone buying them.*

products and processes, it should be seen as a continuous and uniform whole, a stream including suppliers as well as customers.

The concepts were brought to mass Western audiences thanks to work carried out at the Massachusetts Institute of Technology as part of its International Motor Vehicle Program. The MIT research took five years, covered 14 countries and looked exclusively at the worldwide car industry.

The research concluded that while American car makers remained fixed in the mass production techniques of the past, Japanese car makers managed to square the manufacturing circle – management, workers and suppliers worked to the same goals, resulting in increased production, high quality, happy customers and lower costs. The research spawned the 1990 bestseller by James Womack, Daniel Jones and Daniel Roos, *The Machine That Changed the World*. (Womack and Roos were from MIT while Jones was from Cardiff Business School.) From lean production, Womack and Jones went on to propose the "lean enterprise" (based on research covering 25 American, Japanese and German companies) and "lean management."[8]

Lean production became fashionable. As with most management fads, it was wilfully misinterpreted. It became linked to reengineering and, more worryingly, with downsizing.

The reality is that lean production is a highly effective concept. "Lean production is a superior way for humans to make things," argue Womack and Jones. They are right. If, as Toyota has largely done, you get it right, lean production gives you the best of every world – the economies of scale resulting from mass production; the sensitivity to market and customer needs usually associated with smaller companies; and job enrichment for employees.

The trouble is that getting it right has proved difficult. In many cases, Western organizations were so committed to their very different ways of working that the changes required were impossibly all-embracing. The obese cannot transform themselves into sylphs overnight.

But it is not only that lean production requires large-scale changes in practice and attitude. The West continues to equate leanness with numbers. Lean production is seen as a means of squeezing more production from fewer people. This is a fundamental misunderstanding. Reduced numbers of employees is the ends rather than the means. Western companies have tended to reduce numbers and then declare themselves as lean organizations. This overlooks all three of the concepts which underlie genuine lean production (just-in-time manufacturing; responsibility for quality; and the company as value stream). Womack argues that while lean production requires fewer people, the organization should then accelerate product development to tap new markets to keep the people at work.

Inevitably, lean production is not without its downside. The most obvious one is that its natural home is the mass manufacturing world of car making. It has been translated into other industries – retailing, for example – but there are other areas where it is more difficult to apply. It is not a universal panacea.

The second obvious problem with lean production is that it fails to embrace innovation and product development. It is one thing being able to make a product efficiently, but how do you actually originate exciting and marketable products in the first place? Womack and Jones would suggest that "the critical starting point for lean thinking is value," but this is effectively one stage beyond the initial one of generating ideas.

Even so, lean production has moved the debate about quality forwards. It has raised awareness, provided a new benchmark and brought operational efficiency to a wider audience. "Organizations did well to employ the most up-to-date equipment, information technology and management techniques to eliminate waste, defects and delays," says Harvard Business School's Michael Porter. "They did well to operate as close as they could to the productivity frontier. But while improving operational effectiveness is necessary to achieving superior profitability, it is not sufficient."[9]

Key books

Monden, Yasuhiro, *Toyota Production System*, Institute of Industrial Engineers, 1988

Ohno, Taichi, *Toyota Production System*, Productivity Press, 1988

Womack, James and **Jones, Daniel T**, *Lean Thinking*, Simon & Schuster, New York, 1996

Womack, James, **Jones, Daniel T** and **Roos, Daniel**, *The Machine That Changed The World*, Rawson Associates/Macmillan, 1990

References: the quality revolution

1 Quoted in Griffith, Victoria, "Corporate fashion victim," *Financial Times*, 12 April 1995.
2 Schonberger, Richard, *Building a Chain of Customers*, Free Press, New York 1990.
3 Heller, Robert, "Fourteen points that the West ignores at its peril," *Management Today*, March 1994.
4 Juran, Joseph M, "Why quality initiatives fail," *Journal of Business Strategy*, Vol. 14, No. 4, July–August 1993.
5 Juran, Joseph M, "Why quality initiatives fail," *Journal of Business Strategy*, Vol. 14, No. 4, July–August 1993.
6 Binney, George, *Making Quality Work – Lessons from Europe's Leading Companies*, Economist Intelligence Unit, London, 1993.
7 Albrecht, Karl, *The Only Thing That Matters*, Harper Business, New York, 1993.
8 Womack, James, Jones, Daniel and Roos, Daniel, *The Machine That Changed the World*, Rawson Associates/Macmillan, 1990.
9 Porter, Michael, "What is strategy?," *Harvard Business Review*, November–December, 1996.

8

Reinventing marketing

"Markets are not created by God, nature or by economic forces, but by businessmen."

Peter Drucker[1]

"The marketing view of the business process requires that all innovations be thought of as intended to help get and keep customers, in short, to make the firm more competitive."

Ted Levitt[2]

Hard selling – the rise of marketing

Few would now question that marketing is a core activity of any organization. Its role is critical to success. Marketing involves planning and executing all customer-related activities (apart from the actual process of selling). Marketing identifies customer needs, suggests products to satisfy the demand and then operates a follow-up support system to ensure consumer satisfaction. The marketing department is the mouthpiece of the customer in the organization.

The origins of modern marketing can be traced back to the early 1960s. (Marketing itself is ancient, effectively beginning as soon as goods were bartered or sold.) Until that time the vast majority of Western companies were production led. They concentrated on producing goods as efficiently as they could. With the produced goods piled in the warehouse they could then turn their attention to actually selling them in the marketplace. The trouble was that often the marketplace was disinterested. Undeterred, the company carried on manufacturing in the hope and expectation that the market's interest would, sooner or later, be captivated by one means or another.

The end result was labelled **marketing myopia** by Harvard Business School's marketing guru **Ted Levitt** (born 1925). In a 1960 *Harvard Business Review* article, Levitt propelled marketing to center stage. He argued that instead of concentrating on production, companies should become "customer-satisfying," marketing led. Levitt's argument marked an important turning point. Inspired by the success of Henry Ford, businesses had remained intent on giving customers what they thought they needed and wanted. Ford had succeeded in creating a market for his cars, but it was a strategy which was inappropriate to the vast majority of products and services. As Levitt pointed out, Ford was soon outstripped by General Motors which gave customers what they actually wanted – more choice, more colors, regularly changing models.

> ## TED LEVITT
>
> Born Germany, 1925
>
> American
>
> Educator
>
> **Career:** Professor at Harvard Business School.
>
> **Books:** *Innovation in Marketing,* McGraw-Hill, New York, 1962; *The Marketing Mode,* McGraw-Hill, New York, 1969; *The Marketing Imagination,* Free Press, New York, 1983; *Thinking About Management,* Free Press, New York, 1991.

Levitt's message still holds considerable attraction for the modern business. He pre-empted the current fascination with customers by over 30 years. The only drawback of his popular article was its examples – Levitt castigated railroad companies for not moving into the airline business, a move which would have undoubtedly ended in disaster for both.

While Levitt's message was avidly consumed, its effect was minimal. It was only in the 1980s that marketing was rediscovered and companies began to shift their emphasis from production to marketing. They did so with commendable enthusiasm. So much so, that the 1980s saw the apotheosis of marketing. Its importance was more widely recognized than ever before. Companies championed themselves as being market driven. Budgets swelled and senior marketing managers were given a place on the board of many organizations.

A great deal of this was a case of throwing money at a problem with little overall change in emphasis or behavior. Investing in a marketing department proved far easier than changing a company from being production to marketing led.

The quest to become market driven

Harvard Business School's Benson Shapiro argues that truly market driven companies have three characteristics:

- information on all important buying influences permeates every corporate function
- strategic and tactical decisions are made inter-functionally and inter-divisionally
- divisions and functions make well coordinated decisions and execute them with a sense of commitment.[3]

Wharton's George S Day provides another slant on what it means to be market driven.

He says that firms which fail to become market driven usually fall prey to three traps. First, some become "self-centered." The archetypal example of this is what happened to IBM during the 1980s. It became distant from its customers. Customer information was poorly captured and distributed. Senior managers became ever more distant from what was happening in the marketplace. In addition, its undoubted centers of excellence existed in isolation. IBM continued to sustain superb standards, but lacked any means of delivering such excellence on a broader scale. IBM also began to concentrate on cost reduction to achieve short-term financial results rather than on long-term development.

Unfortunately, the next pitfall identified by George Day, "the customer compulsion trap" is also epitomized by IBM – though this time in the early 1990s. In effect, IBM sought to redress the balance by listening to each and every one of its customers. The result was confusion and disillusionment. Which leads to the final trap: skepticism. Companies can regard customers as an unwelcome distraction arguing that customers should be led rather than followed.

Day concludes that the route to becoming market driven is likely to involve a number of characteristics: offering superior solutions and experiences; focussing on superior customer value; converting satisfaction to loyalty; energizing and retaining employees; anticipating competitors' moves; viewing marketing as an investment, not a cost; and nurturing and leveraging brands as assets. In the end, the companies which succeed will have some – though not all – of these characteristics.

In order to work, marketing must truly permeate an organization's values and practice. It is not an isolated function, but a *raison d'être*. The beginning of the 1990s saw a shift in attitudes and practice.

Some organizations realized that, despite their talk of being *market driven* and *market focussed*, they had become *marketing driven* and *marketing focussed*. Marketing is not any less important but, instead of dispensing blank checks to marketing

> **In order to work, marketing must truly permeate an organization's values and practice.**

departments, companies are beginning to question and examine the role and achievement of marketing managers in attaining their objectives. No resource is an island and organizations need to establish how marketing best fits and relates to the rest of the organization and, most importantly, how effective it is in meeting the needs of customers. There is no point in having a corporate lubricant if all it does is support cyclical motion in a narrowly defined area.

The malaise now identified in the marketing operation of many organizations is a functional one. Often, marketing departments have not only failed to build close relationships with customers, but have isolated themselves within their own organizations. A survey of 100 UK companies by management consultants Coopers & Lybrand[4] found huge disparities between what marketing departments think they contribute and what everyone else feels. A third of marketing directors think they are entirely or mainly responsible for strategic planning; but only one fifth of managing directors agree.

The Coopers & Lybrand report also demonstrated that most procedures for measuring the effectiveness of marketing activity are irrelevant and result in a lack of accountability. A total of 57 per cent of companies used sales revenue to measure effectiveness; 53 per cent used market share; and 39 per cent used net profit. The report concluded that the effective marketing department of the future will:

- have within its remit all the processes that contribute to managing the customer and consumer interface
- have clear and defined responsibility for these processes
- focus on activities that demonstrably add value
- be measured, and judged against these measures.[5]

Some companies are already reorganizing their marketing resources so that they become more truly aligned to the needs of customers; interact more effectively with the rest of the organization and are treated as a process rather than as an unwieldy and often isolated department. Marketing needs to redefine its role and organization for the future. In *Tomorrow's Competition*, Mack Hanan writes that the modern marketing challenge is to "make your business competitive by making the businesses of your customers more competitive."[6]

Philip Kotler provides three key aphorisms for shaping the future:

- **Invest in the future** – "Companies pay too much attention to the cost of doing something. They should worry more about the cost of not doing it."

- **Move fast** – "Every company should work hard to obsolete its own product line... before its competitors do."

- **Excel at everything you do** – "Your company does not belong in any market where it can't be the best."

The message is that marketing must become part of the mainstream of all an organization's activities. The word "marketing" is notably absent from Tom Peters' exhortations for organizations to become customer oriented. The reason is simple – everyone must be involved in marketing in the same way as everyone must be dedicated to quality. In the best organizations marketing is left unsaid, but not undone.

Key books

Hill, Sam and **Rifkin, Glenn**, *Radical Marketing*, Harper Business, New York, 1998

Kotler, Philip, *Marketing Management: Analysis, Planning and Control*, Prentice Hall, New Jersey, 1993

Webster, FE, *Market-Driven Management*, John Wiley, New York, 1994

The Four Ps of marketing

Among the central functions of business, marketing probably holds the distinction of being the one most bedevilled by fashionable acronyms and vacuous managerial mantras. From the marketing audit to megamarketing and marketing warfare, the majority emerge meteorically, only to disappear just as quickly into the obscurity of empty seminar rooms. Some, a small minority, have proved to be more robust.

In 1960, E Jerome McCarthy introduced a new concept to the world of business theory. McCarthy took the marketing mix (defined by marketing's *éminence grise*, Philip Kotler, as "the set of marketing tools that the firm uses to pursue its marketing objectives in the target market") and identified its critical ingredients as product, price, place and promotion. This became known as the Four Ps of marketing. It is a mantra which has stood the test of time. It is still recited by students and known by virtually everyone in business. (The renown of marketing's Four Ps is such that purchasing sought to follow its example with its own Four Os.)

Despite its popularity and longevity, it would be wrong to view the idea of the Four Ps as anything other than a catchy, and fairly accurate, *aide memoire*. Knowing what the Four Ps are is unrelated to your ability or willingness to do anything with them. In the same way as the Seven S framework is not going to transform a company's performance, the Four Ps are unlikely to turn a company into a marketing superstar

Even so, at the time of their inception, the Four Ps encapsulated the essence of traditional marketing. A company which successfully focused its attention on all of the Four Ps *could* develop a soundly based marketing strategy. A company which failed to do so – or which allowed its focus to shift – was unlikely to excel at marketing.

> **At the time of their inception, the Four Ps encapsulated the essence of traditional marketing.**

Examining the four categories, first there is the product (or the service) being offered. This appears straightforward enough –

though Philip Kotler noted, "The idea of a product seems intuitive; yet there is a real problem in knowing exactly what it embraces." Kotler eventually settled for a definition of a product as: "a bundle of physical services and symbolic particulars expected to yield satisfaction or benefits to the buyer." (This has since been distilled down to: "A product is something that is viewed as capable of satisfying a want.")

Next comes the self-explanatory issue of pricing. In recent years this has become ever more complex with the appearance of an array of pricing strategies covering everything from premium pricing to seasonal or even daily pricing.

The other two elements, place and promotion, are more wide ranging. Place embraces how and where the company makes the product accessible to potential customers. This includes, therefore, distribution and logistics.

Promotion hides a multitude of activities, all of which have enjoyed an explosion of growth over the last 20 or so years. These include communication, personal selling, advertising, direct marketing, sales promotion and public relations.

The attraction of the Four Ps is that they give four easily remembered categories under which marketing activities can be considered. While, at a basic level, this may be useful, it is less useful in a complex modern organization – especially one which is in a service industry. The Four Ps suggests that that the categories can be viewed in isolation. In reality, there are a myriad relationships between the various components of any marketing mix. To religiously follow the Four Ps structure runs the risk of overlooking such relationships.

Over the years since the Four Ps were first introduced, a series of thinkers have regularly offered alternative classifications. Indeed, there is an endless array of potential combinations. Albert Frey, in *Advertising*, advocates separation between the offering (made up of product, packaging, brand, price and service) and methods and tools (distribution channels, personal selling, advertising, sales promotion and publicity). In their book *Managerial Marketing*, William Lazer and Eugene Kelly suggest three mixes – the goods and service mix; the distribution mix; and the communications mix.

Others, including Philip Kotler, have correctly pointed out that the Four Ps is essentially a seller's mix rather than a buyer's mix. They suggest that more attention be paid to a buyer's marketing mix – the Four Cs of customer needs and wants, cost to the customer, convenience and communication. Similarly, it has been suggested that the provision of customer service should be added to the list. (Philip Kotler counters this, arguing that customer service is an aspect of product strategy.) While yet another author suggests that people, physical evidence and processes should supplement the original Four Ps. More recently, two academics have moved up the alphabet, suggesting the "RS-model" of content, context and infrastructure.

Emulation is largely futile. The Four Ps were a useful summary of the dominant parts of the marketing mix in the 1960s when mass industrial marketing was the order of the day. However, the nature of business has changed. No longer is the emphasis on volumes, but on customer delight. No longer does a company blindly start with the product and then attempt to find a market; rather, the customer is the starting point.

The nature of marketing has also fundamentally changed. The divisions between the Four Ps are increasingly blurred, sometimes non-existent. For example, the Four Ps are of limited value if you are marketing and selling your products over the Internet. Despite great technological leaps forward, product, price, place and promotion are still important. The trouble is that defining their exact meaning, role and potential is more and more difficult.

Key books

Kotler, Philip, *Principles of Marketing*, Prentice Hall, Englewood Cliffs, 1996 (7th edition)

Kotler, Philip, *Marketing – An Introduction*, Prentice Hall, Englewood Cliffs, 1987

McCarthy, E Jerome, *Basic Marketing: A Managerial Approach*, Irwin, Homewood, Illinois, 1981 (9th edition)

Relationship marketing

Everyone in business has been told that success is all about attracting and retaining customers. It sounds reassuringly simple and achievable. But, in reality, words of wisdom are soon forgotten. Once companies have attracted customers they often overlook the second half of the equation. In the excitement of beating off the competition, negotiating prices, securing orders and delivering the product, managers tend to become carried away. They forget what they regard as the humdrum side of business – ensuring that the customer remains a customer.

Failing to concentrate on retaining as well as attracting customers costs businesses huge amounts of money annually. It has been estimated that the average company loses between 10 and 30 per cent of its customers every year. In constantly changing markets this is not surprising – what is surprising is the fact that few companies have any idea how many customers they have lost

Only now are organizations beginning to wake up to these lost opportunities and calculate the financial implications. Cutting down the number of customers a company loses can make a radical difference in its performance. Research in the US found that a five per cent decrease in the number of defecting customers led to profit increases of between 25 and 85 per cent.

Rank Xerox takes the question of retaining customers so seriously that it forms a key part of the company's bonus scheme. In the US, Domino's Pizzas estimates that a regular customer is worth more than $5,000 over ten years. A customer who receives a poor quality product or service on their first visit, and as a result never returns, is losing the company thousands of dollars in potential revenue (more if you consider how many people they are liable to tell about their bad experience).

In the car market, customer loyalty has long been recognized as a vital ingredient in long-term success. Research in the US showed that a satisfied customer usually stays with the same car manufacturer for 12 years, buying another four cars within that time. Not surprisingly, buying a car now guarantees a steady deluge of information and sales literature from the car maker as they try to ensure that you are not tempted elsewhere.

Once on the road, customer loyalty programs can be seen at every petrol station. The simple purchase of petrol is not really affected by price – left to their own devices, customers would stop at the nearest petrol station and fill up. Customer loyalty programs make it a more complex matter. Customers must choose between them.

The logic behind nurturing customer loyalty is impossible to refute. "In practice most companies' marketing effort is focused on getting customers with little attention paid to keeping them," says Adrian Payne of Cranfield University's School of Management and author of *The Essence of Services Marketing*. "Research suggests that there is a high degree of correlation between customer retention and profitability. Established customers tend to buy more, are predictable and usually cost less to service than new customers. Furthermore, they tend to be less price sensitive and may provide free word-of-mouth advertising and referrals. Retaining customers also makes it difficult for competitors to enter a market or increase their share of a market."[7]

> **The logic behind nurturing customer loyalty is impossible to refute.**

Payne points to a ladder of customer loyalty. On the first rung, there is a prospect. They are then turned into a customer, then a client, supporter and finally, if the relationship is successful, into an advocate persuading others to become customers. Developing customers so they travel up the ladder demands thought, long-term commitment and investment.

Customer loyalty programs cover a multitude of activities from customer magazines to vouchers and gifts. Basically, a customer loyalty program aims to persuade a person to use a preferred vendor in order to take advantage of the benefits on offer, whether a trip to Acapulco or a price-reduction voucher for a calorie-controlled canned drink. Skeptics may mutter that there is nothing new in this. Indeed, businesses have been giving long-standing customers discounts and inducements since time immemorial. What is now different is the highly organized way in which companies are attempting to build relationships and customer loyalty.

Technology means that customer loyalty programs are becoming ever more sophisticated. When it comes to creating loyal customers, the database is king. When diaper makers introduced trainer pants to the UK they were relying on the power and accuracy of their databases to steal a march on their rivals. Procter & Gamble, Kimberly-Clark and Peaudouce each has a database which identifies families with children of potty-training age. The families were then deluged with special offers and various other inducements – Procter & Gamble's Pampers brand helped its publicity campaign along with an achievement chart ("I can poo in my potty" being the primary goal).

Databases mean that companies can target audiences more effectively. One DIY chain, for example, has a discount card which entitles holders to an annual payout – which comes in the form of a voucher to be spent at the shop. The details of the cardholders enable the store to send out regular mailings to customers giving them advance warning of special offers and giving them an extra 5 per cent discount on certain days.

Technology also means that one customer loyalty program tends to blend into another. "The cycle is never ending with loyalty to one product or service being bolted on to another," says management consultant and author Tim Foster. "The rapid expansion of customer loyalty programs is proof that if they are well thought-out then they can have a great impact. If they are poorly constructed, the effect can be disastrous."[8]

In fact, putting the simple idea into practice has become increasingly complex. Customers are now more highly demanding and fickle than ever before. They are organized and use their lobbying power more effectively. Expectations are high, but companies are quickly realizing that customers with a conscience create new markets.

Companies are now developing loyalty programs which are directly related to the conscience of their customers. There is a plethora of products which pledge to donate money to help save the rain forests or support medical research, if you buy them. One supermarket chain, for example, gives customers vouchers which they can take to their children's schools to save up for a computer. Such loyalty building creates a situation in which all sides appear to win – though, of course, the supermarket wins the most through creating a loyal customer.

Customer loyalty programs are likely to become ever more ambitious. The potential for mutually beneficial link-ups is never ending. A credit card from General Motors would have been unthinkable a few years ago. Now, it is the tip of an expanding iceberg. Some American supermarkets already give customers a "smart card" which means the company knows the contents of each customer's weekly shopping basket.

> *Customer loyalty programs are likely to become ever more ambitious.*

Amid the enthusiasm for customer loyalty, the issue of which programs are effective – if any – has tended to be forgotten as managers have joined yet another in a long line of bandwagons. Research by Australian-based academics, Grahame Dowling and Mark Uncles, does not provide good news for organizations which have invested heavily in loyalty programs (or for consulting companies which have hyped customer loyalty).[9] In fact, Dowling and Uncles argue that there is little evidence to suggest that programs change the structure of markets. Instead, they tend to involve increased expenditure with little added brand loyalty. Indeed, loyalty appears depressingly thin on the ground – research has shown that a mere 10 per cent of buyers are 100 per cent loyal to a particular brand. Customers appear cynically opportunistic and are "loyal" to a variety of products at differing times.

Given this fickleness, nurturing customer loyalty is an ambitious task. Dowling and Uncles suggest that success requires that a program "leverage the value of the product to the customer." To do so, it must include a "perception of value." It must offer something tangible and worthwhile which can be attained in the near future. An instant cash prize is preferable to a distant prize of something of limited value or use.

As well as offering genuine benefits, a customer loyalty program needs to: enhance the value proposition of the product or service; be fully costed; maximize the buyer's motivation to buy again; and consider market conditions when it is planned. The trouble is, as Dowling and Uncles point out, it may not even be worth that much effort. "Loyal" customers are as fickle as any others and you cannot assume that they cost less to service, are less price sensitive or that they recommend products to others.

The battle of the future lies in utilizing customer information more effectively than the competition and in building relationships with customers which generate value. The bottom line is simple: while 30 per cent of customers are price sensitive, 70 per cent are more sensitive to value.

To take advantage of this, companies need to ensure that they take the lead in building up knowledge about their customers. If they are fully informed and take advantage of that knowledge, they are less likely to be beaten to the punch by new entrants. Companies must also focus on "sources of new value for the industry, not just redistributing or even destroying value." Imaginative use of differentiated pricing and better targeted offerings can create new value. Those who make do with old value will find it withering in their arms.[10]

Key books

Christopher, Martin, Payne, Adrian and **Ballantyne, D**, *Relationship Marketing*, Butterworth-Heinemann, Oxford, 1991

Cram, Tony, *The Power of Relationship Marketing*, FT/Pitman, London, 1995

Payne, Adrian, *The Essence of Services Marketing*, Prentice Hall, New Jersey, 1993

Reichheld, Frederick, *The Loyalty Effect*, Harvard Business School Press, Boston, 1996

Brand management

At its simplest, branding is a statement of ownership. Cows are branded and, in the commercial world, branding can be traced back to trademarks placed on Greek pots in the seventh century BC and, later, to medieval tradesmen who put trademarks on their products to protect themselves and buyers against inferior imitations. (Of course, in the modern world people are adept at copying trademarks – whether they are Lacoste, Sony, Rolex or Le Coq Sportif – and producing imitations, which are often highly accurate.) Trademarks remain highly effective prompts – there are now some 50 million registered worldwide.

In the beginning came the product. Branding was a mark on the product – a signature or symbol – signifying its origin or ownership. The traditional view of what constitutes a brand is summed up by marketing guru Philip Kotler in his classic text book *Marketing Management*. Kotler writes: "(A brand name is) a name, term, sign, symbol or design, or a combination of these, which is intended to identify the goods or services of one group of sellers and differentiate them from those of competitors."[11]

The trouble with older definitions of brands is that they remain preoccupied with the physical product. The product stands alone; the brand exists within corporate ether. The product comes first and the brand does little more than make it clear which company made the product and where.

A more recent definition comes from Richard Koch in his book *The Dictionary of Financial Management*. Koch defines a brand as: "A visual design and/or name that is given to a product or service by an organization in order to differentiate it from competing products and which assures consumers that the product will be of high and consistent quality."[12] Reflecting the emphasis of our times, Koch stresses differentiation – making your product or service different (or seeming to be different) – and achieving consistent quality.

Consultants, Sam Hill, Jack McGrath and Sandeep Dayal define branding as "creating a mutually acknowledged relationship between the supplier and buyer that transcends isolated transactions or specific individuals." Again, it is a significant sign of our times that the brand is now pinned around a "relationship."[13]

If we think of brands we inevitably begin with the great American brands – Marlboro, Coca-Cola, McDonald's, Budweiser and many, many more. They are the garish, colorful icons of our times. Many have become cultural touchstones. Often, our image of these great icons bears little relation to the product or reality. Wearing a pair of Levi's does not give you freedom.

That the iconic brands of the twentieth century are American owes a great deal to the fact that American businesses have continually developed brands at a faster pace than their European counterparts. This can partly be attributed to geography. American companies had (and have) a huge homogeneous national market; Europe does not. While American companies could launch massive advertising and marketing campaigns across the US and the English-speaking world, European companies learned to adapt (or not) to the cultural nuances of individual countries.

> **American businesses have continually developed brands at a faster pace than their European counterparts.**

The rise of brands

Trailers once traveled the American countryside laden with every possible known cure, stimulant, medicine or treatment. The medicine jamborees may have had an indifferent medical record, but their contribution to the success of brands cannot be overlooked. They played a small but significant part in the development of national branding during the late nineteenth century. Patent medicines and tobacco set the trend. Though distributed only regionally, they developed recognizable brand names and identities.

The increase of brands on a regional basis provided the foundation for growth on a much greater scale. Instead of being restricted to low quality, regionally distributed products, brands took the great leap forward into the high quality mass market. The conditions were fertile. Efficient pan-American transportation had emerged so that a successful product in Chicago could be sold in St Louis cost effectively.

But improvements weren't limited to transport – production processes and packaging improved and advertising became almost respectable. There were also changes in trademark laws and increasing industrialization and urbanization. While the brands expanded, their management remained resolutely set in its ways. Company owners and directors took responsibility. The array of tools at their disposal – from premiums and free samples, to mass advertising – grew quickly.

The period after the First World War cemented the place of brands. Advertising became increasingly prevalent and the acquisition of brands became identified with success and development. Consumers wanted Fords not motor cars; they bought from Sears rather than elsewhere.

Success brought complexity. Companies began to own a number of brands which they were able to produce, distribute and sell *en masse*. In 1931 Procter & Gamble took functional organization a stage further when it created a new function: brand management. With brands like Ivory and Camay bath soaps, P&G believed that the best way to organize itself would be to give responsibility to a single individual: a brand manager.

The system did not transform the world overnight, but gradually brand management became an accepted functional activity, an adjunct to sales and marketing – and often a fairly junior adjunct at that. Its popularity was fueled by the economic boom of the 1950s which brought a plethora of new products and brands. These were supplemented by developments such as shopping centers and the emergence of television advertising. We had never had it so good and never had so much. Brand management provided some hope of order amid the confusion introduced by prosperity.

By 1967, 84 per cent of large manufacturers of consumer packaged goods in the United States had brand managers. Though titles have changed, this system largely prevails today. It was only in the 1990s that the brand management system began to be questioned through trends such as reengineering which sought to break down long-established functional barriers.

Tom Peters argues that Marlboro Friday in 1993 (when Philip Morris slashed the prices of its premium cigarette brand) marked the end of a generation of big brands.[14] The new world of brands is radically different. The big names still exist but they no longer have a monopoly over the art of branding. Peters points to the rise of the Internet as evidence of a new, more personal brand generation. After all, you return to the Web site you trust and gain the most value from. Increasingly we need to promote our own personal brands through such things as developing our contacts or updating our CVs. Self-creation is the order of the day.

The new and emerging issues facing brands are, for many, a matter of life and death.

Fragmentation

Thanks to the likes of Heinz and Nestlé, markets have become highly fragmented. This means that there is always the possibility of an interloper stealing a march on bigger rivals by finding a small and lucrative niche.

Targeting

The obvious repercussion of this is that targeting the right market and then the right part of that market is crucial. A large amount of information is now available on buying habits as well as a host of other factors. The only difficultly for organizations is deciding how they can plough through all the data to find the right information and at the same time move speedily to fill smaller and smaller niches.

Innovation and speed

The answer in many markets is to develop new products and services more quickly than has ever been done before. This means that development times have to be slashed. The big brands of recent years have been those which deluge the market with new ideas – companies like Compaq, Rubbermaid (which boasts a new product every day) and Swatch.

Cost squeeze

To make matters more challenging, organizations have to achieve these things within reduced budgets. Gone are the days when a brand could be pushed to the top simply through an expensive advertising campaign. Consumers are more sophisticated and advertising costs have soared. Even a household name like Unilever's Persil only has around 25 per cent of its past amount of television advertising. But, not only have advertising costs soared, there is now also a profusion of media. Growing numbers of TV and radio stations allow companies unprecedented levels of access to audiences which are becoming progressively smaller and more fragmented.

Margins squeeze

In many sectors of business profit margins are being squeezed dry. Supermarkets are engaged in a perpetual price war with discounters entering the fray throughout Europe having already wreaked havoc in the United States.

Performance squeeze

If margins are down and costs reduced the performance of individuals and organizations has to be improved. From being an ostentatious, decadent world, branding has become obsessed with leveraging performance everywhere and anyhow.

Creating value

The end result is, in the phrase of our times, added value. Companies must add value throughout every single process they are involved in and then translate this into better value for consumers.

A *Financial Times* editorial on the soap wars between Unilever and Procter & Gamble sums it up: "It does not matter how mundane the product. Consumers are more demanding than ever before – and competitors more ruthless. The manufacturer that fails to appreciate these facts will go to the wall."[15]

The good news is that, in the age of brands, nothing is beyond branding – witness the way branding techniques are now routinely applied to football teams, pop groups, political parties and even countries. Two management consultants from Booz-Allen & Hamilton and Sam Hill of Helios Consulting have even presented an approach to branding sand – as well as any other "lowly differentiated" product or service.[16]

They say that the first step in branding is simply to "carve up the market from every angle – profits, needs, behaviors – to identify those customers who are responsive to differentiation." Taking as their starting point the belief that no market is completely homogeneous, the authors argue that customers can be divided into three groups – gold standard customers (willing to pay premium prices if their, sometimes exacting, requirements are met); potentials (more interested in price, but perspectives can be moved); and incorrigibles (short term and price fixated).

With greater understanding of customers – there is no substitute for knowing the market – companies can move onto the second stage of branding: differentiation. This was once entirely product related. Now, service-based differentiation is increasingly important.

Differentiatiors can then be "bundled" together to make up a brand which is communicated consistently and strongly. Finally, a company must align itself "to reinforce and defend the brand and the underlying sources of differentiation." "The key is to take a disciplined, deliberate approach that begins with the market, understands how to create and deliver value and, most importantly, figures out how to get paid for it," they conclude. "Getting paid for it requires branding, extending the relationship beyond the transaction to encompass the full organisation."

Key books

Aaker, David, *Managing Brand Equity*, Free Press, New York, 1991

Crainer, Stuart, *The Real Power of Brands*, FT/Pitman, London, 1995

Kapferer, Jean-Noel, *Strategic Brand Management*, Kogan Page, London, 1992

References: Reinventing marketing

1 Drucker, Peter, *The Practice of Management*, Harper & Row, New York, 1954.
2 Levitt, Ted, *Thinking About Management*, Free Press, New York, 1991.
3 Shapiro, Benson, "What the hell is market oriented?," *Harvard Business Review*, November–December 1988.
4 Coopers & Lybrand, *Marketing at the Crossroads*, Coopers & Lybrand, 1993.
5 Coopers & Lybrand, *Marketing at the Crossroads*, Coopers & Lybrand, 1993.

6 Hanan, Mack, *Tomorrow's Competition*, AMACOM, New York, 1991.
7 Author interview.
8 Author interview.
9 Dowling, Grahame R and Uncles, Mark, "Do customer loyalty programmes really work?," *Sloan Management Review*, Vol. 38, No. 4, Summer 1997.
10 Glynn, Simon, Caufield, Simon and César, Jacques, "Making customer relationships make money," *Mercer Management Journal*, No. 9, 1997.
11 Kotler, Philip, *Marketing Management: Analysis, Planning and Control*, Prentice Hall, Engelwood Cliffs, 1993 (8th edition).
12 Koch, Richard, *The Dictionary of Financial Management*, Financial Times Pitman Publishing, London, 1994.
13 Hill, Sam I, McGrath, Jack and Dayal, Sandeep, "How to brand sand," *Strategy & Business*, Second Quarter 1998.
14 Peters, Tom, "The brand called you," *Fast Company*, August–September 1997.
15 "Soap and chips," *Financial Times*, 21 December 1994.
16 Hill, Sam I, McGrath, Jack and Dayal, Sandeep, "How to brand sand," *Strategy & Business*, Second Quarter 1998.

9

Leadership

"Our prevailing leadership myths are still captured by the image of the captain of the cavalry leading the charge to rescue the settlers from the attacking Indians. So long as such myths prevail, they reinforce a focus on short-term events and charismatic heroes rather than on systemic forces and collective learning."

Peter Senge, MIT[1]

"A leader is a man who has the ability to get other people to do what they don't want to do, and like it."

Harry Truman[2]

"To survive in the twenty-first century we're going to need a new generation of leaders not managers."

Warren Bennis[3]

The rise of the new model leader

Leadership is one of the great intangibles of the business world. It is a skill most people would love to possess, but one which defies close definition. Ask people which leaders they admire and you are as likely to be told Gandhi as John Kennedy, Jack Welch as Anita Roddick. Yet, most agree that leadership is a vital ingredient in business success and that great leaders make for great organizations.

When considering leadership in the business context most roots lead to the military world. Management, long used to the concept of divide and rule, has perennially sought its leadership role models from the military. The temptation to view the business world as a battlefield is, even now, highly appealing. Indeed, the success of Sun-Tzu's *The Art of War* as a management text points to the continuing popularity of this idea.

Another key historical text, and one which is increasingly referred to, is Machiavelli's *The Prince*. Amid the grey-suited pantheon of management greats, **Niccolò Machiavelli** (1469–1527) holds an unlikely, but undeniable, place. A Florentine diplomat and writer, his career was colorful – punctuated by interludes of indulgence in "petty dissipations," torture on the rack and farming. His abiding relevance to the world of management rests on a slim volume, *The Prince*.

The Prince is a sixteenth-century equivalent of Dale Carnegie's *How to Make Friends and Influence People*. Embedded beneath details of Alexander VI's tribulations, lie a ready supply of aphorisms and insights which are, perhaps sadly, as appropriate to many of today's managers and organizations as they were nearly 500 years ago.

"It is unnecessary for a prince to have all the good qualities I have enumerated, but it is very necessary to appear to have them," Machiavelli advises, adding the suggestion that it is useful "to be a great pretender and dissembler." But *The Prince* goes beyond such helpful presentational hints. Like all the great books, it offers something for everyone. Take Machiavelli on managing change: "There is nothing more difficult to take in hand, more perilous to conduct, or more uncertain in its success, than to take the lead in the introduction of a new order of things." Or on sustaining motivation: "He ought above all things to keep his men well-organised and drilled, to follow incessantly the chase."

Above all, Machiavelli is the champion of leadership through cunning and intrigue, the triumph of force over reason. An admirer of Borgia, Machiavelli had a dismal view of human nature. Empowerment was not in his vocabulary. Unfortunately, as he sagely points out, history has repeatedly proved that a combination of being armed to the teeth and devious is more likely to allow you to achieve your objectives. It is all very well being good, says Machiavelli, but the leader "should know how to enter into evil when necessity commands."

"Like the leaders Machiavelli sought to defend, some executives tend to see themselves as the natural rulers in whose hands organizations can be safely entrusted," says psychologist Robert Sharrock of consultants YSC. "Theories abound on their motivation. Is it a defensive reaction against failure or a need for predictability through complete control? The effect of the power-driven Machiavellian manager is usually plain to see."[4]

In companies addicted to internal politics, Machiavelli remains the stuff of day-to-day reality. But, warns Robert Sharrock, Machiavellian management may have had its day. "The gentle art of persuasion is finding fashion with managers. The ends no longer justify the means. The means, the subtle management of relationships, are the ends by which future opportunities may be created. Also, most managers now recognize that organizations have purposes other than the maximization of profit. There is a return to the age of reason against which Machiavalli rebelled."

> *In the corporate trenches, Machiavelli remains useful reading.*

For many, the age of reason has yet to dawn. Managers may not have read *The Prince* but will be able to identify with Machiavelli's observation that "a prince ought to have no other aim or thought, nor select anything else for his study, than war and its rules and discipline." In the corporate trenches, Machiavelli remains useful reading.

Military models

Leadership reemerged on the management agenda in the 1980s after a period of relative neglect. A great many books were produced purporting to offer essential guidance on how to become a leader. These tended to follow military inspirations with the business leader portrayed as a general, inspiring the corporate troops to one more effort.

Even so, there are some useful inspirations in the military world for today's corporate leaders. One of the most persuasive, and underestimated, is Field Marshall William Slim. Slim believed that the leadership lessons he had learned in the army could readily be applied to the business world. In his book, *Defeat Into Victory*, Slim described his thoughts on raising morale:

> *"Morale is a state of mind. It is that intangible force which will move a whole group of men to give their last ounce to achieve something, without counting the cost to themselves; that makes them feel they are part of something greater than themselves. If they are to feel that, their morale must, if it is to endure – and the essence of morale is that it should endure – have certain foundations. These foundations are spiritual, intellectual, and material, and that is the order of their importance. Spiritual first, because only spiritual foundations can stand real strain. Next intellectual, because men are swayed by reason as well as feeling. Material last – important, but last – because the highest kinds of morale are often met when material conditions are lowest."[5]*

The doyen of the military-inspired approach is the UK leadership writer and practitioner, **John Adair**, who was himself in the army (as well as spending time on an Arctic trawler and various other adventures). Adair has identified a list of the basic functions of leadership: planning, initiating, controlling, supporting, informing and evaluating. Central to Adair's thinking is the belief that leadership is a skill which can be learned like any other. This is one of the fundamentals of the military approach to leadership – leaders are formed in the crucible of action rather than through chance genetics.

In the management world there is a tendency to fluctuate between the two extremes. On the one hand, managers are sent on leadership development courses to nurture, and discover, leadership skills. On the other hand, there is still a substantial belief that leaders have innate skills which cannot be learned.

Modern leadership writers tend to suggest that leadership as a skill or characteristic is distributed generously among the population. "Successful leadership is not dependent on the possession of a single universal pattern of inborn traits and abilities. It seems likely that leadership potential (considering the tremendous variety of situations for which leadership is required) is broadly rather than narrowly distributed in the population," wrote Douglas Macgregor in *The Human Side of Enterprise*.[6] The American, Warren Bennis, inspired by Macgregor, has studied leadership throughout his career. Bennis also concludes that each of us contains the capacity for leadership and has leadership experience. He does not suggest that actually translating this into becoming an effective leader is straightforward, but that it can be done, given time and application.

While such arguments are impressively optimistic about human potential, they are disappointed by reality. The dearth of great leaders is increasingly apparent. This suggests that either innate skills are not being effectively developed or that the

> **The dearth of great leaders is increasingly apparent.**

business world simply does not encourage managers to fulfil their potential as leaders.

The evolution of leadership

Leadership thinking has moved rapidly from one theory to another. The main schools of thought can be divided into the following.

Great Man Theory

Great Man theories were the stuff of the late nineteenth and early twentieth centuries, though their residue remains in much popular thinking on the subject. The Great Man Theory is based round the idea that the leader is born with innate, unexplainable and, for mere mortals, incomprehensible leadership skills. They are, therefore, elevated as heroes.

Trait Theory

This theory continues to fill numerous volumes. If you know who the Great Men are, you can then examine their personalities and behavior to develop traits of leaders. This is plausible, but deeply flawed. For all the books attempting to identify common traits among leaders there is little correlation.

Power and Influence Theory

This approach chooses to concentrate on the networks of power and influence generated by the leader. It is, however, based on the assumption that all roads lead to the leader and negates the role of followers and the strength of organizational culture.

Behaviorist Theory

In some ways the behaviorist school continues to hold sway. It emphasizes what leaders actually do rather than their characteristics. Its advocates include Blake and Mouton (creators of the Managerial Grid) and Rensis Likert.

Situational Theory

Situational Theory views leadership as specific to a situation rather than a particular sort of personality. It is based round the plausible notion that different circumstances require different forms of leadership. Its champions include Kenneth Blanchard and Paul Hersey whose influential book, *Situational Leadership Theory,* remains a situationalist manifesto.

Contingency Theory

Developing from Situational Theory, contingency approaches attempt to select situational variables which best indicate the most appropriate leadership style to suit the circumstances.

Transactional Theory

Increasingly fashionable, Transactional Theory places emphasis on the relationship between leaders and followers. It examines the mutual benefit from an exchange-based relationship with the leader offering certain things, such as resources or rewards, in return for others, such as the followers' commitment or acceptance of the leader's authority.

Attribution Theory

This elevates followership to new importance, concentrating on the factors which lie behind the followers' attribution of leadership to a particular leader.

Transformational Theory

While transactional leadership models are based on the extrinsic motivation of an exchange relationship, transformational leadership is based on intrinsic motivation. As such, the emphasis is on commitment rather than compliance from the followers. The transformational leader is, therefore, a proactive, innovative, visionary.

The new leader

The increasing emphasis in recent years has been on leaders as real people managing in a consensus-seeking manner. "Today's leaders understand that you have to give up control to get results – they act as coaches not as 'the boss'," observed Robert Waterman in *The Frontiers of Excellence*.[7] Instead of seeing leadership as being synonymous with dictatorship, this view sees leadership as a more subtle and humane art. It also breaks down the barrier between leadership and management. Traditionally, in theory at least, the two have been separated. "Men are ripe for intelligent, understanding, personal leadership, they would rather be led than managed," observed Field Marshal Slim.

Increasingly, management and leadership are seen as inextricably linked. It is one thing for a leader to propound a grand vision; but this is redundant unless the vision is managed into real achievement. While traditional views of leadership tend eventually to concentrate on vision and charisma, the message now seems to be that charisma is no longer enough to carry leaders through. Indeed, leaders with strong personalities are just as likely to bite the corporate dust. The new model leaders include people like Percy Barnevik, formerly at Asea Brown Boveri, Virgin's Richard Branson and Jack Welch at GE in the United States.

Contemporary trends were partly anticipated in the work of psychologist and researcher **Rensis Likert** (1903–1981). Likert identified four types of management style:

- *Exploitative authoritarian* – management by fear.
- *Benevolent autocracy* – top-down but with an emphasis on carrots rather than sticks.
- *Consultative* – communication both up and down, with decisions largely coming from the top.
- *Participative* – decision making in working groups which communicate with each other via individuals who are linking pins, team leaders or others who are also members of one or more other groups.

Beyond these four "systems" Likert also anticipated System 5 where all formal authority had disappeared.

The magic which marks such executives has been analyzed by INSEAD leadership expert **Manfred Kets de Vries**. "They go beyond narrow definitions. They have an ability to excite people in their organizations," he says. "They also work extremely hard – leading by example is not dead – and are highly resistant to stress. Also, leaders like Branson or Barnevik are very aware of what their failings are. They make sure that they find good people who can fill these areas."[8]

Leonard Sayles, author of *Leadership: Managing in Real Organizations* and *The Working Leader*, is representative of a great deal of the new thinking. Sayles suggests that leadership affects managers at all levels, not simply those in the higher echelons of management. "It is leadership based on work issues, not just people issues, and is very different from the method and style of managing that has evolved from our traditional management principles."

Sayles argues that the leader's role lies in "facilitating co-ordination and integration in order to get work done." Sayles is dismissive of the perennial concept of the great corporate leader. Instead his emphasis is on the leader as the integrator of corporate systems. The leader is a kind of fulcrum "adapting, modifying, adjusting and rearranging the complex task and function interfaces that keep slipping out of alignment." Instead of being centred around vision and inspiration, Sayles regards the leader's key role as integrating the outputs of his or her work unit with those of the rest of the organization. To Sayles, "managers who are not leaders can only be failures."

Interestingly, and unhelpfully for the practising manager, leadership attracts such aphorisms rather than hard and fast definitions. Indeed, there is a plethora of definitions of what constitutes a leader and the characteristics of leadership. In practice, none has come to be universally, or even widely, accepted.

The very individualism associated with leadership is now a bone of contention. The people we tend to

> *The people we tend to think of as leaders – from Napoleon to Winston Churchill – are not exactly renowned for their teamworking skills.*

think of as leaders – from Napoleon to Winston Churchill – are not exactly renowned for their teamworking skills. But, these are exactly the skills management theorists insist are now all-important.

"In some cases, the needs of a situation bring to the fore individuals with unique qualities or values, however, most leaders have to fit their skills, experience and vision to a particular time and place," says psychologist Robert Sharrock. "Today's leaders have to be pragmatic and flexible to survive. Increasingly, this means being people rather than task-oriented. The 'great man' theory about leadership rarely applies – if teams are what make businesses run, then we have to look beyond individual leaders to groups of people with a variety of leadership skills."[9]

Indeed, Indiana University's Charles Schwenk contends that the times call for weak leadership. According to Schwenk, the call from management thinkers for strong visions could be the first step towards corporate totalitarianism. (He overlooks the fact that corporate dictatorship has been a fact of life for decades.) Schwenk believes that decision making needs to build from diversity of opinion rather than a simplistic statement of corporate intent. This requires "weaker leadership" and that "top management's vision needs to be less clearly communicated (and less strongly enforced) than the advocates of management vision recommend."[10]

Though it flies in the face of conventional wisdom there is much good sense in Schwenk's argument. He points persuasively to the example of Microsoft's slow endorsement of the Internet. Originally, the Internet was not looked upon as fertile ground. Bill Gates' apparently all-encompassing vision did not include entering the Internet fray. Eventually, after much internal lobbying, Gates changed his mind and the company moved into Internet services. By traditional yardsticks this was an act of weak leadership. Visions are worthless if they are so easily changed. Surrender is not in the vocabulary of the John Wayne-type leader. Think again. What if Gates was wrong? Should a single view of the future always prevail? Schwenk thinks not: "Without tolerance for eccentricity it is unlikely that any technique for encouraging the expression of diverse views will improve decision making in a firm."

Another valuable perspective comes from Ron Heifetz of Harvard Business School and consultant Don Laurie. They contend that corporate leaders and organizations are now facing "adaptive challenges." The technical know-how to meet these challenges often exists, but that does not necessarily make life any easier. "Adaptive work is required when our deeply held beliefs are challenged, when the values that made us successful become less relevant, and when legitimate yet competing perspectives emerge," they write.[11]

Adaptive work requires leadership (a skill in perennial short supply). Heifetz and Laurie suggest that the kind of leadership best suited to adaptive change is based on six principles. First is what they label "getting on the balcony." Business leaders must be able to involve themselves in the nitty-gritty while maintaining an overall perspective. This is the prerequisite for success.

The second leadership skill lies in identifying the adaptive challenge. This is a somewhat nebulous term for getting beneath the surface and really identifying where cultural problems lie. The third facet is regulating distress. The leader must recognize that change causes stress and distress. Moving too quickly or not giving people an opportunity to relieve the pressure is counter-productive. Fourth, leaders must "maintain disciplined attention." "People need leadership to help them maintain their focus on the tough questions. Disciplined attention is the currency of leadership," write Heifetz and Laurie. Leaders steer people to confront the really tough questions they would rather ignore.

The final two principles of adaptive leadership are closely linked: "give the work back to people" and "protect voices of leadership from below." People must be involved in any process of change and must be allowed to express their opinions – even if they are discordant. What links all these elements is the perpetual need for questioning. "Leaders do not need to know all the answers. They do need to ask the right questions," say Heifetz and Laurie neatly concluding that "One can lead with no more than a question in hand."

Shouting orders is out, listening is in. Indeed, the pendulum has swung so far that there is growing interest in the study of followers. Once the humble foot soldier was ignored as commentators sought out the commanding officer, now the foot soldiers are encouraged to voice their

> *Shouting orders is out, listening is in.*

opinions and shape how the organization works. Today's corporate leaders expend a great deal of effort in communicating directly with their employees. Roger Enrico, vice chairman of PepsiCo, spends half his time "coaching" executives. Body Shop's Anita Roddick has installed bulletin boards, faxes and video recorders in each of the 700 Body Shops so that staff can communicate more effectively and she can communicate directly with them.

Richard Pascale has reported on a new breed of leadership used by Royal/Dutch Shell: "grassroots leadership."[12] This addition to the management vocabulary is attributed to Steve Miller, group managing director of Shell. Miller observed the difficulties the company was experiencing in becoming more creative, innovative and faster moving. It was attempting to transform itself one layer of management at a time. Change quickly became becalmed.

Miller cut out the middlemen and went straight to employees. In small groups, the people from filling stations and the like were brought in for intensive training. Miller concentrated half his time on talking to, meeting with and involving "grassroots" people. "As people move up in organizations, they get further away from the work that goes on in the field – and as a result, they tend to devalue it," he says. "People get caught up in broad strategic issues, legal issues, stakeholder issues. But what really drives a business is the work that goes on down at the coal face. It's reliability, it's producing to specification, it's delivering to the customer."[13]

A degree of selflessness is now expected from leaders. "Effective leaders recognize that the ultimate test of leadership is sustained success, which demands the constant cultivation of future leaders," says Noel Tichy of the University of Michigan.[14] Leaders must, therefore, invest in developing the leaders of tomorrow and they must communicate directly to those who will follow in their footsteps.

Tichy cites a number of American examples. Larry Bossidy, CEO of Allied Signal, put all the company's 86 000 employees through a development program and managed to speak to 15 000 of them during his first year in the job. Along the way, Bossidy also increased the market value of the company by 400 per cent in six years. Other exemplars are the usual suspects – including Andy Grove of Intel, GE's Jack Welch and Lew Platt of Hewlett-Packard.

Manfred Kets de Vries contends that leaders, like products, have a life cycle.

Knowing when to let go has become an integral part of the skills of the modern leader. There are many examples of leaders who stay on in organizations and in governments far beyond their practical usefulness. Manfred Kets de Vries contends that leaders, like products, have a life cycle. De Vries identifies three stages in this: entry and experimentation; consolidation; and decline, and estimates that life cycles for leaders are shortening.[15]

Noel Tichy believes that being able to pass on leadership skills to others requires three things. First, a "teachable point of view" – "You must be able to talk clearly and convincingly about who you are, why you exist and how you operate." Second, the leader requires a story. "Dramatic storytelling is the way people learn from one another," Tichy writes, suggesting that this explains why Bill Gates and the like feel the need to write books. When business leaders were men with a nifty line in regression analysis and the stamina of mules on stimulants, mention of storytelling would have provoked loud laughter. "Forget bullet points and slide shows. The best leaders use stories to answer three simple questions: Who am I? Who are we? Where are we going?" writes Elizabeth Weil in *Fast Company*.[16]

Weil's case is supported by Tichy: "Leadership is about change. It's about taking people from where they are now to where they need to be. The best way to get people to venture into unknown terrain is to make it desirable by taking them there in their imaginations."[17]

Weil cites examples of companies which have used stories to help build strong cultures. Most famously, there is the example of Hewlett-Packard's Bill Hewlett who found a storeroom door padlocked and returned to rip the padlock off and post a notice warning against anyone locking the door again. The message? Openness and trust are the way to do business.

This sort of spontaneous behavior is now the stuff of corporate legend. But, it was never planned that way. Bill Hewlett did not think that breaking the padlock would be a great way of building corporate culture. It annoyed him so he just did it. The danger must be that storytelling creates mythological leaders or rewrites history. (Even so, storytelling is of emerging interest – writer and researcher, Art Kleiner, has worked extensively on corporate histories.)

The third element in passing on the torch of leadership is teaching methodology – "To be a great teacher you have to be a great learner." The great corporate leaders are hungry to know more and do not regard their knowledge as static or comprehensive.

Phil Hodgson, of Ashridge Management College, has analyzed the behavior of a number of business leaders. His conclusion is that the old models of leadership are no longer appropriate. "Generally, the managers interviewed had outgrown the notion of the individualistic leader. Instead, they regarded leadership as a question of drawing people and disparate parts of the organization together in a way that made individuals and the organization more effective." He concludes that the new leader must add value as a coach, mentor and problem solver; allow people to accept credit for success and responsibility for failure; and must continually evaluate and enhance their own leadership role. "They don't follow rigid or orthodox role models, but prefer to nurture their own unique leadership style," he says. "And, they don't do people's jobs for them or put their faith in developing a personality cult." The new recipe for leadership, says Hodgson, centers on five key areas: learning, energy, simplicity, focus and inner sense.

In the age of empowerment, the ability to delegate effectively is critically important. "Empowerment and leadership are not mutually exclusive," says INSEAD's de Vries. "The trouble is that many executives feel it is good to have control. They become addicted to power – and that is what kills companies."

> *In the age of empowerment, the ability to delegate effectively is critically important.*

Warren Bennis provides another link between empowerment and leadership. "Leadership can be felt throughout an organization. It gives pace and energy to the work and empowers the workforce. Empowerment is the collective effect of leadership."[18]

The growing interest and belief in the human side of leadership is, in itself, nothing new. Leadership thinker **James McGregor Burns** coined the phrases **transactional** and **transformational** leadership. Transactional leadership involves leaders who are very efficient at giving people something in return for their support or work. Followers are valued, appreciated and rewarded. Transformational leadership is concerned with leaders who create visions and are able to carry people along with them towards the vision.

The ability to create and sustain a credible vision remains critical. Harvard's **John Kotter** identifies three central processes in leadership: establishing direction; aligning people; motivating and inspiring. The way in which these core elements are put into practice is continually being refined. But, at its heart, is an appreciation that the leader cannot act alone. Peter Drucker has observed that leaders habitually talk of "we" rather than "I." The great leaders appear to be natural teamworkers, a fact overlooked by heroic models of leadership. In *The Tao of Leadership*, John Heider produces another aphorism – but one which cuts to the heart of modern leadership: "Enlightened leadership is service, not selfishness."[19]

Key books

Adair, John, *Effective Leadership: A Modern Guide to Developing Leadership Skills*, Pan, London, 1988

Burns, James McGregor, *Leadership*, Harper & Row, New York, 1978

Kotter, John, *A Force for Change: How Leadership Differs From Management*, Free Press, New York, 1990

Maucher, Helmut, *Leadership in Action: Tough Minded Strategies from the Global Giant*, McGraw-Hill, New York, 1994

Syrett, Michel and **Hogg, Clare** (editors), *Frontiers of Leadership: An Essential Reader*, Blackwell, Oxford, 1992

White, Randall P, Hodgson, Philip and **Crainer, Stuart**, *The Future of Leadership*, FT/Pitman, London, 1996

Zaleznik, Abraham, *The Managerial Mystique: Restoring Leadership in Business*, Harper & Row, New York, 1990

Warren Bennis
Doing the right thing

In many ways, Warren Bennis is the epitome of the modern-day management thinker. Now based at the University of Southern California, he has a lengthy academic pedigree – beginning as a protégé of Douglas Macgregor, author of *The Human Side of Enterprise*, to become the *éminence grise* of contemporary leadership, advising four US presidents. His work has become steadily more populist and popular.

The most widely read of Bennis' numerous publications is *Leaders: The Strategies for Taking Charge* (1985), co-written with Burt Nanus.[20] This examined the behavior and characteristics of 90 leaders and sought to reach general conclusions. The leaders studied were a truly electic – and somewhat eccentric – group, including Neil Armstrong and Karl Wallenda, a tightrope walker. Bennis concluded that the leaders possessed four vital competencies:

1 **Management of attention** – the vision of the leaders commanded the attention and commitment of those who worked for and with them in attempting to achieve it.

2 **Management of meaning** – the leaders were skilled communicators, able to cut through complexity to frame issues in simple images and language. They were expert distillers of information.

3 **Management of trust** – "Trust is essential to all organizations," observes Bennis. For the leaders, trust was expressed through consistency of purpose and in their dealings with colleagues and others. Even though people sometimes disagreed with what they said or did, the leaders were admired for their consistency of purpose.

4 **Management of self** – the leaders were adept at identifying and fully utilizing their strengths; and accepting and seeking to develop areas of weakness.

WARREN BENNIS

Born 1925

American

Educator

Education: Antioch College; MIT.

Career: Army during the Second World War; provost at SUNY, Buffalo 1967–71; President, University of Cincinnati, 1971–78; University of Southern California since 1979.

Books: *Leaders: The Strategies for Taking Charge* with Burt Nanus, Harper & Row, New York, 1985; *On Becoming a Leader*, Addison Wesley, Reading, 1989; *Why Leaders Can't Lead*, Jossey-Bass, San Francisco, 1989; *An Invented Life: Reflections on Leadership and Change*, Addison Wesley, Reading, 1993.

To Bennis, leadership is a skill which can be learned by the manager willing to put in substantial effort. It is, however, fundamentally different from management. "To survive in the 21st century we're going to need a new generation of leaders, not managers. The distinction is an important one. Leaders conquer the context – the volatile, turbulent, ambiguous surroundings that sometimes seem to conspire against us and will surely suffocate us if we let them – while managers surrender to it." He goes on to list the fundamental differences between the two as:

- the manager administers; the leader innovates
- the manager is a copy; the leader is an original
- the manger maintains; the leader develops
- the manager focusses on systems and structure; the leader focusses on people
- the manager relies on control; the leader inspires trust
- the manager has a short-range view; the leader has a long-range perspective
- the manager asks how and when; the leader asks what and why
- the manager has his eye on the bottom line; the leader has his eye on the horizon
- the manager accepts the status quo; the leader challenges it
- the manager is the classic good soldier; the leader is his own person
- the manager does things right; the leader does the right thing.[21]

The last element has become something of a catch-phrase, another in a long line of neat aphorisms which don't, in the end, bring the practitioner nearer to understanding how to actually develop leadership skills.

Bennis has to some extent become a victim of pigeon-holing. His work actually covers a far wider span of issues than leadership. In the 1950s, for example, he studied group dynamics and was involved in the teamworking experiments at the US National Training Laboratories. In the 1960s he developed a reputation as a student of the future – in a 1964 *Harvard Business Review* article, Bennis and co-author Philip Slater accurately predicted the downfall of communism ("Democracy is inevitable," they wrote).

In the mid-1960s, he was predicting the demise of the modern organization – a prediction which has taken 30 years to begin to be fulfilled. "Bureaucracy emerged out of the organization's need for order and precision and the workers' demands for impartial treatment. It was an organization ideally suited to the values and demands of the Victorian era. And just as bureaucracy emerged as a creative response to a radically new age, so today new shapes are surfacing before our eyes."[22]

Curiously, Bennis' career actually follows many of the patterns of Douglas Macgregor's. Macgregor was president of Antioch College during the time Bennis was an undergraduate and advised Bennis to move on to MIT. In 1959, when Bennis was teaching at Boston University and Harvard, Macgregor recruited him to MIT to establish the new organization studies department. Macgregor moved from being an academic to an administrator before returning to academic life. Bennis has done the same – his academic career was interrupted by a spell as provost at the State University of New York at Buffalo and as president of the University of Cincinnati. This proved disappointing. "The very time I had the most power, I felt the greatest sense of powerlessness," Bennis observes in the autobiographical *An Invented Life*. In practice, Bennis found that his ambitious intentions were hamstrung by the very organization he purported to lead. Despite the power attributed to him through his job title, in practice he was powerless.

Bennis then returned to academic life, attempting to understand the lessons learned and to convert them into more general lessons about the nature of leadership and the relationship between the individual leader and the organization. His search has not, however, been for the perfectly formed, one-line summation, but rather an enduring study of the humanity behind leadership.

Teamworking

Teamworking is not a skill traditionally associated with leaders. Indeed, the assumption has usually been that teamworking is the preserve of the factory floor rather than the office. Yet, in recent years, teamworking has become highly fashionable – it is significant that Warren Bennis' most recent work focusses on groups rather than individual leaders.

Teamworking is a side effect of the increasing concentration on working across functional divides and fits neatly with the trend towards empowerment. A project team may draw on people from throughout the organization to achieve the best results. Instead of passing reports and paperwork from one department to another, teams provide a dynamic meeting place where ideas can be shared and expertise more carefully targeted on important business issues.

That teamworking is growing cannot be doubted. A survey by the Industrial Society of 500 personnel managers found that 40 per cent worked in organizations with self-managed teams. The average team in this survey had around eight people

> *That teamworking is growing cannot be doubted.*

and the main reasons cited for their use were improved customer service, increased staff motivation and quality of output.[23]

Despite the extensive literature about teams and teamworking, the basic dynamics of teamworking often remain clouded and uncertain. What is a team? Is a team simply a fancy word for a group of people? What is the difference between a team and a task force? What is the difference between a team and a committee? Is a team simply a group of people with different skills aiming for the same goal?

Teams occur when a number of people have a common goal and recognize that their personal success is dependent on the success of others. They are all interdependent. In practice, this means that in most teams people will contribute individual skills many of which will be different. It also means that the full tensions and counter-balance of human behavior will need to be demonstrated in the team.

It is not enough to have a rag-bag collection of individual skills. The various behaviors of the team members must mesh together in order to achieve objectives. For people to work successfully in teams, you need people to behave in certain ways. You need some people to concentrate on the task at hand (**doers**). You need some people to provide specialist knowledge (**knowers**) and some to solve problems as they arise (**solvers**). You need some people to make sure that it is going as well as it can and that the whole team is contributing fully (**checkers**). And you need some people to make sure that the team is operating as a cohesive social unit (**carers**).

Teamworking: Who's Who?[24]

Solver
Role: helps the team to solve problems by coming up with ideas or finding resources from outside the team. Can see another way forward.
Characterized by: innovation, ideas generation, imagination, unorthodox, good networking skills, negotiates for resources.

Doer
Role: concentrates on the task, getting it started, keeping it going, getting it done or making sure it is finished. Some may focus on only one aspect of the task. Making sure it is finished is the most rare.
Characterized by: high energy, high motivation, push others into action, assertiveness, practical, self-control, discipline, systematic approach, attention to detail, follow through.

Checker
Role: concern for the whole process, tries to ensure full participation while providing a balanced view of quality, time and realism.
Characterized by: prudence, reflection, critical thinking, shrewd judgments, causing others to work towards shared goals, use of individual talents.

Carer
Role: concern for the individuals in the team and how they are developing and getting along.
Characterized by: supportive, sociable, concerned about others, democratic, flexibility.

Knower
Role: provider of specialist knowledge or experience.
Characterized by: dedication, standards, focus.

Modern management thinking suggests that organizations need a balance of behaviors for any change management activity – they may have to slightly unbalance the team in favor of the type of change they are trying to undertake.

It is also worth noting that for all the research into effective teamworking, teams remain a law unto themselves. Managers who sit down and play at human engineering by trying to select exactly the right sort of combination usually end up in a state of confusion. Effective teams often come about spontaneously or include an unusual combination of specialists. The key to success does not appear to lie in the selection of team members – you only have to look briefly at team sports to find examples of talented individuals working together poorly as a team. Instead, success is often characterized by the genuine granting of power and responsibility to teams so they can solve their own problems.

One notable example of teams at work is Microsoft which fosters creativity, both individually and in teams, at the same time as meeting commercial deadlines and demands. The Microsoft product development philosophy is labeled "synch-and-stabilize." This involves focussing creativity by evolving features and "fixing" resources; and doing everything in parallel with "frequent synchronizations."[25]

What is striking about the Microsoft approach is that the company is not the free-wheeling ideas factory it is often portrayed as. Pizzas may be delivered directly to desks, but there is also a great deal of control – or discipline – at work. It may appear jolly and collegiate, but it is deadly serious. For example, the scope and ambition of each and every project is carefully delineated. The numbers of people involved and the time they spend on a particular project are also carefully controlled. Some rules are unbending – bugs have to be immediately repaired – to ensure that work is coordinated.

But, as MIT's Michael Cusumano points out, this is simply good project management as applicable to software development as to any other business where product development is continuous. People are given responsibility and allowed to determine their own working patterns and schedules – up to a point. The boundaries are very clear and simple. People know where they stand, how the system works and what is expected from them. Of course, textbooks on parenting suggest that you treat children in exactly the same way.

References: Leadership

1 Senge, Peter, *The Fifth Discipline*, Doubleday, New York, 1990.
2 Quoted in Prior, P, *Leadership is not a Bowler Hat*, David & Charles, Newton Abbot, 1977.
3 Bennis, Warren, "Managing the dream," *Training Magazine*, 1990.
4 Author interview.
5 Slim, William, *Defeat Into Victory*, Buccaneer Books, New York, 1991.
6 Macgregor, Douglas, *The Human Side of Enterprise*, McGraw-Hill, New York, 1960.
7 Waterman, Robert, *The Frontiers of Excellence*, Nicholas Brealey, London, 1994.
8 Author interview.
9 Author interview.
10 Schwenk, Charles, "The case for *weaker* leadership," *Business Strategy Review*, Autumn 1997.
11 Heifetz, Ronald A and Laurie, Donald L, "The work of leadership," *Harvard Business Review*, January–February 1997.
12 Pascale, Richard, "Grassroots leadership," *Fast Company*, April/May 1998.
13 Pascale, Richard, "Grassroots leadership," *Fast Company*, April/May 1998.
14 Tichy, Noel M, "The mark of a winner," *Leader to Leader*, Fall 1997.
15 de Vries, Manfred Kets, "CEOs also have the blues," *European Management Journal*, September 1994.
16 Weil, Elizabeth, "Every leader tells a story," *Fast Company*, June–July 1998.
17 Weil, Elizabeth, "Every leader tells a story," *Fast Company*, June–July 1998.
18 Bennis, Warren, *An Invented Life*, Addison Wesley, Reading, 1993.
19 Heider, John, *The Tao of Leadership*, Wildwood House, Aldershot, 1986.
20 Bennis, Warren and Nanus, Burt, *Leaders: The Strategies for Taking Charge*, Harper & Row, New York, 1985.
21 Bennis, Warren, "Managing the dream," *Training Magazine*, 1990.
22 Bennis, Warren, "The coming death of bureaucracy," *Think Magazine*, 1966.
23 Industrial Society, *Self-Managed Teams*, Industrial Society, London, 1995.
24 Obeng, Eddie, *All Change!*, FT/Pitman, London, 1994.
25 Cusumano, Michael, "How Microsoft makes large teams work like small teams," *Sloan Management Review*, Vol. 39, No. 1, Fall 1997.

10

Learning and development

"The days of an MBA degree in general management are over. Our new curriculum says that we think that the best way to get to the top of a company is to start off after business school with a jump on the competition – have a special competence, not just know a little bit about everything."

Lester Thurow[1]

The rise of the learning business

In the beginning learning and development simply happened. Executives weren't dispatched on expensive courses, they learned by coming through the ranks. The job taught them everything they needed to know

This view appears to be an artefact of ancient history. It isn't. The process of developing people in organizations remains in its infancy. Though the world is crowded with business schools, management development is a relatively new science.

Indeed, in Europe, France's INSEAD offered an MBA for the first time in 1959. It was not until 1965 that the UK's first two public business schools (at Manchester and London) were opened. Elsewhere, management has been seriously studied (at least in academic terms) for a longer period. In the US, Chicago University's business school was founded in 1898; Amos Tuck at Dartmouth College, New Hampshire – founded in 1900 – was the first graduate school of management in the world; and Harvard offered its first MBA as long ago as 1908 and established its graduate business school in 1919.

Of course, these statistics pale into insignificance when set against the centuries spent educating lawyers, clerics, soldiers, teachers and doctors in formal, recognized institutions. But, during this century, management has begun to claw back the ground lost during past centuries.

Business schools have generally followed the American model with a traditional emphasis on finance and strategy rather than the "softer" side of management. While business schools have become a massively successful industry, recent years have seen increasingly vociferous criticism of their methods and, more fundamentally, of their role in management development.

> *Management is the art of the moment, immediate and spontaneous, how can it be taught distant from the workplace?*

The chief gripe against them is that as management is the art of the moment, immediate and spontaneous, how can it be taught distant from the workplace?

Indeed, some suggest that learning and development must be enshrined in day-to-day activities rather than being something you do for two weeks of the year on a marketing course. This has prompted the emergence of the **learning organization** or, at least, the concept of the learning organization. In the learning organization the act of learning is continuous and affects, and involves, everyone.

The rise in interest in developing people throughout the organization can be attributed to a number of factors. First, in leaner organizations people are taking on broader ranges of responsibility. Managers, in particular, are faced with a completely new environment. They are responsible for more people, often working in a process-oriented organization, and the skills and behaviors which previously served them well no longer work. They have to make fundamental changes or fail.

Second, the growth in numbers of, what Peter Drucker labels, knowledge workers means that there is a premium on possessing high quality skills and expertise. The marketplace is teeming with highly qualified people.

Third, there has been a somewhat belated recognition of the importance of recruiting, retaining and developing talented people. In a turbulent environment it has never been more important to have the right people for the job – and to keep them, motivate them and develop them. There is a need to constantly develop skills, no matter who you are, what you do, who you do it for or where you do it.

Key books

Cunningham, Ian, *The Wisdom of Strategic Learning*, McGraw-Hill, Maidenhead, 1994

Mumford, Alan, *How Managers Can Develop Managers*, Gower, Aldershot, 1993

Pedler, Mike, Burgoyne, John and **Boydell, Tom**, *The Learning Company*, McGraw-Hill, Maidenhead, 1991

Chris Argyris
The learning challenge

A superficial look at Chris Argyris' work and career gives an impression of the classic academic. Argyris has spent his entire working life at some of the leading centers of American academic excellence – at Yale in the 1950s and 1960s, at Harvard Business School since 1968. But, the scope of his thinking defies conventional academic strictures. "Working in academia is both exhilarating and infuriating," he admits. His work is driven by high quality academic research, rather than unsubstantiated opinion. It is also, he admits, not highly accessible. "My books are not easy to read. It is the way I think," he says. "I write articles based on anecdotes and books based on research. I don't want to research, raise basic questions and then stop."[2]

Underpinning Argyris' career has been a humane desire to develop and nurture individuals within organizations. "I am interested in social sciences in organizations of any kind," he says. "Discipline-oriented people can feel I'm a traitor." Argyris' intellectual armory includes a Baccalaureate in psychology, a masters in economics and a doctorate in organizational behavior.

CHRIS ARGYRIS

Born 1923

American

Educator

Education: Baccalaureate in psychology; masters in economics; doctorate in organizational behavior.

Career: Taught at Yale in the 1950s becoming Beach Professor of Administrative Finance in 1965; joined Harvard Business School, and became James Bryant Conant Professor of Education and Organizational Behavior in 1971.

Books: *Personality and Organization,* Harper & Row, New York, 1957; *Overcoming Organizational Defences,* Allyn & Bacon, Boston, 1990; *Organizational Learning: A Theory of Action Perspective,* with Donald Schon, Addison Wesley, Wokingham, 1978; *On Organizational Learning*, Blackwell, Cambridge, 1993; *Knowledge for Action*, Jossey-Bass, San Francisco, 1993.

Tracing his *raison d'être* back through his career, Argyris observes: "What drives me now has motivated me for the last 40 years. It sounds corny but I love learning for its own sake and, after serving in World War Two, I wanted to do something when I got back. I am optimistic, believing there can be a better, more just world. Though I am an unabashed romantic, I have always been connected with reality. A true romantic has a vision without it being operational. Being a soft-hearted romantic is deadly. In my case, research and theory provide the quality control. Success has always to be compared with your values."

For Argyris research has gone hand in hand with teaching and consultancy. He does not compartmentalize his interests in the way of some other management thinkers. Instead, the three strands support and interrelate with each other. His work is based around the fundamental belief that if organizations allow and encourage individuals to develop to their full potential this will be mutually beneficial. Argyris' research constantly challenges his natural optimism. Executives are often poor communicators, unwilling to challenge the status quo or able to learn from their experiences. "Some executives can't cope with changing anything. When new ideas are implemented the old theory of control is left intact. This is a source of continual disappointment, but my disappointment is tempered with a sense of understanding," says Argyris. "I am not angry, but just think let's face reality. Disappointment is an opportunity for leverage for change."

What Argyris has constantly observed is a mismatch between people and organizations. To fit people into organizational structures, they have been limited rather than developed, constrained and contained. People have, in turn, failed to develop themselves or accept responsibility for

> *To fit people into organizational structures, they have been limited rather than developed, constrained and contained.*

their actions. "Responsibility is not a one-way process," he says. "We are personally responsible for our behavior but, unfortunately, many companies change their parking space and not people's sense of responsibility."

The origins of the development of the now popular concept of the learning organization can be traced to Argyris. "Any company that aspires to succeed in the tougher business environment of the 1990s must first resolve a basic dilemma: success in the marketplace increasingly depends on learning, yet most people don't know how to learn. What's more, those members of the organization who many assume to be the best at learning are, in fact, not very good at it," he wrote in a 1991 *Harvard Business Review* article. "Because many professionals are almost always successful at what they do, they rarely experience failure. And because they have rarely failed, they have never learned how to learn from failure."[3]

His pleasure in the growing interest in the role of learning is combined with fears that it might be short lived. "I am pleased that organizational learning is in vogue but I worry that if we are not careful it will become another fad," he says. "I have little difficulty in talking about organizational learning to chief executives but, as you go down the hierarchy, it is regarded as being a bit dreamy."

Argyris' contribution to the debate was the seminal work, *Organizational Learning* (1978), which he co-wrote with MIT's Donald Schön.[4] Together with Schön, Argyris developed the concept of **single-loop** and **double-loop learning**. Argyris later explained the idea: "Learning may be defined as occurring under two conditions. First, learning occurs when an organization achieves what it intended; that is, there is a *match* between its design for action and the actual outcome. Second, learning occurs when a *mismatch* between intention and outcome is identified and corrected; that is, a mismatch is turned into a match... Single-loop learning occurs when matches are created, or when mismatches are corrected by changing actions. Double-loop learning occurs when mismatches are corrected by first examining and altering the governing variables and then the actions."[5]

In short, single-loop learning does not question underlying assumptions while double-loop learning tackles basic assumptions and beliefs. The vast majority of learning falls into the category of single-loop learning, though Argyris believes that double-loop learning is now more widely recognized – "Double-loop learning is gaining credence as a practical thing." Indeed, the preoccupations of the early 1990s suggest that managers are more willing to tackle (or at least to contemplate) the big issues and to question and re-establish first principles.

Argyris believes that IT has a crucial role to play in furthering the acceptance and practice of learning within organizations. "In the past the one-way, top-down approach gained strength from the fact that a lot of behavior is not transparent. IT makes transactions transparent so that behavior is no longer hidden. It creates fundamental truths where none previously existed."

Argyris' ability to dedicate time and energy to getting under the skin of organizations is forcefully demonstrated in *Knowledge for Action* (1993). In this book Argyris examines the behavior of one of his consultancy clients, itself a consultancy group. The consultancy arose when seven successful consultants decided to establish their own company. They hoped that it would be free from the Machiavellian political wrangles they had encountered in other organizations. In practice, their dreams were disappointed. Indeed, by the time Argyris was called in, internal wrangling consumed too many of its productive energies.

The company preferred to remain anonymous. "I have always advocated not naming the companies I carry out research in," says Argyris, recalling, "When I worked with IBM Thomas Watson Junior said name the company – at a stockholder meeting someone asked why the company employed Communist consultants!"

The consultants featured in *Knowledge for Action* were, in fact, falling prey to what Argyris calls **defensive routines**. Faced with a personally threatening problem, the executives were adept at covering it up or bypassing it entirely. Board meetings, therefore, concentrated on trivial topics – there was always one person keen to avoid discussion of an important issue. Outside the boardroom the big issues were discussed and blame apportioned so that divisions built up relentlessly between the original founders. This approach affected the behavior of the rest of the organization – others consciously kept information to a minimum so that executives weren't forced to face up to something new.

The fact that Argyris' client is a group of management consultants helps convey the importance of his message. If highly trained, intelligent executives fall into such traps, what chance have ordinary mortals?

Argyris' work forms a bridge between theory and practice in a way few other academics have managed. "In education it is important that students connect what they learn to what they actually do. Executive education goes on every day, not simply by sending executives to a classroom. Too much formal executive education reinforces the status quo of the organization and too many academics are romantic in the pejorative sense. They run away from developing new approaches so you read 600 pages on leadership and it adds up to what? There are academic standards, but theories need to be tested," says Argyris. "Academics and executives have a love-hate relationship. Academics say that executives are too shallow; while executives are interested in the pay-off. What executives now complain about is not the newness of the concepts but that the new concepts don't keep implementation in mind. You get unconnected fads and ideas so that managers can't use them."

While critical of formal processes of executive development, he points out that practising managers have a negligible record when it comes to developing important ideas. "Practitioners don't come up with the ideas, the great theories which influence and create best practice. There have been people like Sloan and Barnard, but they were exceptional."

Even so, Argyris identifies strongly with managers. "I feel sorry for managers to some extent. There tends to be a fundamental assumption that if anything needs correcting it is management. And they are now being asked to deal with a lot of information. But I don't think they will ever be asked to deal with an amount beyond their competence. The amount is not the issue. The human mind is finite though managers sometimes act as if it wasn't."

The learning organization

With his 1990 book, *The Fifth Discipline*, Peter Senge propeled the term "the learning organization" to the forefront of the corporate – and the conference – agenda.[6] The expression has since gone on to rival excellence, vision and empowerment as useful phrases that have now been almost completely stripped of any consistent meaning.

In *The Fifth Discipline*, Senge uses examples drawn from his workshops at MIT to describe how organizations suffer from learning disabilities that prevent them from recognizing threats and opportunities. He then describes the disciplines that individuals and organizations need in order to turn disabled organizations into learning organizations.

The learning disabilities that he describes relate to the inability of individuals and their organizations to see patterns – the "invisible fabric of inter-related actions, which often take years to fully play out their effects on each other." He applies these failures to "think systematically" to specific business situations, for example, showing how systems thinking saved Royal Dutch/Shell and how the failure

PETER SENGE

Born 1947

American

Educator

Education: Engineering degree from Stanford; PhD on social systems modelling, MIT.

Career: Director of the Center for Organizational Learning at MIT; founding partner of Innovation Associates (now part of the Arthur D Little consulting firm).

Books: *The Fifth Discipline*, Doubleday, New York, 1990; *The Fifth Discipline Fieldbook*, with Roberts, Ross, Smith and Kleiner, Nicholas Brealey, London, 1994.

to think systematically doomed People Express Airlines. "The airlines that will excel in the future will be the organizations that discover how to tap people's commitment and capacity to learn," says Senge.

The Fifth Discipline includes five key concepts:

1 **Systems theory** – Senge developed the idea of **systems archetypes**. These can help managers to spot repetitive patterns, such as the way certain kind of problems persist, or the way systems have their own in-built limits to growth.

2 **Personal mastery** – Senge includes within this spiritual growth – opening oneself up to a progressively deeper reality – and living life from a creative as opposed to reactive viewpoint. This involves continually learning how to see current reality more clearly. The resulting gap between vision and reality produces the creative tension from which learning emerges.

3 **Mental models** – these are what Ed Schein calls the "basic assumptions" of the organization. Senge believes managers must recognize the power of patterns of thinking at organizational level and the importance of non-defensive enquiry into the nature of these patterns.

4 **Shared vision** – shared vision can develop from personal vision. Senge argues that shared vision is present when the task that follows from the vision is no longer seen by team members as separate from the self.

5 **Team learning** – this demands dialog and discussion. Dialog is characterized by its exploratory nature and discussion by the opposite process of narrowing down the best alternatives available. The two complement each other, but only if they are separated in the first place.

Success did not come overnight to Senge. He and his team at the Center for Organizational Learning at MIT's Sloan School of Management have been working on the theme for some time. "For the past 15 years or longer, many of us have been struggling to understand what 'learning organizations' are all about, and how to make progress in moving organizations along this path. Out of these efforts, I believe some insights are emerging," says Senge in the multi-authored sequel, *The Fifth Discipline Fieldbook*.[7]

With around 50 contributors, the *Fieldbook* is a tumbling spree of ideas and suggestions. Enthusiasm and energy is apparent on every page. Their underlying message is simple: learning is positive; learning is good for organizations. Skeptics – and there remain many – will continue to doubt the practical wisdom of such wholeheartedness. Indeed, anyone wanting to hear neatly packaged solutions will find it easy to accuse Senge and others in this field of sounding too philosophical and Eastern, and of not being specific enough.

Perhaps the problem is that although the learning organization sounds as if it is a product, it is actually a process. Processes are not suddenly unveiled for all to see. Academic definitions, no matter how precise, cannot be instantly applied in the real world. Managers need to promote learning so that it gradually emerges as a key part of an organization's culture. Being convinced of the merits of the learning organization is not usually a matter of dramatic conversion.

> *Although the learning organization sounds as if it is a product, it is actually a process*

Seven obstacles to creating learning organizations

Turning the learning organization into practice has proved very difficult. Seven of the most significant obstacles are as follows:

1 **Managers are unhappy about handing over power** – in the traditional organization managers controlled training budgets and attending courses was often treated as an occasional perk of the job, dispensed by the manager when he or she saw fit. In the learning organization managers surrender a great deal of this power to the individual.

2 **Learning requires flexibility and a willingness to risk something new and having the authority to try it** – managers are ill at ease with the entire idea of learning from their mistakes. As Chris Argyris has pointed out, they are more likely to attempt to sweep a mistake under the corporate carpet than take it out into the open and attempt to learn from it.

3 **Dealing with uncertainty** – the learning organization creates uncertainty and ambiguity in areas which were previously clear. Managers must learn to manage in this more nebulous and less easily understood environment.

4 **Accepting responsibility** – individuals must take responsibility for learning. They cannot blame others for a lack of development opportunities, but must pursue and create their own.

5 **The learning organization requires new skills** – in particular managers must develop listening skills and be able to act as facilitators. Simply dictating adds no learning value.

6 **Trust** – reared on the concept of divide and rule, trusting people does not come easily to many managers.

7 **Inability to learn from experience** – another obstacle is that explored by Chris Argyris: companies are remarkably inept at learning from experience. Indeed, experience is one of the great mysteries of organizational life. It is assumed that managers benefit from experience. More experience enables better decisions (though only if you learn from experience). But while personal experience is recognized as important, collective corporate experience tends to be overlooked.

In relation to the last point, Art Kleiner, author of *The Age of Heretics* and long-term Senge collaborator, and George Roth, an MIT researcher, have studied how to put experience to work.

They argue that "managers have few tools with which to capture institutional experience, disseminate its lessons and translate them into effective action." To do so, they suggest using a tool called the *learning history* – "a narrative of a company's recent set of critical episodes, a corporate change event, a new initiative, a widespread innovation, a successful product launch or even a traumatic event like a downsizing." The histories can be anything from 25 to 100 pages in length and are arranged in two columns. In one column the people involved in the events describe what happened. In the opposite column are comments and observations from grandly titled, "learning historians." These are consultants and academics from outside the organization though people from inside the corporation may also comment. The commentary draws out the lessons, trends and conclusions which can be drawn from the narrative. The history can then be discussed by groups.[8]

While this may all sound remarkably flaky – Kleiner and Roth believe it is related to ancient community storytelling – the observed benefits are worthy of consideration. The method, they say, builds trust. People are asked about their version of events. They can speak out without fear on subjects which may have concerned them for years – the contributions are anonymous. Most importantly, learning histories can allow an organization to transfer experience from one division to another. The end result could be organizations which genuinely learn from experience and "a body of generalizable knowledge about management."

The changing role of business schools

In the 1980s the world's business schools could do no wrong. Managers sought them out, anxious to arm themselves with MBAs; major corporations invested heavily in developing their executives for the future. Their numbers mushroomed, especially in Europe where there are now 400 business schools.

Times change and business schools have come under intensifying scrutiny from managers and their companies. Under the harsh glare of unexpected examination, business schools have been fighting to deliver the kind of training now demanded by businesses – rather than the training business schools think managers should have.

In many ways the challenges now facing business schools mirror those facing the rest of the business world. The 1990s have seen major companies struggling with the twin demons of achieving global presence while being locally responsive. The management development world has been facing a parallel paradox – how to deliver general management education; as well as courses and programs continually tailored to the specific requirements of companies and, increasingly, to the needs of individuals.

The situation is further complicated by the fact that, under pressure to "reinvent" themselves and their organizations, as well as managing constant change, managers can often afford to spend little time on developing vital competencies for the future. "Workloads are substantial and if you are sent away on a course, you do think of the work piling up on your desk," says Sheila Dawson, head of business services at the international banking arm of the Bank of Ireland. "We are going through radical business re-design and process improvement, so training must put things in context and help our managers to deliver core objectives."

Changed times, demand new approaches to development. "While classroom-based and distance learning are clearly valuable, they cannot avoid being formulaic or relying on a 'one best way' approach. There is a growing need for local learning – learning which is continuously adapted and fitted around the immediate needs of managers. If access to learning is immediate it becomes a far more valuable managerial currency," says Eddie Obeng of Pentacle – The Virtual Business School.

The standard criticism of business schools tends to repeatedly focus on the same points. Business schools, it is said, are out of touch with the harsh world of recession and hyper-competition. They provide standardized off-the-shelf teaching which is often inappropriate for individual managers and their companies; and they are too narrow in their outlook when companies and managers increasingly demand an international perspective.

One of the most influential critics of the traditional business school format is management thinker, Henry Mintzberg. "Regular full-time MBA programs with inexperienced people should be closed down. It's wrong to train people who aren't managers to become managers," he argues. "MBA programs are confused between training leaders and specialists. At the moment, we train financial analysts and then expect them to become leaders."

Mintzberg believes that the conventional approach is limiting rather than expanding. "To be superbly successful you have to be a visionary – someone with a very novel vision of the world and a real sense of where they are going. If you have that, you can get away with the commercial equivalent of murder. Alternatively, success can come if you are a true empowerer of people, are empathetic and sensitive." These, he makes clear, are not qualities which most business schools are likely to nurture. "MBA programs generally attract neither creative nor generous people and the end result is trivial strategists."

Mintzberg is not alone in calling for major changes in the approach of business schools. Time is tight, corporate budgets are even tighter and expectations are growing. Under pressure to "reinvent' themselves and their organizations, as well as managing constant change, managers can often afford to spend little time on developing vital competencies for the future. They look to business schools for practical support.

> *Mintzberg is not alone in calling for major changes in the approach of business schools.*

Not surprisingly, given the regularity of its airing, it is a message which many business schools have taken on board. Change is in the air. Some business schools now claim to be "reengineering" themselves though for some this is more of a question of paying lip-service to change than genuinely transforming themselves.

Even so, a blueprint for the business school of the future is now emerging. Instead of providing set courses, it will tailor programs to the particular needs of companies. It will cater to the development needs of individual executives and be truly international in perspective and practice. It will be at the leading edge of technology, harnessing IT to deliver programs throughout the world. It will be outward looking – in constant contact with real business – rather than inward looking and academic. The list is apparently endless and constantly expanding. But is it achievable?

The shift to tailored corporate programs is already underway. This is especially the case in the UK and the US. At the Wharton and Duke University in the US, tailored work accounts for 65 per cent of executive education; at the prestigious Kellogg School it has reached 40 per cent.

The emerging business school

In the same way as business schools are having to meet the increased demands of companies, they are also having to cater to the individual requirements and aspirations of managers. Increasingly managers and executives are taking the major development decisions for themselves, seeking out the school which is best for them rather than accepting the nearest or cheapest.

> *Today's managers know what they want and are willing to go and find it.*

Today's managers know what they want and are willing to go and find it – rather than automatically taking what they are offered. In response, business schools have to consider and cater for the development needs of individual managers.

This presents a golden opportunity for business schools – as well as teaching and developing managers, much of their future role is likely to be diagnosing which skills are needed by which organization and which individual manager. To achieve this, business schools must return to their roots in the real, and increasingly harsh, world of business.

A survey by the European Foundation for Management Development (EFMD) of business schools and major companies in 18 European countries, found that 65 per cent anticipated that the future demand for management education would expand, with 23 per cent expecting it to remain stable. Only 10 per cent anticipated a decline and, perhaps more significantly, companies were more optimistic than the business schools themselves.

Four generic themes underpinning the future demand emerged from the EFMD survey – internationalization; changes in technology; changes in corporate structure; and changes in economic conditions. The EFMD survey showed that companies now expect business schools to put greater emphasis on providing tailored or in-company programs. Indeed, this was identified as the top priority in a business school portfolio.

The business school of the future

The business school of the future is likely to be characterized by:

- close links with client organizations and industry generally with businesses heavily involved in research projects;
- an emphasis on lifetime and continuous learning with business schools in regular contact throughout a person's career rather than for brief, but intense, periods;
- an emphasis on developing managers into facilitators;
- being learning centers and resources rather than providers of standard business "solutions" taught by resident experts;
- networks. Increasingly, business schools are developing networks among themselves and with businesses. This can be seen in the rise of consortium programs involving a number of companies;
- multicultural and international. They will be truly international in terms of course content and outlook;
- use of the latest technology to facilitate continuous learning.

Action learning

Action learning is one of those blissfully simple, commonsensical ideas which has consistently been derided for being just that. While the essence of action learning is very simple, it is deceptively so.

> **Action learning is one of those blissfully simple, commonsensical ideas which has consistently been derided for being just that.**

The man who has done most to champion action learning is the British thinker, Reg Revans. Revans is feted in countries as far apart as Belgium and South Africa, and fans of action learning include Sir Peter Parker and GE's Jack Welch whose Workout program is a form of action learning. Revans is a former Olympic athlete who worked at the Cavendish Laboratories and for the National Coal Board alongside EF Schumacher of "small is beautiful" fame. "The essence of action learning is to become better acquainted with the self by trying to observe what one may actually do, to trace the reasons for attempting it and the consequences of what one seemed to be doing," says Revans.[9]

To explain action learning, Revans created a simple equation: $L = P + Q$. Learning occurs through a combination of programed knowledge (P) and the ability to ask insightful questions (Q). In essence, action learning is based around releasing and reinterpreting the accumulated experiences of the people in a group. Working in a group of equals (rather than a committee headed by the chief executive), managers work on key issues in real-time. The emphasis is on being supportive and challenging, on asking questions rather than making statements.

While programed knowledge is one-dimensional and rigid, the ability to ask questions opens up other dimensions and is free flowing. The process is a continuous one of confirmation and expansion. Action learning is no quick fix. It requires a fundamental change in thinking.

The structure linking the two elements of knowledge and questions is the small team or set, defined by Revans as a "small group of comrades in adversity, striving to learn with and from each other as they confess failures and expand on victories."

Clearly, action learning is the antithesis of the traditional approach to developing managers. Revans argues that educational institutions remain fixated with programed knowledge instead of encouraging students to ask questions and roam widely around a subject. He is contemptuous of business schools and of the flourishing guru industry.

Action learning demands flexibility and fluidity. For many, reared on a diet of chalk and talk, this is a daunting prospect. Typically, there is no formal structure with facilitators acting as catalysts rather than as leaders. While some executives are attracted to this, others are wary that action learning cannot be measured in the conventional sense. Indeed, it is impossible at the beginning of a program to forecast exactly what benefits each participant will take away with them. Nor can the benefits of action learning be easily related to the bottom line of business performance. But, if it is working effectively, action learning should involve a continuous process of self-evaluation.

To a large extent, action learning involves an admission that participants face complex problems and would benefit from the views of others. It encourages us to learn from the unusual. Familiarity breeds contempt; unfamiliarity breeds learning. Historically, in the managerial ranks, admissions of fallibility have been interpreted as weakness. The thought of admitting weaknesses and confusion to a group is, for some, anathema. This is particularly true among managers who tend to believe that they deal in answers and solutions rather than questions and imponderables.

The reality is that, if it is to work, learning involves taking a risk and taking risks makes us vulnerable. People are afraid to make themselves more vulnerable, to expose themselves to potential loss of face, loss of opportunity or simply loss. Yet, in the continuing environment of tumultuous change, fallibility is a fact of life. Indeed, fallibility must be turned into an opportunity for others to take responsibility and for executives to develop new skills and insights.

Asking questions and listening to answers is an increasingly important managerial skill. Action learning encourages both. Contrast this with executives "forced" to go on training courses. When learning is work it is ineffective.

> *Asking questions and listening to answers is an increasingly important managerial skill.*

The potential benefits of action learning cannot disguise the challenge it presents. Unused to concentrating on their own development, it can take a protracted period for managers to fully understand and utilize action learning. Many are handicapped by a mental model which insists that learning is a passive activity. Also, most top managers are used to displaying their self-confidence and competence rather than admitting they feel insecure, vulnerable or anxious. Most are good at parading their strengths and rarely have the opportunity – or willingness – to discuss their weaknesses with people who understand the pressures but have no direct business relationship with them.

Action learning appears to be attracting greater attention. There is now a Revans Centre for Action Learning and Research at Salford University. Business schools now utilize action learning – Ashridge Management College, for example, has an action learning program for chief executives.

The most substantial and sustained example of action learning in practice took place, somewhat strangely, in Belgium. In the late 1960s Revans, ignored in the UK, led an experiment launched by the Foundation Industrie-Université with the support of Belgium's leading business people and five universities. The Belgians responded to the idea of action learning with enthusiasm. Top managers were exchanged between organizations to work on each other's problems. People from the airline business talked to people from chemical companies. People shared knowledge and experience. With minimal attention from the rest of the world, the Belgian economy enjoyed a spectacular renaissance – during the 1970s Belgian industrial productivity rose by 102 per cent, compared with 28 per cent in the UK.

Key books

Dotlich, David and **Noel, James L**, *Action Learning: How the World's Top Companies are re-creating their Leaders and Themselves*, Jossey-Bass, San Francisco, 1998

Mumford, Alan (editor), *Action Learning at Work*, Gower, London, 1997

Pedler, Mike (editor), *Action Learning in Practice*, Gower, London, 1997 (3rd edition)

Revans, Reg, *Action Learning*, Blond & Briggs, London, 1979

References: Learning and development

1 Crainer, Stuart and Dearlove, Des, *Gravy Training*, Capstone, Oxford, 1998.
2 Author interview.
3 Argyris, Chris, "Teaching smart people how to learn," *Harvard Business Review*, May–June 1991.
4 Argyris, Chris and Schön, Donald, *Organizational Learing*, Addison Wesley, Reading, Mass., 1978.
5 Argyris, Chris, "Problems in producing usable knowledge for implementing liberating alternatives," Address to the International Congress of Applied Psychology, July 1982.
6 Senge, Peter, *The Fifth Discipline: The Art and Practice of the Learning Organization*, Doubleday, New York, 1990.
7 Senge, Peter, Roberts, C, Ross, R, Smith, B and Kleiner, Art, *The Fifth Discipline Fieldbook: Strategies and Tools for Building a Learning Organization*, Nicholas Brealey, London, 1994.
8 Kleiner, Art and Roth, George, "How to make experience your company's best teacher," *Harvard Business Review*, September–October 1997.
9 Author interview.

11

Global management

"Think globally, act locally, think tribally, act universally."

John Naisbitt[1]

"Tough domestic rivalry breeds international success."

Michael Porter[2]

"Almost all our problems, and their solutions, are recognizable all over the world. Internationally-operating managers are in the middle of these dilemmas."

Fons Trompenaars[3]

Discovering the world

Management and business are more international than ever before. The 1990s have seen the rise of the truly global organization. Currently, some 37 000 parent companies control over 200 000 subsidiaries abroad. Some 40 per cent of the total assets of the world's 100 largest companies are already located outside their home countries. The UN estimates that the sales of international corporations accounted for one quarter of the world's GDP in 1991 (and a higher proportion of *private sector* output).[4] The sales of these international corporations in 1991 were estimated at $US 5.5 trillion.

Globalization is all-embracing – even for organizations which are not global in their operations. "Their company will now face greater competition from others selling into many different markets, who have an advantage over the national manager in that they have the ability to pick up on new ideas and experience from other markets," says Annik Hogg, co-author of *The Marketing Challenge*.[5] "Marketing, after all, is all about good ideas, and you shouldn't be constantly reinventing the wheel." The national organization is likely to be fighting off competitive threats from companies which are organized on a global scale.

> *Globalization is all-embracing – even for organizations which are not global in their operations.*

Key drivers behind globalization

Globalization has been spurred on by a number of forces.

Technology

Harvard's **Ted Levitt** has argued that technology is the most potent force towards homogenization. Technology is clearly a driving force behind globalization in markets such as drugs and cosmetics. In the 1980s Unilever identified cosmetics as an area of potential growth – it backed its enthusiasm with investment in Elizabeth Arden ($1.5 billion), Chesebrough-Pond's and Calvin Klein Cosmetics ($306 million). P&G also followed this route with the purchase of Max Factor. While learning that cosmetic brands behave in different ways from soap powder, Unilever has rationalized and reorganized distribution so that there is a single distribution point in Europe for Elizabeth Arden products (rather than 12). The products are made in Virginia and a small number of European sites. The global structure of the company matches the global nature of the brand.

Cost savings

Globalization tends, in corporate terms, to be synonymous with rationalization. Economies of scale mean that someone somewhere is out of a job. Typically, companies with extensive brand portfolios have closely examined the cost of running and promoting large numbers of brands. If one brand costs $X to promote and ten brands costs $10X, then surely it makes sense to put all ten under a single corporate umbrella brand and concentrate the marketing expenditure there.

The rise of homogenous markets

With increased international travel, technology and the mass media, markets are now more similar than ever before. Our spending and consumption habits have an increasing amount in common no matter where we live. The logic is straightforward: homogenous markets lead inexorably to homogenous products.

Globalization, it is thought, brings speed, flexibility and cost savings. The company is in tune with and close to all of its markets no matter where they are located. Says Carnegie-Mellon's Bruce McKern: "Firms evaluate a foreign country for investment in terms of its attractiveness (adjusted for risk) as a *market* for the firm's products or services, as a source of *resources* (such as labor), or as a *center for rationalization* of the firm's worldwide operations in its drive to achieve global efficiency."[6]

The attractions of organizing a company's activities on a global basis tend to fall into a number of categories:

1 **Research and development** – if R&D is organized on a global basis and aimed toward global markets this should allow an organization to simplify its product range; move more quickly to meet market needs; and be more efficient through mutual cooperation.

2 **Purchasing** – global purchasing can allow companies to respond quickly to changes in the markets for their raw materials; to move more quickly to meet customer needs and to flex their purchasing power more effectively (such as in making the most of currency dealings).

3 **Production** – if production is organized on a global basis to better meet the needs of customers it can bring economies of scale and cost reductions.

4 **Marketing** – in theory, global marketing can allow a company to make more cost-effective use of global media; save costs by eliminating duplication and share knowledge and experience more easily.

5 **Distribution/sales** – with systems geared to servicing a global market, a company's range of products and services should be more readily and more quickly available anywhere in the world. In addition, after-sales service should be improved – no more long waits of three months for a spare part – plus IT should enable speedy problem solving.

While there are many convincing arguments pointing to the advantages of globalization, the process also produces a number of paradoxes, which organizations are finding increasingly difficult to come to terms with. Globalization may be fashionable, but it is far from straightforward – "All you need is the best product in the world, the most efficient production in the world and global marketing. The rest takes care of itself," said former Sony chairman, Akio Morita. It is simply as complex as that.

The most often observed complexity is that between being globally and locally responsive. The truly global organization runs the risk of losing its local identity. People are reassured by local presence, products specially tailored for their local tastes. But they also want a wide range of competitively priced products to choose from. Customers want the best of both worlds and organizations have to meet this apparently paradoxical challenge.

The answer lies in **glocalization**, an unwieldy phrase to describe the ability to reap the benefits of global production, IT, R&D and marketing resources, while still being locally responsive.

It is a difficult, and commercially dangerous, balance. Former ABB chief executive, Percy Barnevik is one of the few executives who have taken on the challenge. "You want to be able to optimize a business globally – to specialize in the production of components, to drive economies of scale as far as you can, to rotate managers and technologists around the world to share expertise and solve problems," he says. "But you also want to have deep local roots everywhere you operate – building products in the countries where you sell them, recruiting the best local talent from the universities, working with the local government to increase exports. If you build such an organization, you create a business advantage that is damn difficult to copy."[7]

Making the global company work

Professor Hans Wüthrich of Munich's Universität der Bundeswehr says that a global company:

- operates with one global strategy in place of diverse strategies oriented to national markets;
- acts within a homogeneous or increasingly homogeneous market;
- markets a standardized product globally, and makes consistent use of the opportunities offered by the international division of labor with the aim of realizing economies of scale and synergy effects.

The global company does not happen overnight, though many organizations persist in believing that a single acquisition will thrust them into the global league. Indeed, Nancy Adler and her colleagues at McGill University in Canada suggest that companies move through different phases of international evolution and that each phase demands a different strategy and structure, different approaches to cultural interaction, and different kinds of international manager:[8]

1 A **domestic stance** – in which the company operates primarily in its home market and is structured as a centralized hierarchy. Here, few managers (if any) are sent abroad, although export skills may be needed when the firm starts to go international.

2 A **multi-domestic phase** – where the company has expanded internationally and each country in which it operates is managed separately within the decentralized hierarchy. Here, expatriate managers from the home country need country-specific skills for adapting culturally to a single country abroad.

3 A **multinational phase** – where the company integrates domestic and foreign operations into worldwide lines of business but headquarters tightly controls major decisions worldwide through a centralized hierarchy. Here, international management roles are focussed on top managers who are drawn from all parts of the worldwide organization and whose role is to integrate the company. Managers in the international cadre require a greater understanding of the world business environment and the cross-cultural skills needed to deal with a multiplicity of cultures. Cultural differences will be minimized by assimilating them into the dominant organizational culture.

4 A **transnational stage** – where companies, structured as non-hierarchical "networks of equals," are both globally integrated and locally responsive and depend on worldwide organizational learning. In companies of this kind the old distinctions between local and expatriate managers become obsolete because people from all over the world must constantly communicate and work with each other and consciously manage their cultural diversity. The overwhelming majority of managers have international responsibilities and require the ability to move between local responsiveness and the global perspective. They need to be able to integrate worldwide diversity and create cultural synergy, collaboration and learning.

On its emergence into the harsh light of the transnational stage, the organization faces challenges on a broad variety of fronts:

1 **The global company must deliver benefits to consumers** – it must bridge the paradox of producing standardized products which are customized.

2 **The global company must provide customer service** – customers will not accept indifferent service. The global organization has to be responsive.

3 **Presence is essential** – being a global company cannot be interpreted as meaning that the company does not require offices or representation in its markets.

4 **Market information** – homogenous markets cannot be assumed to be so in every way. Their nature needs to be continually evaluated and monitored.

5 **Constant utilization of global cost efficiency** – while global cost efficiencies are highly attractive, they are in a constant state of flux. This requires that purchasing and employment patterns need to be continually evaluated. The end result can be highly complex – the intermediary products for the Ford Escort car are obtained from 15 countries.

6 **Avoidance of repetition and duplication** – global operations can result in activities and information being generated by different parts of the same organization. Mechanisms need to be in place to avoid costly replication, for example, through the use of IT.

7 **Management efficiency** – the global company must have a dynamic and flexible management structure which enables information and skills to be shared speedily. This may require a federal structure, as championed by Charles Handy, and demands an excellent system of communications – as well as a willingness to communicate.

8 **Rethinking strategy** – clearly, globalization has important implications for strategy. These have been explored by **Kenichi Ohmae**. Ohmae suggests that global strategies require companies to return to first principles. "The essence of business strategy is offering better value to customers than the competition, in the most cost-effective and sustainable way," Ohmae writes. "But today, thousands of competitors from every corner of the world are able to serve customers well. To develop effective strategy, we as leaders have to understand what's happening in the rest of the world, and reshape our organization to respond accordingly. No leader can hope to guide an enterprise into the future without understanding the commercial, political and social impact of the global economy."[9]

Ohmae believes that the global economy is the result of a number of forces. First, there are booming regional economies. Instead of talking about countries as economic units, we need to begin thinking in terms of regions. To Ohmae, the question is whether to invest in, say, Catalonia, Wales or Alsace-Lorraine rather than in Spain, the UK or France.

The second factor is the much reported growth in new media and information technology. Ohmae points out that full utilization of technology requires "new laws, policies and relationships among business, government, individuals and communities." There is more to technology than sitting in the same place doing the same things quicker.

> **There is more to technology than sitting in the same place doing the same things quicker.**

The third factor is the rise of universal, consumer cultures. Technology and the global dominance of certain products means that we are all Californians now. The obvious corollary of this is that there are huge economies of scale to be made. Global standards "lay the groundwork for enormous generation of wealth." Though Ohmae adds that small companies can still succeed by imaginatively nipping at the heels of their larger competitors.

To meet these challenges, Ohmae suggests that corporate leaders should concentrate on building networks. "We have to learn to share, sort and synthesize information, rather than simply direct the work of others. We have to rethink our basic approach to decision making, risk taking and organizational strategy. And we have to create meaning and uphold values in flatter, more disciplined enterprises," Ohmae concludes. We will, it seems, have to forget the past in order to create the future.

It is worth noting that the rush to globalization has not been universally celebrated. Enthusiasm for the obvious plus side of globalization has tended to overshadow discussion of its implications. Making globalization work is, in fact, far more demanding than its champions would sometimes have us believe. Harvard University's Dani Rodrik, for example, has identified three sources of tension.[10]

First, in terms of employment, globalization accentuates the divide between the skilled who are increasingly mobile and the unskilled who are increasingly vulnerable. The second source of tension is that globalization "engenders conflict within and between nations over domestic norms and the social institutions that embody them." One example of this is Western unease with the consumption of products made by children in underdeveloped countries. Finally, tension is caused by the difficulties globalization presents governments in providing social insurance and the like. Globalization makes government a highly demanding task. If the owners of capital are more mobile, then their earnings are likely to be similarly mobile and elusive. Governments, therefore, face the unpalatable alternative of increasing taxation on those who can afford it least.

The risk, says Rodrik, is that "the social pressures unleashed by global economic integration will likely result in bad economics and bad governance." To face – and perhaps overcome – such challenges requires responses from government, business and society. "Responses need to be based on pragmatism and be guided by political entrepreneurship, imagination, patience here, impatience there, and other varieties of *virtu* and *fortuna*." Globalization, it seems, demands some form of global stakeholding.

Ten steps to being world class

Work at London Business School provides a ten-point agenda for companies aspiring to become world class:[11]

1 *Think before using the next faddish idea.* Just copying what other companies are doing is inadequate: the aim is to find new ideas to beat competitors, not ape them. Success comes from incorporating the best ideas into distinctly local solutions.

2 *The role of the chief executive in pushing forward change is crucial.* But one person is rarely enough. The chief executive needs to galvanize the people around him so that leadership comes from the whole top team.

3 *Financial measurements are a misleading guide to a company's strategic health.* Non-financial measures – customer satisfaction, employee morale, quality – are vital warning signs for problems three or four years ahead.

▶

4 *Set ambitious goals.* Survival is not enough. Unless you are aware of what other companies worldwide are doing and strive to be the best, you will not survive.

5 *Most firms put the emphasis on efficiency* – cutting costs, improving utilization rates and so on. *More ambitious firms aim to combine efficiency with effectiveness* – improving skills and capabilities relative to competitors.

6 *Strategic innovation is crucial.* Today the only sustainable competitive advantage is a company's ability to achieve continuous improvement. This means freeing up innovation and creativity at all levels, particularly in middle management. To survive, a company must become a moving target.

7 *Becoming world class demands continuous building of capabilities.* Develop long, medium and short-term objectives, identify capabilities needed to reach them, then determine strategies to acquire or develop them.

8 *Good management is a process of balancing dilemmas*: achieving effectiveness and efficiency; differentiation and low cost; financial goals and long-term vision; consistency and flexibility.

9 *Look outward.* The international dimension is vital even for companies which are not striving to be global. Nothing less than the best international standards is sufficient in the increasingly open and competitive home market.

10 *A bias for action.* Effective firms remove the hidden disincentives to risk taking, allow people to make mistakes and learn from failure.

Key books

Bartlett, Christopher and **Ghoshal, Sumantra**, *Managing Across Borders*, Harvard Business School Press, Boston, 1989

Bennett, S and **Wallace, T**, *World Class Manufacturing*, Oliver Wight, 1994

Robock, SH and **Simmonds, K**, *International Business and Multinational Enterprises*, Irwin, Homewood, Illinois, 1989

Fons Trompenaars
Cosmopolitan man

While other management thinkers rant and rave about the intricacies of strategic management and marketing, Dutch consultant and author, Fons Trompenaars paints on a larger canvas. Not for Trompenaars the world of miniatures. His subject is the universal one of cultural diversity. How do we think? How do we behave in certain situations? How does that affect the way we manage businesses? And, what are the skills essential to managing globally?

"Basic to understanding other cultures is the awareness that culture is a series of rules and methods that a society has evolved to deal with the recurring problems it faces," says Trompenaars. "They have become so basic that, like breathing, we no longer think about how we approach or resolve them. Every country and every organization faces dilemmas in relationships with people; dilemmas in relationship to time; and dilemmas in relations between people and the natural environment. Culture is the way in which people resolve dilemmas emerging from universal problems."[12]

The roots of his interest in the perils, practice and potential of cross-cultural life go back to Trompenaars' childhood. Brought up by a Dutch father and a French mother, he later studied at top American business school, Wharton, which played a part in convincing him that the American management model was neither perfect nor universally applicable.

Now in his mid-forties, Trompenaars continues to have a troubled relationship with the American business world which tends to regard his work as concerned with diversity, racial and sexual, rather than to do with different cultures. Undeterred, Trompenaars remains more cosmopolitan man than

> *Trompenaars remains more cosmopolitan man than corporate man.*

corporate man. He is still dismissive of the American (or any other) managerial model – "It is my belief that you can never understand other cultures. I started wondering if any of the American management techniques I was brainwashed with in eight years of the best business education money could buy would apply in the Netherlands, where I came from, or indeed in the rest of the world." The answer he provides is simply that they do not.

This is not just opinion or intuition. To the ethereal world of culture, Trompenaars has brought enthusiastic vigor. His books are based around exhaustive and meticulous research. Typically, *Riding the Waves of Culture* drew from over 900 seminars, presented in 18 countries. The Trompenaars database is a large and impressive beast – his latest book emerged from a 58-item questionnaire among 34 000 middle and senior managers from some 58 countries. This produced two million responses. The complexity of the research, in Trompenaars' eyes, matches the complexity of the subject. "Management is beyond simple rationalization," he says. (The corollary of this is that anyone who simplifies or rationalizes the world of business is an impostor.)

For all the nationalistic nerves it touches, at the heart of Trompenaars' research is a relatively simple proposition: the only positive route forward for individuals, organizations, communities and societies is through reconciliation. "Our hypothesis is that those societies that can reconcile better are better at creating wealth," says Trompenaars. The rich don't get even; they get on with each other.

As a result, how international managers reconcile differences is the very essence of their job. "The international manager needs to go beyond awareness of cultural differences," Trompenaars argues. "He or she needs to respect these differences and take advantage of diversity through reconciling cross-cultural dilemmas. The international manager reconciles cultural dilemmas."

Of course, it is easy to make such statements but managing in the global environment – even for Trompenaars' most fervent of disciples – remains fraught with difficulty. With reference to this complexity, in his earlier work Trompenaars presented a number of fundamentally different cultural perspectives while acknowledging that within a country attachment to any given cultural trait varies widely. The first of these intriguing pairings is the conflict between what Trompenaars labels the "universalist" and the "particularist." Universalists (including Americans, Canadians, Australians and the Swiss) advocate "one best way," a set of rules that applies in any situation. Particularists (South Koreans, Chinese and Malaysians) focus on the peculiar nature of any given situation.

Trompenaars examines the extremes by way of archetypal situations. In the universalist-particularist conflict, he presents the following dilemma: You are in a car with a close friend who has an accident in which a third party is injured. You are the only witness, and he asks you to falsely testify about his driving speed. In such a situation, universalists won't lie for their friend while particularists will. The difference becomes even more pronounced if the injury is severe. The universalist becomes even more adherent to the rules while the particularist's sense of obligation grows. (In this example, 74 per cent of South Koreans would assist their friend and lie, compared to just 5 per cent of Americans.)

Such results allow Trompenaars to provide advice on how business dealings between the two parties might work. Universalists doing business with particularists should, for example, "be prepared for meandering or irrelevancies that do not seem to be going anywhere"; moreover, we should not "take get to know you chatter as small talk." It is important to particularists. Particularists doing business with universalists should "be prepared for rational and professional arguments and presentations."

The cultural imponderables and wide range of basic differences in how different cultures perceive the world provides a daunting picture of the world ridden with potential pitfalls. "We need a certain amount of humility and a sense of humor to discover cultures other than our own; a readiness to enter a room in the dark and stumble over unfamiliar furniture until the pain in our shins reminds us of where things are," says Trompenaars. Most managers, it seems, are more intent on protecting their shins than blundering through darkened rooms.

Honing in on the great imponderables is Trompenaars' latest book, *Mastering the Infinite Game*, written with Charles Hampden-Turner of Cambridge's Judge Institute of Management Studies. Hampden-Turner was also co-author of the 1994 book *The Seven Cultures of Capitalism*.

The duo argue that the massive and dramatic success of the East Asian "tiger economies" can be attributed to "seven major integrations." Central to these are cultural differences which mean that the lost managerial souls of the West find themselves "playing Finite Games in which individuals win or lose by specific criteria in universal contests." In contrast, the East Asians are playing an Infinite Game "with rules which are adapted by the exceptions they encounter, with contests from which all players learn co-operatively."

Not surprisingly, Trompenaars and Hampden-Turner identify fundamental differences in Western and Eastern values. The West believes in rule by laws (universalism) while the East believes in unique and exceptional circumstances (particularist); winning is opposed by negotiating consensus; success is good opposes the belief that the good should succeed. The differences between West and East have been much debated and there is little to disagree about in Trompenaars and Hampden-Turner's list. But that is not their argument. Instead, their argument remains the same: reconciling different values is key to success – and it is something which Eastern cultures have proved marvellously adept at achieving. While the East settles the difference, the West remains obsessed with splitting the difference. It is a cultural imponderable which is enough to make even Fons Trompenaars despair.

> *While the East settles the difference, the West remains obsessed with splitting the difference.*

FONS TROMPENAARS

Born 1952

Dutch

Consultant

Education: Masters in business economics; PhD at Wharton.

Career: Shell; founded Center for International Business Studies; Trompenaars-Hampden-Turner Group.

Books: *Riding the Waves of Culture* with Charles Hampden-Turner, Nicholas Brealey, London, 1993; *The Seven Cultures of Capitalism*, with Charles Hampden-Turner, Piatkus, London, 1994; *Mastering the Infinite Game* with Charles Hampden-Turner, Capstone, Oxford, 1997.

The rise of the global brand

In terms of globalization brands have, to a large extent, led the way. Their flexibility and increasingly international nature mean that it has been automatically assumed in many quarters that particular brands are ripe for a global approach. Many are. To prove the point, any major international sporting event will feature an array of global brands whether they are Mars, Coke, whiskies or cigarettes.

Brands travel well and global brands have now penetrated virtually every country on earth. The last bastions against global brands are gradually falling. Research by Gallup into the brand awareness of the Chinese found that Coke was already the second most popular brand, following Hitachi. While the Chinese don't, as yet, have the money

> *Brands travel well and global brands have now penetrated virtually every country on earth.*

or the opportunity, they do have the aspirations. They are also fully aware of the power of brands as the profusion of imitation and copying shows. (In a sign of the times, the Japanese dominated the top ten brands identified by the Chinese and only one European company, Nestlé, managed to get into the top 20.)

Globalization is nothing new to brand managers. Take the story behind Hilton hotels. The realization of the group's founder Conrad Hilton was that hotels were not just used by holiday makers, but were temporary homes and offices for the travelling foot soldiers of the business world. In response, Hiltons offered high quality standardized service. While other hotels crumbled through the competition from motels, Hilton invented a lucrative business. Senior managers still flock to Hiltons. The global and standardized brand remains firmly in place – the Hilton in Miami is the same as that in Rome or elsewhere. Indeed the company's advertising features a taxi in a city with the caption "Take me to the Hilton" – the assumption is that any major city will have a Hilton "where you can be your self again."

More and more companies are seeking to follow the Hilton's example. The importance of global brands was summed up by Unilever chairman Michael Perry:

> *"The first question to be asked of any successful brand today anywhere is, will it travel? And how fast will it travel? Because you have no time to take this process slowly but surely. If you don't move that successful brand around the world rapidly you can be sure your competitor will take the idea, lift it and move it ahead of you. Speed to market is of the essence. But the point... central to all of this is a global brand is simply a local brand reproduced many times."[13]*

For some, it is a simple argument of economy of scale. If the same advertisement will work in Italy as it does in Finland, you don't need to make two. A television commercial can cost hundreds of thousands of pounds so making one or two rather than 12 represents a huge saving. Similarly, if the Spanish product can have the same packaging as the French, then there is a substantial cost saving. The only thing the company needs to ensure is that the advertising or packaging works successfully in particular countries and markets. This essential detail is often one which is overlooked by companies intent on cost savings rather than brand development.

While its repercussions are widespread, clearly global branding also comes with an array of potential problems. From a logistical point of view, legislative differences are still major factors in global brand management. Broadcasting laws are many and varied throughout the world. What is acceptable in one country may well be anathema elsewhere. In France, for example, supermarket petrol stations cannot advertise on television thanks to a ban on advertising by the distribution sector.

The rise of mass customization

The issue of the homogenous nature of markets is also contentious. In Europe, for example, the entire issue of sovereignty and national identity is deeply political. In a nationally splintered area like Europe most brands inevitably began life as local brands. Local brands either remain thoroughly local or develop outwards. There is no middle ground. Those which choose the latter route are pushing Europe towards a greater degree of homogenization. This process can be contrasted to what has happened in the United States where companies had a huge fairly homogenous market on their doorstep and were quick to attempt to satisfy it. Often their attempts at developing brands in Europe quickly ran aground as they tried to enforce the same level of homogenization on the diverse European market. Now American companies tend to be more realistic and concentrate on more localized marketing and advertising – typically, the management of Playtex in Europe is now separate from the US and there is a far greater degree of autonomy in European subsidiaries than was previously the case.

Global brands can be interpreted as uniform, unbending solutions to the needs of particular markets. But, ultimately, uniformity is not what makes brands succeed. They do have to be consistent, but they also have to be flexible and responsive to local needs. People have different expectations and requirements.

Indeed, the way people use a particular product may fundamentally differ from one country to the next. Schweppes, for example, is used as a mixer in the UK and Ireland, but as a straight drink in France and Spain. Finding a neat approach which suits the needs of both markets is practically impossible.

As Interbrand founder John Murphy says in his book, *Brand Strategy*: "The trend towards international branding of goods and services is likely to continue and indeed strengthen. This, however, by no means precludes the need for sensitive brand positioning to suit local conditions."[14]

Any brand which places uniformity ahead of local responsiveness is taking a substantial risk. Organizations may easily master globally organized mass production, but may find it harder to achieve the **mass customization** now required. The customer is king and demanding more and more. At Panasonic Bicycle in Japan, for example, customers can specify the size, shape and color of their chosen bike. The computer-controlled production line then does the work.

> *Any brand which places uniformity ahead of local responsiveness is taking a substantial risk.*

Meeting the growing demands of consumers while benefitting from global production using the latest technology is the new challenge for companies and brands. Customization requires local and personal contact. Brands which are based on contacts with people – such as hotels and retail brands – tend to be the most locally responsive. Ironically, they are also among the pace setters in creating global organizations.

References: Global management

1 Crainer, Stuart, *The Ultimate Book of Business Quotations*, Capstone, Oxford, 1997.
2 Porter, Michael, *The Competitive Advantage of Nations*, Free Press, New York, 1990.
3 Author interview.
4 UNCTAD, Program on Transnational Corporations, *World Investment Report: Transnational Corporations and Integrated International Production*, New York, 1993.
5 Hogg, Annik and Mazur, Laura, *The Marketing Challenge*, Addison Wesley, Reading, Mass., 1993.
6 McKern, Bruce, "The transformation of the international economy," in *The Financial Times Handbook of Management*, Financial Times Pitman Publishing, London, 1995.
7 Taylor, W, "The logic of global business: an interview with ABB's Percy Barnevik," *Harvard Business Review*, March–April 1991.
8 Adler, NJ and Bartholomew, S, "Managing globally competent people," *Academy of Management Executive*, Vol. 6, No. 3, 1992; and Adler, NJ and Ghadar, F, "Strategic human resource management: a global perspective" in Pieper, R (ed.), *Human Resource Management: an International Comparison*, de Gruyter, Berlin, New York, 1990.
9 Ohmae, Kenichi, "Strategy in a world without borders," *Leader to Leader*, Winter 1998.
10 Rodrik, Dani, "Has globalization gone too far?," *California Management Review*, Vol. 39, No. 3, Summer 1997.
11 Stopford, J, *et al.*, *Building Global Excellence*, London Business School, 1994.
12 Author interview.
13 Quoted in *AdWeek*, 14 December 1992.
14 Murphy, John, *Brand Strategy*, Prentice Hall, Hemel Hempstead, 1990.

Glossary of management thinkers

John Adair

The leading UK thinker on the subject of leadership. He has had an interesting career and his books have proved influential. His key phrase is **action-centered leadership**. Susceptible to gung-ho interpretations of leadership, but notable for his persuasive insistence that leadership is a skill which can be developed.

Key Work: *Effective Leadership* (1983)

Igor Ansoff

The doyen of **strategic management**. His books are far from being light reading, indeed they have a tendency to become tortuously academic. Yet, Ansoff's contribution is undoubted. His book, *Strategic Management* remains an important stage in the development of strategy. His later work has lacked its impact. He has brought the world the **Ansoff Matrix** and added **synergy** to the management vocabulary.

Key Works: *Corporate Strategy* (1965); *Strategic Manage-ment* (1979); *Implanting Strategic Management* (1984)

Chris Argyris

The father of the learning organization though MIT's Peter Senge tends to receive most of the plaudits. Argyris' work has never become populist though it has retained its popularity. He has pursued an admirably independent line, coaxing ideas along rather than detonating them in front of gasping audiences. His best work has a knack of infiltrating the underside of organizations – and, more depressingly, human behavior. A convinced romantic, he believes people's potential can – and should – be fulfilled. Introduced the concepts of **single-loop** and **double-loop learning**.

Key Works: *Personality and Organization* (1957); *Organizational Learning* (with the late Donald Schön, 1978)

Chester Barnard (1886–1961)

Unlike most influential management theorists, Barnard was actually a manager. His books on organizational and executive behavior have proved important, despite their inaccessibility.

Key Works: *The Functions of the Executive* (1938); *Organization and Management* (1948)

Percy Barnevik

The former chief executive of Asea Brown Boveri deserves mention simply because of the vast amount of management literature he and his company have spawned. ABB is venerated as the way a modern global company should be run. Barnevik has proved that headquarters don't need to be huge buildings filled with staff, but can be small, dynamic and still do the job. He introduced a complex **matrix structure** which reaped impressive results.

Christopher Bartlett

Harvard Business School professor and co-author, with Sumantra Ghoshal, of *Managing Across Borders* (1989) – one of the key books in understanding the new world of the global organization. They argue that there is now an emergent organization form – **the entrepreneurial organization** – taking the place of the multi-divisional structure. *The Individualized Corporation* further cemented their reputations.

Key Works: *Managing Across Borders* (1989); *The Individualized Corporation* (1997)

Warren Bennis

Unfortunately, Bennis is automatically associated with leadership. Yet, his career has been more broad ranging. He brought the world **adhocracy** and has predicted many of the issues which are only now emerging. His best read book is one co-authored with Burt Nanus, *Leaders*. It is not his best, but provides idiosyncratic examples of leadership in practice from Neil Armstrong to a tightrope walker.

Key Works: *The Temporary Society* (1968); *The Unconscious Conspiracy* (1976); *Leaders* (with Burt Nanus, 1985); *Organizing Genius* (with Patricia Ward Biederman, 1997)

Robert Blake

The joint creator of the **managerial grid** with Jane Mouton. This was fashionable in the 1960s. (See **Jane Mouton**)

Edward de Bono

The Maltese-born creator of **lateral thinking** has forged a brilliant career from an idea which is more intriguing than it is practical. His output numbers 43 books. He now argues that competition is no longer enough and "sureption" (which concerns the creation of value monopolies) is going to be the game of the future. He has his own private island of Tessera in Venice, from which he organizes "creativity projects."

Key Work: *The Use of Lateral Thinking* (1968)

James McGregor Burns

Highly influential leadership theorist. Invented the terms **transactional** (focused on immediate events) and **transformational leadership** (long-term and visionary).

Key Work: *Leadership* (1978)

Andrew Campbell

The UK academic is nothing if not versatile. His books include one on Scottish country dancing as well as others covering topics as weighty as the role of vision and corporate-level strategy. Formerly with McKinsey he is now at the London-based Ashridge Strategic Management Centre. In *Strategies and Styles*, Campbell and co-author Michael Goold identify three approaches a parent company can take to its businesses: financial control; strategic planning and strategic control. In *Corporate-Level Strategy*, Campbell attacks the performance of most parent companies, describing them as "value destroyers" rather than value creators.

Key Works: *Strategies and Styles* (with Michael Goold, 1987); *Corporate-Level Strategy* (with Michael Goold and Marcus Alexander, 1994)

James Champy

Co-author of the highly successful *Reengineering The Corporation* (with Michael Hammer). The book is evangelical and passionate about the need for reengineering. Doubts remain about its long-term impact. A consultant, he was co-founder of CSC Index and now runs the consulting operations of Perot Systems.

Key Work: *Reengineering The Corporation* (with Michael Hammer, 1993)

Alfred D Chandler Jr.

The economic historian whose work formed a highly effective bridgehead in the examination of strategy and the evolution of strategic management. He championed the **decentralized organizational form** and was an advocate of Alfred Sloan's strategy at General Motors.

Key Work: *Strategy and Structure* (1962)

Philip Crosby

One of the leading quality consultants. Formerly with ITT, his catch-phrase, in a business of catch-phrases, is "Quality is free."

W Edwards Deming (1900–1993)

Deming's rejection in the US and his success in Japan is one of the great business stories. It took a TV documentary to propel Deming to overnight fame in the world's boardrooms. He spent the last years of his life desperately travelling the world preaching his gospels, built around his famed, almost biblical, 14 points.

Key Work: *Out of the Crisis* (1982)

Peter Drucker

Born in Austria, though he has spent most of his life in California, Drucker is the pre-eminent management thinker of the twentieth century. His work is all-encompassing and always worth reading. Even in his eighties, he remains a shrewd and perceptive commentator on virtually every aspect of management and business.

Key Works: *The Practice of Management* (1954); *The Age of Discontinuity* (1969); *Management: Tasks, Responsibilities, Practices* (1974); and virtually all other of his many books.

Henri Fayol (1841–1925)

Sadly, Fayol is now virtually unacknowledged, yet he was Europe's first significant management thinker. A French businessman he distilled the core functions of management down to 14 elements.

Key Work: *General and Industrial Management* (1949)

Mary Parker Follett (1868–1933)

The American political scientist has recently been rediscovered. Among the first to describe the importance of teamworking, her work had some impact in Japan but was largely neglected in the United States.

Key Work: *Mary Parker Follett: Prophet of Management* (1995)

Henry Ford (1863–1947)

The first to translate scientific management into practice. He is best known for his achievements in mass production. This tends to overshadow an extraordinary life and his extraordinary business success.

Jay Forrester

MIT academic who invented **core memory** during the first wave of modern digital computers, also pioneered the field of **system dynamics** – analysis of the behavior of systems.

Harold Geneen (1910-97)

The legendary leader of ITT during the 1960s. He was the archetypal numbers man, driven by an unquenchable desire for information. Though he expanded ITT rapidly and recorded excellent results, the company floundered after his departure. Among modern managers who acknowledge Geneen as an influence are Sir Colin Marshall, chairman of British Airways.

Key Works: *Managing* (1984); *The Synergy Myth* (1997)

Sumantra Ghoshal

Now Professor of Strategic Leadership at London Business School, after spells at INSEAD and MIT. Working with Harvard's Christopher Bartlett he has become one of the most respected business gurus of the 1990s.

Key Works: *Managing Across Borders: The Transnational Solution* (1988); *Transnational Management* (1990); *Organization Theory and the Multinational Corporation* (1993); *The Individualized Corporation* (1997)

Gary Hamel

Visiting Professor of Strategic Management at London Business School and formerly with the University of Michigan. Author and co-author of a number of highly influential *Harvard Business Review* articles and, with CK Prahalad, of *Competing for the Future*. Founder of the consulting firm, Strategos.

Key Work: *Competing for the Future* (1994)

Michael Hammer

Former MIT and computer science professor and joint author, with James Champy, of the best-selling *Reengineering The Corporation*. Hammer is derisory of companies which take only gradual or cautious steps to improve customer service, when they should be making striking improvements in their basic operations. "We've had the same answer for 40 years, but the questions have changed. If the taxicab engine is broken, I don't care if the driver is friendly," he says.

Key Work: *Reengineering The Corporation* (with James Champy, 1993)

Charles Handy

Irish-born Handy has seen his reputation burgeon in recent years. His increasingly bleak perspectives on the nature of work and organizations are essential reading. He developed the concept of the **Shamrock Organization** and continues to argue the case for federalism.

Key Works: *The Age of Unreason* (1989); *The Empty Raincoat* (1994)

Frederick Herzberg

Now based at the University of Utah, Herzberg was a major figure in management thinking during the 1960s. He took Abraham Maslow's work a stage further, identifying **motivator** and **hygiene** factors as the two sides of motivation.

Key Work: *The Motivation to Work* (with Mausner and Snyderman, 1959)

Geert Hofstede

The Dutch-based anthropologist and academic is increasingly recognized for his work on corporate and international cultures.

Key Work: *Cultures and Organizations* (1991)

Joseph Juran

The "other" quality guru. Juran has lived somewhat in Deming's shadow. Their careers followed similar paths and Juran continues to try to get his quality message across. Less statistical in his orientation than Deming, Juran foresaw the rise of empowerment, some 40 years ago.

Key Work: *Juran on Planning for Quality* (1988)

Rosabeth Moss Kanter

Harvard Business School's Moss Kanter possesses a formidable intellect. A former editor of the *Harvard Business Review*, her work is based on humane, liberal premises. She championed empowerment and has contributed some of the best books on managing change.

Key Works: *Change Masters* (1984); *When Giants Learn to Dance* (1989); *World Class* (1995); *Rosabeth Moss Kanter on the Frontiers of Management* (1997)

Philip Kotler

"Marketing takes a day to learn. Unfortunately it takes a lifetime to master," says Kotler. He is a prolific author and his texts are now seminal reading for anyone wishing to understand the intricacies of modern marketing. *Marketing Management: Analysis, Planning and Control* is widely used in business schools and his many other books are similarly rigorous. Kotler is Professor of International Marketing at the JL Kellogg Graduate School of Management at Northwestern University.

Key Work: *Marketing Management* (1993)

John Kotter

Professor of Organizational Behavior at Harvard Business School and world-renowned expert on leadership, culture and managing change. His published output is prodigious.

Key Work: *A Force for Change* (1990); *Corporate Culture and Performance* (with James Heskett, 1992)

Theodore Levitt

The German-born marketing thinker peaked early in his career with the massively influential *Harvard Business Review* article, "Marketing myopia." It exposed the limitations of conventional thinking on marketing and exhorted companies to become marketing led rather than production led. Levitt's later work has largely failed to match the impact of "Marketing myopia." However, his work on **globalization** has proved critical in developing an understanding of the forces now at work.

Key Work: *Thinking About Management* (1991)

Douglas Macgregor (1906–1964)

From 1954 until his death Macgregor was a Professor at MIT. He is best known for his development of **Theories X** and **Y**. Theory X was the motivational stick (people don't really want to work and need to be constantly cajoled) and the carrot (give them an incentive and they will work and enjoy it).

Key Work: *The Human Side of Enterprise* (1960)

Abraham Maslow (1908–1970)

Labeled "The father of humanist psychology", Maslow was head of the psychology department at Brandeis University. He developed the **hierarchy of needs** which proved highly influential on a number of thinkers.

Key Works: *Motivation and Personality* (1954); *Towards a Psychology of Being* (1962); *Maslow on Management* (1998)

Elton Mayo (1880–1949)

Prodigiously talented and perpetually underrated. Mayo received medical training in London and Edinburgh. He moved on to an Adelaide printing company and then taught moral and mental philosophy at Queensland University. Along the way he pioneered a new treatment for victims of shell shock and was the driving force behind the Hawthorne experiments in Chicago.

Key Works: *The Human Problems of an Industrial Civilization* (1933); *The Social Problems of an Industrial Civilization* (1945)

Henry Mintzberg

Mintzberg's work is rigorous, eclectic and studiously eccentric. Deeply researched in classic academic style, it takes unusual directions which make it essential reading. His 1973 book, *The Nature of Managerial Work*, encouraged an entirely new perspective on what managers actually do. Since then Mintzberg has cast his intellectual net wide. He works at McGill University in Canada and INSEAD in France; this does not prevent him being one of the most vehement critics of the modern MBA.

Key Works: *The Nature of Managerial Work* (1973); *The Rise and Fall of Strategic Planning* (1994)

Jane Mouton (1930–1987)

A social scientist who, together with Robert Blake, developed the idea of the **managerial grid**. This measured management styles on two dimensions – concern for production and concern for people. The concept was refined and developed over numerous books.

Key Work: *The Managerial Grid* (1964)

Kenichi Ohmae

Formerly head of McKinsey's Tokyo office, Ohmae is a brilliant thinker whose range and aspirations have increasingly expanded – they now embrace politics. His views on strategy embrace the apparent opposites of rational analysis and the irrational world of intuition. His later work covers globalization, and what he labels the Inter-Linked Economy of the US, Europe and Japan/Asia.

Key Works: *The Mind of the Strategist* (1982); *The Borderless World* (1990)

C Northcote Parkinson (1909–1993)

An academic who spent time at universities in the US, the UK and Malaysia. He is best known for his cynical, but all too accurate, **Parkinson's Law** which observed that work expanded to fill the time allotted to it.

Key Work: *Parkinson's Law* (1958)

Richard Pascale

Unlike many of his contemporaries, Pascale is not a prolific writer. His books only number two – *The Art of Japanese Management* (with Anthony Athos) and *Managing on the Edge* (1990) – but both were bestsellers. Pascale's approach manages to combine heavyweight theory with clarity. His message, unpalatable to many managers, is that change is not enough. He calls for transformation, discontinuous shifts in financial performance, key industry benchmarks and company culture. Organizations must reinvent themselves.

Key Work: *Managing on the Edge* (1990)

Tom Peters

Amid Peters' exuberant stage technique and expansive writing style lie many great examples and vital messages which can be overlooked. The former McKinsey consultant champions the customer-focussed, responsive, dynamic, fast moving, humane organization. Peters believes in people; that people make a difference and that people make things happen. Unfairly criticized for the failure of some of the companies featured in *In Search of Excellence*, Peters' achievement is to put the humane into management.

Key Works: *In Search of Excellence* (1982); *Liberation Management* (1992)

Michael Porter

Harvard's Michael Porter is the man who brought the world the concept of **competitive advantage**. A prodigiously talented individual, his books are required but demanding reading. Since his first success with *Competitive Strategy* in 1980, Porter's audience has grown with each new book – as has his ambition. Porter has carried academic rigor and analysis to new extremes which, according to your preference, are exactly what businesses need or a rational leap too far.

Key Works: *Competitive Strategy* (1980); *Competitive Advantage* (1985); *Competition in Global Industries* (1986); *The Competitive Advantage of Nations* (1990)

CK Prahalad

Professor of Corporate Strategy and International Management at the University of Michigan. In partnership with London Business School's Gary Hamel, Prahalad is setting the new agenda for management. Their *Harvard Business Review* articles "Strategic intent" and "Competing with core competencies" proved highly influential and readable. Author of *The Multinational Mission* (with Yves Doz of INSEAD) and author (with Hamel) of *Competing for the Future*, the most compelling business book of the 1990s.

Key Work: *Competing for the Future* (1994)

Reg Revans

The idiosyncratic Reg Revans has ploughed a lonely furrow, taking his concept of **action learning** to a variety of relatively obscure countries. Action learning appears blindingly obvious – it emphasizes learning from doing in groups (though putting this into practice is more demanding than it seems). Its very simplicity appears to have put off other academics from embracing it.

Key Work: *Action Learning* (1979)

Edgar Schein

Schein has been with MIT for nearly 40 years and during that time has become a pioneer of organizational development. In *Organizational Culture and Leadership*, he clarified the concept of organizational cultures and showed its relationship to leadership. He is also the inventor of the terms **career anchor** and the **psychological contract** which have attracted increasing attention.

Key Work: *Organizational Culture and Leadership* (1985)

Ricardo Semler

One of the more unlikely gurus, Semler has transformed his family business from a staid and traditional one into a model of empowerment and employee participation. Criticized by some as an eccentric rather than a maverick, Semler is a highly persuasive speaker and writer.

Key Work: *Maverick!* (1993)

Peter Senge

Director of the Center for Organizational Learning at MIT and author of *The Fifth Discipline: The Art and Practice of the Learning Organization*. Senge, almost single-handedly, propelled the concept of the **learning organization** onto the management agenda. Since then there has been something of a backlash with attempts at implementing Senge's theories proving disappointing.

Key Work: *The Fifth Discipline* (1990)

EF Schumacher (1911-77)

Schumacher's *Small is Beautiful* is one of those books which can be found on bookshelves the world over. It has entered into the argot of management as surely as *Catch-22* has penetrated popular consciousness. Yet few have actually read the book and fewer still have turned Schumacher's theories into reality.

Key Work: *Small is Beautiful* (1973)

Alfred P Sloan (1875–1966)

Highly influential role model of the **decentralized organization.** His work at General Motors revolutionized the company – allowing it to quickly out-perform Ford – and provided a much emulated organizational model. Only now, says Sumantra Ghoshal, are organizations shaking off Sloan's legacy.

Key Work: *My Years with General Motors* (1963)

Frederick Winslow Taylor (1856–1917)

When he wasn't winning tennis tournaments or developing new ways to throw a baseball, Taylor developed the first coherent theory of management: **scientific management**. Now, it is routinely derided for its inhumane attitude to those who carry out the work, but as Peter Drucker points out, Taylor was the first man to actually begin to think about the nature of the work.

Key Work: *The Principles of Scientific Management* (1913)

Fons Trompenaars

Dutch expert on cultural diversity.

Key Works: *Riding the Waves of Culture* (1993); *The Seven Cultures of Capitalism* (with Charles Hampden-Turner, 1994)

Lyndall Urwick (1891–1983)

Chief European champion of Frederick Taylor's scientific management. He fulfilled this role to great effect, creating a classical interpretation of management.

Key Work: *The Making of Scientific Management* (with EFL Brech, 1946)

Manfred Kets de Vries

Leadership expert, based at France's INSEAD. Voted one of Europe's top business school gurus by the *Financial Times*. He has unparalleled access to some of the world's foremost business leaders. His interest lies in the interface between international management, psychoanalysis and dynamic psychiatry.

Robert Waterman

Most famously Tom Peters' co-author for *In Search of Excellence*, Waterman has since faded into the background. His books remain forceful reminders that excellence does exist.

Key Works: *The Renewal Factor* (1987); *Frontiers of Excellence* (1994)

Thomas Watson Sr. (1874–1956)

Indomitable figure behind the rise of IBM. His lasting legacy was the creation of IBM's corporate culture which stood the test of time, until the disasters of the 1980s.

Max Weber (1864–1920)

Unfortunately saddled with responsibility for the invention of bureaucracy. This is a harsh interpretation of his observation that a "rational-legal" organizational form was the best for the times.

Index